DEATH and BEREAVEMENT

DEATH and
BEREAVEMENT

WITHDRAWN

Edited by

AUSTIN H. KUTSCHER

In Collaboration with

49 Contributors and 122 Consultant—Respondents

SECOND PRINTING

CHARLES C THOMAS • **PUBLISHER**
Springfield • *Illinois* • *U.S.A.*

Published and Distributed Throughout the World by

CHARLES C THOMAS • PUBLISHER

Bannerstone House

301-327 East Lawrence Avenue, Springfield, Illinois, U.S.A.

©*1969, by* CHARLES C THOMAS • PUBLISHER

(cloth) ISBN 0-398-01070-6
(paper) ISBN 0-398-03293-9

Library of Congress Catalog Card Number: 73-77930

First Printing, 1969
Second Printing, 1974

With THOMAS BOOKS careful attention is given to all details of
manufacturing and design. It is the Publisher's desire to present books that are
satisfactory as to their physical qualities and artistic possibilities and
appropriate for their particular use. THOMAS BOOKS will be true to those
laws of quality that assure a good name and good will.

Printed in the United States of America

R-1

To the memory of
HELENE WALD KUTSCHER
DR. HARVEY I. GOLDBERG
SAMUEL BLUMBERG
ROSE MOLLIS MEILEN

ABOUT THE AUTHOR

Austin H. Kutscher is an Associate Professor in the Division of Stomatology of the School of Dental and Oral Surgery of Columbia University. He is the President of the Foundation of Thanatology, a multidisciplinary organization with a Professional Advisory Board composed of psychiatrists, nonpsychiatric physicians, clergymen, psychologists, sociologists and representatives of many other fields. The Foundation is devoted to scientific and humanistic inquiries as well as to the application of knowledge to the subjects of the psychological aspects of dying, reactions to death, loss and grief, and recovery from bereavement.

Dr. Kutscher has published widely in the professional literature of medicine and dentistry, is the co-editor of four books in the field of pharmacotherapeutics and diagnosis of oral disease, has edited two other multicontributor books in the area of death, grief, and recovery from bereavement, and is a co-editor of a volume for the health professions entitled *Loss and Grief: Psychological Management in Medical Practice* (Columbia University Press).

CONTRIBUTORS

Gene E. Bartlett, D.D., President, Colgate–Rochester Divinity School, Rochester, New York.

Joseph Bess, D.O., Private Practice, West Hollywood, Florida.

Sandra Bess, Classical Literature, West Hollywood, Florida.

H. Robert Blank, M.D., Private Practice, Psychiatry, White Plains, New York.

James P. Cattell, M.D., Assistant Clinical Professor, Department of Psychiatry, College of Physicians and Surgeons, Columbia University; and Assistant Attending Psychiatrist, The Presbyterian Hospital in the City of New York.

Paula J. Clayton, M.D., Assistant Professor of Psychiatry, Department of Psychiatry, Washington University, School of Medicine, St. Louis, Missouri.

Reverend Walter Debold, Englewood Cliffs College, Englewood, New Jersey.

Charles S. Ferber, District Manager, Social Security Administration, Department of Health, Education and Welfare, New York, New York.

Regina Flesch, Ph.D., Eastern Psychiatric Institute, Philadelphia, Pennsylvania.

Jean E. Fox, R.N., B.S., Prelatura Nullius de Sicuani, Sicuani, Peru.

Rose N. Franzblau, Ph.D., Psychology, Columnist New York Post, New York, New York.

J. T. Frazer, Secretary, International Society for the Study of Time, Pleasantville, New York.

Thomas Gonda, M.D., Psychiatry, Associate Dean, College of Medicine, Stanford University, Palo Alto, California.

Fred Heller, Chartered Financial Analyst, Assistant Vice-President, Nuveen Corporation, New York, New York.

Frederic Herter, M.D., Professor and Chairman, Department of Surgery, College of Physicians and Surgeons, Columbia University; Attending Surgeon, The Presbyterian Hospital in the City of New York.

Dorothy Howard, Librarian, University of Windsor, Windsor, Ontario, Canada.

George A. Hyman, M.D., Assistant Clinical Professor, Department of Medicine, College of Physicians and Surgeons, Columbia University; Assistant Attending Physician, The Presbyterian Hospital in the City of New York.

Edgar N. Jackson, D.D., Former Pastor, Mamaroneck Methodist Church, Mamaroneck, New York; Chairman, Advisory Board, Guidance Center of New Rochelle, New Rochelle, New York.

Richard A. Kalish, Ph.D., Associate Professor, School of Public Health and Associate Director, Gerontology Training Program, University of California, Los Angeles, California.

Robert Kastenbaum, Ph.D., Professor, Department of Psychology, Wayne State University, Detroit, Michigan.

James R. Kinney, D.V.M., Private Practice, New York, New York.

Donald F. Klein, M.D., Director of Research, Hillside Hospital, Glen Oaks, New York.

Gilbert Kliman, M.D., Director, The Center for Preventive Psychiatry, White Plains, New York.

James A. Knight, M.D., Associate Dean and Professor of Psychiatry, Tulane University, School of Medicine, New Orleans, Louisiana.

Austin H. Kutscher, D.D.S., Associate Professor, Division of Stomatology (Therapeutics and Clinical Pharmacology), School of Dental and Oral Surgery, Columbia University, New York, New York.

Joseph C. Landrud, Th.D., Minister, St. Paul's Lutheran Church, Monrovia, California; El Monte Counseling Service, El Monte, California.

Boris M. Levinson, Ph.D., Professor of Psychology, Department of Educational Psychology and Guidance, Ferkauf Graduate School of Humanities and Social Sciences, Yeshiva University, New York, New York.

Austin Mehrhof, B.A., M.A., New York, New York.

Robert Michels, M.D., Instructor, Department of Psychiatry, College of Physicians and Surgeons, Columbia University; Assistant Attending Psychiatrist, The Presbyterian Hospital in the City of New York.

Glenn R. Mosley, D.D., Associate Minister, Unity Temple, Detroit, Michigan.

Gardner Murphy, Ph.D., The Menninger Foundation, Topeka, Kansas.

Sidney Nathanson, D.D., Rabbi, Temple Sholom, Plainfield, New Jersey.

Jacob Needleman, Ph.D., Professor of Philosophy, San Francisco State College, San Francisco, California.

Ralph Ober, LL.B., Former Executive Director, Parents Without Partners, Inc., New York, New York.

John F. O'Connor, M.D., Assistant Director, Vanderbilt Clinic, The Presbyterian Hospital in the City of New York; Assistant Clinical Professor, Department of Psychiatry, College of Physicians and Surgeons, Columbia University, New York, New York.

Lee M. Olson, Conference Coordinator, Oakland University, Rochester, Michigan.

Norman L. Paul, M.D., Private Practice, Psychiatry, Cambridge, Massachusetts.

Elizabeth L. Post, Editor, Emily Post's Etiquette, Funk and Wagnalls, New York, New York.

Elizabeth R. Prichard, M.S., Assistant Professor, Department of Medicine (Medical Social Service), College of Physicians and Surgeons, Columbia University, New York, New York.

W. Dewi Rees, M.D., General Practice, Llanidlees, Wales, United Kingdom.

Robert B. Reeves, Jr., Chaplain, The Presbyterian Hospital in the City of New York, Columbia-Presbyterian Medical Center, New York, New York.

Paul J. Reiss, Ph.D., Chairman, Department of Sociology and Anthropology, Fordham University, Bronx, New York.

Alan Rosell, B.A., New York, New York.

Bernard B. Schoenberg, M.D., Assistant Clinical Professor, Department of Psychiatry, College of Physicians and Surgeons, Columbia University; Associate Attending Psychiatrist, The Presbyterian Hospital in the City of New York.

Frederick J. Stare, M.D., Professor of Nutrition, Chairman of the Department of Nutrition, Harvard University, School of Public Health, Boston, Massachusetts.

Jerome Steiner, M.D., Instructor, Department of Psychiatry, College of Physicians and Surgeons, Columbia University; Assistant Attending Psychiatrist, The Presbyterian Hospital in the City of New York, New York.

Lenore O. Stern, Research Assistant, Department of Pediatric Psychiatry, Babies Hospital, Columbia-Presbyterian Medical Center, New York, New York.

Paul E. Steward, B.A., Secretary-Treasurer, Bergen County Funeral Directors Association, New Jersey.

Helen Wargotz, M.S., Certified Social Worker; Director, Allied Teen-Age Guidance Service; Chief Psychiatric Social Worker, Fifth Avenue Center for Counseling and Psychotherapy, New York, New York.

CONSULTANT—RESPONDENTS

Richard B. Adams, Episcopalian Clergyman, Bath, Maine.

James R. Albano, M.D., General Practitioner, Norwalk, California.

Kring Allen, Disciples of Christ Clergyman, Los Angeles, California.

Sherman Arnold, M.D., General Practitioner, Chicago, Illinois.

Jack Austin, Disciples of Christ Clergyman, Peoria, Illinois.

Loren Avery, M.D., Psychiatrist, Chicago, Illinois.

George Russell Barber, Disciples of Christ Clergyman, Los Angeles, California.

Gene E. Barlett, D.D., Protestant Clergyman, Rochester, New York.

Allison Baxter, M.D., General Practitioner, Batavia, Illinois.

Gustav Beck, M.D., Internal Medicine, New York, New York.

Philip Becker, M.D., Analyst, Beverly Hills, California.

Gerhard L. Belgum, Lutheran Clergyman, Lakewood, California.

Stephen Berte, M.D., Internal Medicine, Brooklyn, New York.

Gordon K. Blunt, United Church of Christ Clergyman, Ontario, California.

Gerald Boyle, Catholic Clergyman, Goshen, New York.

Erika Briggs, M.D., Psychiatrist, Togus, Maine.

John Briggs, M.D., Psychiatrist, Tarrytown, New York.

Carl B. Camp, Baptist Clergyman, Glenview, Illinois.

Michael Carlozzi, M.D., Internal Medicine, New York.

Caroll Carlson, M.D., Analyst, Beverly Hills, California.

Arne Christianson, Lutheran Clergyman, San Diego, California.

James Cimino, M.D., Internal Medicine, White Plains, New York.

Robert C. Clark, Disciples of Christ Clergyman, Blue Mound, Illinois.

Arthur Clinco, M.D., Analyst, Los Angeles, California.

William Closson, M.D., Psychiatrist, San Jose, California.

William Coats, M.D., General Practitioner, Chickasaw, Alabama.

Austin Coe, Disciples of Christ Clergyman, Downey, California.

John L. Colburn, United Church of Christ Clergyman, Los Angeles, California.

Paul Crantz, M.D., General Practitioner, Antioch, California.

James Curtis, M.D., Analyst, Brooklyn, New York.

Carlos Dalmau, M.D., Psychiatrist, New York, New York.

Gilbert Daniel, Pastor, Cameron, Illinois.

George A. Detor, Episcopalian Clergyman, Buena Park, California.

Joel Duffield, Pastor, Hamilton, Illinois.

Charles Duncan, Baptist Clergyman, Joliet, Illinois.

Robert Edgar, M.A., D.D., Presbyterian Clergyman, New York, New York.

Frank Ewers, M.D., General Practitioner, Ottawa, Illinois.

Samuel Feder, M.D., Analyst, Scarsdale, New York.

Herman Feifel, Ph.D., Psychologist, Los Angeles, California.

Alfred Fein, M.D., Psychiatrist, Chicago, Illinois.

Solomon Fische, M.D., Internal Medicine, New York, New York.

William H. Frederick, M.D., General Practitioner, Eutaw, Alabama.

David Friedman, M.D., Psychiatrist, New York, New York.

Roald Grant, M.D., Surgeon, New York, New York.

W. B. Greenough III, M.D., Internal Medicine, Bethesda, Maryland.

James Grotstein, M.D., Psychiatrist, Beverly Hills, California.

Curtis Grove, M.D., General Practitioner, Bell, California.

William Gutknecht Jr., Lutheran Clergyman, Lodi, California.

Gerald C. Hammon, Disciples of Christ Clergyman, Winters, California.

Donald H. Harter, M.D., Neurologist, New York, New York.

Max Hayman, M.D., Analyst, Los Angeles, California.

Emeline Hayward, M.D., Analyst, Kingston, New York.

Henry O. Heinemann, M.D., Internal Medicine, New York, New York.

Richard C. Hertz, D.D., Rabbi, Detroit, Michigan.

Douglas R. Hill, M.D., General Practitioner, South Portland, Maine.

E. Holland, Lutheran Clergyman, Freemont, California.

James Hutton, M.D., Internal Medicine, Chicago, Illinois.

David Johnson, M.D., General Practitioner, Downey, Illinois.

Leonard Jourdonais, M.D., Internal Medicine, Evanston, Illinois.

Mark Kanzer, M.D., Analyst, Harrison, New York.

Avraam Kazan, M.D., Analyst, Ardsley, New York.

Walter Kearns, M.D., Surgeon, Canoga Park, California.

Walter Kitt, M.D., Psychiatrist, Chicago, Illinois.

Wallace O. Klandrud, Lutheran Clergyman, Camarillo, California.

Israel Klein, M.D., General Practitioner, Los Angeles, California.

Abbie Knowlton, M.D., Internal Medicine, New York, New York.

Joseph S. Kootsey, M.D., General Practitioner, San Jose, California.

William Krech, M.D., Surgeon, Westbury, New York.

Lillian G. Kutscher, Foundation of Thanatology, New York, New York.

H. Richard Lamb, M.D., Psychiatrist, Hillsborough, California.

Edward Laramie, Catholic Clergyman, Arlington Heights, Illinois.

Ellsworth Larson, M.D., General Practitioner, Highland, California.

Maimon Leavitt, M.D., Analyst, Beverly Hills, California.

Richard Lose, M.D., General Practitioner, Sonoma, California.

Judd Marmor, M.D., Analyst, Los Angeles, California.

Alva McCord, M.D., Analyst, Albany, New York.

John Mebane, M.D., Psychiatrist, Los Angeles, California.

Robert L. Miles, M.D., Private Practice, Santa Barbara, California.

J. Victor Monke, M.D., Psychiatrist, Beverly Hills, California.

H. Frederick More, Lutheran Clergyman, Augusta, Maine.

Henry Moser, Baptist Clergyman, Granite City, Illinois.

Robert Newhouse, M.D., Analyst, Long Beach, California.

Robert Nixon, M.D., Psychiatrist, Poughkeepsie, New York.

Rudolph Novick, M.D., Psychiatrist, Des Plaines, Illinois.

William O'Neal, M.D., Surgeon, Los Angeles, California.

James O'Reilly, Catholic Clergyman, Birmingham, Alabama.

John Orpen, Episcopalian Clergyman, Chicago, Illinois.

C. Murray Parkes, M.D., D.P.M., Psychiatrist, London, England.

George Paulsen, M.D., Surgeon, Bakersfield, California.

David Peretz, M.D., Psychiatrist, New York, New York.

Nathan A. Perilman, Jewish Clergyman, New York, New York.

Charles H. Perry, Episcopalian Clergyman, Sacramento, California.

DeSaussure Philpot, M.D., Psychiatrist, New York, New York.

Edward Pinney, M.D., Psychiatrist, Brooklyn, New York.

George Pollock, M.D., Psychiatrist, Chicago, Illinois.

Sterling Pollock, M.D., General Practitioner, Los Angeles, California.

Elsa Poslusny, R.N., New York, New York.

Elizabeth L. Post, Editor, Etiquette, New York, New York.

Joseph Powell, M.D., General Practitioner, Macomb, Illinois.

William Prescott, Jr., M.D., General Practitioner, Birmingham, Alabama.

Nathan Rickles, M.D., Psychiatrist, Beverly Hills, California.

Lewis Robbins, M.D., Analyst, Glen Oaks, New York.

Santo L. Ruggero, M.D., General Practitioner, Wonder Lake, Illinois.

Howard Sapiro, M.D., General Practitioner, Portland, Maine.

Geoffrey Selth, Unitarian Clergyman, Santa Rosa, California.

Edwin S. Shneidman, Ph.D., Suicide Prevention, National Institute of Mental Health, Bethesda, Maryland.

Ellen Simon, M.D., Analyst, New York, New York.

Arthur Sohval, M.D., Internal Medicine, New York, New York.

Herman Tannor, M.D., Psychiatrist, New York, New York.

Patricia Tretter, M.D., Radiotherapist, New York, New York.

John Tumelty, Catholic Clergyman, Alexander City, Alabama.

Charles W. Wahl, Psychiatrist, Los Angeles, California.

Stanley Wallach, M.D., Internal Medicine, Brooklyn, New York.

Alfred Walter, M.D., Psychiatrist, West Brentwood, New York.

George Wayne, M.D., Analyst, Bel-Air, California.

Irvin Weiland, M.D., Psychiatrist, Van Nuys, California.

Avery Weisman, M.D., Psychiatrist, Boston, Massachusetts.

Mary Woods, Social Worker, Family Consultation Service, Eastchester, New York.

Charles Wylie, M.D., General Practitioner, Santa Monica, California.

Anthony Zoghby, Catholic Clergyman, Pritchard, Alabama.

Anonymous Catholic Clergyman, Rural New York State.

Anonymous Catholic Clergyman.

PREFACE

This book owes its meaning to the compelling force of its origin. It came into being a few weeks after my young wife's death from cancer. In the silence and solitude of the hospital room to which I was briefly confined following minor surgery, the formulation of certain themes began. With grief as the catalyst and time for contemplation, the concepts of this volume began to evolve.

As the ideological base of the book clarified in my mind, I sought assistance from my visitors, many of whom were long-standing colleagues of the hospital's professional staff—physicians, nurses, chaplains. All assured me of their deep interest and promised their fullest cooperation. They spoke of the obvious need and profound importance of such a venture and appeared to be stimulated by the challenge of involvement with this original idea.

From my own vain search I knew that no book had as yet been published which dealt, from the viewpoint of a variety of disciplines, with both the emotional and practical problems facing a bereaved person. A number of those who had evinced early interest in the volume and its concept later acknowledged that, in past situations, they too had sought and had been unable to find such a detailed work. Indeed, booksellers had made it clear that, although many requests had been made for such a volume, none was available.

To be sure, there are essays in periodicals, pamphlets and monographs, and many excellent compilations of literature in book form (such as *A Treasury of Comfort*, by Dr. Sidney Greenberg). There are, as well, extensive and learned books for professional counselors (*Understanding Grief*, by one of our contributors, Reverend Edgar N. Jackson). Still other works have specific and applicable passages and chapters, profoundly moving in their quality of spirituality, such as the memorable *Peace of*

Mind, by Joshua Loth Liebman. Innumerable articles are scattered throughout the psychological-medical and social science literature, but most of these deal with the subject at the clinical level and are of little practical use to most bereaved persons.

Thus, as my visitors returned, reassuring me of their willingness to contribute to the work, *Death and Bereavement* assumed structure, shape, and substance. Further, our contributors were beginning to discover that for each of them the book offered a challenge to verbalize their own special experiences, perhaps for the first time.

I approached the outline for the book in a somewhat unorthodox way by setting down at random the myriad thoughts and problems which had confronted me. An organized outline finally emerged as the result of literally weeks of conscious (and unconscious) effort, from inner reflections which were crystallized and recorded hour by hour. Because my academic background had included the editing of three multicontributor textbooks, I conceived of this work similarly—two volumes which would bring together in counsel many authorities in their respective fields. The second book was to be But Not to Luse. See page xxi.

There began, then, the rewarding process of searching out additional contributors who were willing to draw upon their experiences and unique talents in order to provide advice for the bereaved and those who anticipated bereavement. Some were asked to address themselves to the spiritual, philosophical and medical needs of the bereaved; others, to the practical problems of everyday existence, to ways in which mental and physical pressures upon the bereaved may be reduced or tempered. Psychiatric-psychologic, prophylactic and therapeutic prescriptions were designed by our professional authors. These, hopefully, would lessen the incidence of depression and psychic maladjustment in the grieving person.

The outline, in this interim period, underwent constant revision. I received many suggestions from authors and consultants, in response to my questions. Consultations with contributors continued. There were many facets of the main topic to be covered, and authorities appeared whose voices could not be overlooked. Many gaps opened in new areas and some of them were hard to fill.

I was to realize later how profoundly important were all of my efforts in terms of "working my *own* way through grief." During this period my energies were being devoted to a cardinal concept of this volume—the concept that *some* form of creativity be coupled with the mourning process itself. And the importance of *understanding* and acceptance of grief came to all of us who worked together on the book. The concept of understanding grief has become another basic tenet of the work and one which had to be fully explored before justice could be done to the subject.

Ultimately, through understanding will come release from many anxieties and much despair. It is necessary that a bridge be built over the painful ground of grief and mourning, a bridge that leads to understanding. This is not an easy concept for the bereaved person to grasp, nor is it one which he is prepared to accept, particularly in the initial stages of acute loss. For this reason, the relationship between the bereaved's comprehension and acceptance of grief and his recovery from it are examined from many points of view.

As the weeks passed and topics were chosen, contributors selected, and the final manuscripts prepared and studied, many contributors were found to be preoccupied with the plight of the dying patient himself. It appeared, therefore, both logical and necessary to explore the reactions of the patient to his own illness and its prognosis.* Among many, many others, such questions arose as, for instance, whether it was better to advise the terminal patient of his condition or not.

Some of our contributors chose topics which seemed, at first,

* In the course of the interest which the preparation of *Death and Bereavement* engendered, a book primarily for medical and paramedical personnel also took shape, entitled *Loss and Grief: Psychological Management in Medical Practice*, which will be published by Columbia University Press, to which many of the same, as well as other, contributors added their professional views. This volume looks upon loss and grief from perspectives far broader than that of grief alone, emphasizing clinical elements of grief, loss of body parts and/or function, representative of problems which are frequently part of the physiologic picture of progressive terminal illness.

to bear only peripherally upon the primary subject. In deference to their skills and talents, their choices were respected, with full confidence that their selections would prove appropriate to our goals. Such varied aspects of the main theme produced material on the nurse's confrontation with the dying patient and his family; the doctor and the dying patient; the reactions and impressions of persons rescued or reprieved from death and so forth. When duly contemplated, all of these topics were found to be closely allied with the broad areas of loss and grief, bereavement and mourning. They have added much to the bereaved's acceptance and understanding of grief and, consequently, will contribute much to the reader in his recovery from bereavement.

Another area of concern, found to be somewhat elusive in relation to its importance and the rewards to be derived from an understanding of it, is the aura of bereavement which surrounds the bereaved-to-be before the death of the chronically ill or terminal patient. This phenomenon of anticipatory grief appears at the time of awareness that an illness will be terminal. A "built-in" timetable, one for which we may indeed be thankful, sequentially relates the period of bereavement to a (more or less) finite period in time. Everyone who has experienced bereavement will, doubtless, agree that neither warning nor grieving in advance can do more than cushion the traumatic shock of death when it does occur, but it is important to recognize that the reactions of the bereaved in these cases will differ significantly from other grief reactions.

In the grief syndrome, a great complex of influences affects the intensity of despair and the difficulties of recovery. Thus, specific differences are to be noted, applicable to recovery from grief following prolonged illness eventuating in death as opposed to sudden death (heart attack) and/or suicide. Singularly unique problems and differing timetables occur in cases of lingering and/or sudden death in childhood, as well as comparable differences in deaths of aged persons. Grief differs markedly with the age, resilience, inner personal resources and vigor of the bereaved; it differs with direct relationship to the age of the deceased loved one. Most importantly, however, there is a correlation between the degree of intensity as well as the depth and the nature of the relationship that existed between the deceased and the bereaved. These many aspects of the grief complex received major consideration in the preparation of this volume.

To sum up, then, we may say that great stress has been placed upon a more profound understanding of bereavement and grief, of dying, of grief as it appears in advance of death, on the relationships between those who minister to the dying and care for the bereaved as well as on what such counselors can do for the bereaved if given the opportunity. Great attention has been paid to practicalities which must be dealt with along the way. If not of immediate value, as in, more than likely, the acutely paralyzing and very traumatic initial stages of bereavement, the concepts covered should be found to be of value soon thereafter and later on in the future. It should be noted, however, that the usefulness thus derived will, to a large extent, be dependent upon those events which occur as the result of action or inaction, the timing of those events, and lastly, upon that course which the bereaved person finally chooses to take in rearranging his own life after the death of his loved one.

It should be acknowledged here that a survey, to which the 122 qualified consultant-respondents listed in the front matter replied, served as the inapparent backbone for many areas discussed in this volume and provided the Editor with a constant resource for monitoring the thoughts introduced throughout the book. The detailed particulars concerning this survey appear in the companion book entitled *But Not To Lose*, published by Frederick Fell, Inc., New York, New York, 1969.

In the preceding pages I have attempted to sketch in the origins and define the dominant themes of this book. I have delegated the expansion of these concepts to the experts. Relevant to all of this material, we recognized the vital importance of extensively broadening these areas of grief to include discussion of regaining the pleasures of living and, ultimately, of the profoundly important question of remarriage—certainly a matter of critical concern to the bereaved spouse or to the parent who is left without a partner. For myself, I have remarried. The remaining fractions of two families once existed as best they could, fragmented and incomplete; they share now with one

another the inexpressible blessing of renewed hope and love.
Two families have united in loving perseverance to see this
project through to completion, even to the extent of incor-
porating The Foundation of Thanatology.*

Two quotations seem to me to embody this book's theme: an
understanding of death and grief in order that the spirit may
heal and flourish again. They express the epitome of understanding, both of life and death. The first quotation is attributed
to Mrs. Colin Kelly, widow of the Air Force hero of World War
II, who commented at the time of *her* remarriage: "Of course,
you can never forget the past and the past will always color the
present. But I do not think that you should let the past affect
the present so much that there can be no future."

The second quotation was written by the eminent Cleveland
Clinic surgeon, Dr. George A. Crile, Jr., and appears in his
moving book, *More Than Booty,* which was written as a memorial to his wife. It is reproduced here as his contribution to our
volume:

A. H. K.

MEMORIAL SERVICE
KENT ROAD
CLEVELAND HEIGHTS

*We are gathered together in memory of Jane Crile. If you seek
her memorial look about you in the hearts of her children, in her
writings and in her home.*

*Life has been given and life has been taken away. Life and death
are one, even as the river and the sea are one. Death is only a horizon and a horizon is but the limit of our sight.*

It is now more than a year since Jane died. For the first few
weeks there was numbness and obsession with sorrow. Some

---

* Devoted to scientific and humanistic inquiries into death, loss, grief and
recovery from bereavement, this non-profit organization will service the inter-
disciplinary needs of workers in the fields of the health professions, theology,
psychology, the social sciences, etc., through an educational and publication
program.

of it may have been because of insecurity. Through the years I had become so dependent on Jane that it did not seem I could find a way to live without her. But gradually I found I was competent to do or arrange for many of the things Jane had always done for me. Interest in my work returned. I began again to find pleasure in people.

As is often the case with those who have been deeply in love and the husband or wife dies, I married again. A new life began, filled with new interests and with a continuation of the old.

I still live in the same house. Many of the same birds, the wood ducks and the swan, are still in our back yard. Many of the relics that Jane and I collected in our travels are about our house. But there are no ghosts. Memories that were for a time inexpressibly sad have once again become a source of deep pleasure and satisfaction.

Since we know nothing of death except that it comes to all, it is not reasonable to be sad for the person who has died. The sorrow that once I felt for myself, in my loss, now has been transformed to a rich memory of a woman I loved and the ways we traveled through the world together.

CONTENTS

PART III

BEREAVEMENT

PART IV

PRACTICALITIES OF RECOVERING
FROM BEREAVEMENT

PART V

CARE OF THE BEREAVED

PART VI

REBIRTH OF THE SPIRIT

DEATH and BEREAVEMENT

PART I

DYING AND DEATH

Chapter 1

TO TELL OR NOT TO TELL THE PATIENT

ROBERT B. REEVES, JR.

To tell the patient or not is rarely in itself the real issue. Most people know when they are about to die, and even those for whom death is still a good while off have a way of putting two-and-two together. I have rarely met a terminally ill patient who did not intimate to me in one way or another that he knew, regardless of the protective fictions spun by staff and family, and often in spite of his own overt denial. The question is hardly ever, Should he be told? but rather, How shall we deal with what we must assume he knows? It is a problem not of fact but of relationship.

In the course of a patient's experience with those who attend him, a moment comes, more often than not, when all the facts are in, all the circumlocutions have been exhausted, and the truth is *there*, as a kind of third party or silent partner. Patient, doctor, family, and pastor all "know," at a level either of rational awareness or intuitive feeling. Each one is aware of the other's knowledge. At that moment, the truth must either be acknowledged or denied. Which it will be depends on the quality of their relationship.

Many factors enter into the shaping of a relationship, but for the kind that affects people's behavior at a "moment of truth" in the hospital, two are of central importance. One is the outlook and life-style of the patient: how, characteristically, he handles trouble, reacts to bad news, responds in a crisis. This will affect the way he relates to the person who is attending him. The other is the outlook and style of the person in attendance, the doctor, family member, or pastor; how he characteristically deals with crisis in his own life, and especially how he feels about death. This will affect the way he relates to the patient.

5

A patient's outlook and manner of response to crisis can range from panic and denial at the thought of death, at one extreme, to confident acceptance, at the other. At the extreme of denial, no matter how obvious the signs, one type of patient is likely not to let himself acknowledge that he knows, and no matter what he is told, he will hear only what he wants to hear. At the extreme of acceptance, another patient is likely to be able to talk about death quietly, and understand what he is told. In between lie all degrees of variation.

There is a similar range among those who attend the patient: at one extreme, the person who is so anxious about death himself that he must screen out all thoughts about it, refusing to hear any hint of death conveyed by the patient, and readily convincing himself that the patient does not know; at the other extreme, the person whose feelings about death are quiet and assured, for whom death has a place in his world of meanings, who will be alert to catch the patient's intimations and ready to listen to any of his thoughts about death.

In the situations wherein both patient and doctor, family or pastor, are ridden by anxiety and denial, the "moment of truth" will come and go quickly, obscured at once by a cloud of evasive cheer, hopeful pretense, sometimes double-talk or outright falsehood. *Both parties want it that way.* Each picks up the other's signals and with almost instant complicity plays out the part required of him. The presence of the invisible truth is simply put out of mind. For many people, this is the only way they know how to handle such fatal knowledge, the only way they can relate to one another under such conditions. Any breach in such a denial would be devastating to them both.

Sometimes they succeed so well in screening out the thought of death, that what, for a moment, they "knew," they now no longer know. Their attention is absorbed entirely by secondary matters, such as food and liquid intake, skin condition, weight, mobility, pain, or plans for the time when the patient has recovered. To maintain hope becomes the dominant aim of both patient and his attendant, and every effort is directed toward that end. As long as neither the patient nor the other person in any way disturbs this philosophy of denial, each can maintain a relatively secure relationship, sometimes right up to the very time of death.

When both the patient and the person attending him are able to think quietly about death, however, they will both be able to acknowledge it when the moment of truth arrives. The acknowledgment is rarely very dramatic. It is usually subdued, somber, often dismayed and tearful, sometimes wry or even flippant. It gives pause, and it may be followed, after the other person has left, by some hours of weeping or days of withdrawn, self-grieving on the patient's part. But because the relationship is open, the other person can support the patient by being a sympathetic, concerned listener, until the patient works his way through to a level where, with the final question answered, he is free to enjoy what days remain.

Usually, once the truth is acknowledged and the grieving is done, little more is likely to be said about it. The patient often acts either as if he did not know, or considers it simply to be "the ways things are" and therefore not a matter for discussion. Frequently, he may build up a little fiction of "getting better," as if to protect his family and friends from worry. When his time finally comes, he usually dies in dignity and peace.

These extremes of denial or acknowledgment are likely to occur only when both the patient and the other person have a similar outlook and feeling about death. Their relationship rests on either their complicity in saying "No" to the truth, or their openness in saying "Yes." In either case, so long as their denial or acknowledgment is consistent, a sustaining relationship can be maintained.

The difficulty is that seldom are patients and those who attend them so well matched in their feelings about death. Much more commonly, there is a difference between them. On the one hand, the patient may be terrified, whereas the doctor, family member, or pastor is willing and ready to voice the truth. Every intimation that is offered by the attending person is blocked, diverted, or twisted out of recognition by the patient; or, if any such subtlety is listened to and understood, it is nearly always catastrophic in its impact. To insist on telling the patient the truth under such conditions could be simply brutal.

On the other hand, it may be the attending person himself who underneath it all is terrified. Every hint the patient may offer of his knowledge of the situation is screened out, evaded, or circumvented by the doctor, family or pastor; and if a direct question is asked, it is likely to be met by vociferous denial.

In either case, the relationship between the patient and the attending person is askew. They do not meet in thought or feeling. Open communication is impossible. Any interaction only becomes a contest between avoidance and confrontation of the truth, between manipulation of and respect for each other as human beings. They have little ease, confidence, or trust in one another. A great deal of the anguish I have seen in the hospital is the result of this kind of skewed relationship.

Telling the truth when the patient does not want to hear it is nowhere nearly as frequent a problem as is withholding of the truth when the patient is ready to hear it. If, at the moment of recognition, when the truth is obvious and the patient hints that he sees it, the doctor, family, or pastor shies away in evasion, double-talk, or falsehood, then the patient's journey from that point on is usually one of increasing fretfulness and misery. It is well to remember, *he knows;* at some level of awareness he has an idea of how things stand. Denial of this fact is hardly ever convincing. The patient may appear to accept it and go along with the fiction that is offered him. But little by little, as his condition worsens, the discrepancy grows between what he is told and what he feels, and the suspected truth comes back like a demon to torment him. The worse he becomes, the more intolerable the fictions he is told. In being denied the truth about himself, *he* is being denied as a man. He is, in effect, dishonored and abandoned. He has no one he can trust. And so he is likely to become embittered, self-pitying and complaining, requiring more frequent and stronger medication to control pain and induce sleep. Eventually, he may even have to be stupefied with drugs in order to be manageable at all.

I see this kind of dying every day in the hospital, and I know that many more people than are permitted to do so could die in peace instead of misery, if those who attended them were less anxious about death themselves, and could see their experience with the patient as an opportunity to share the truth, rather than a battle of wits to avoid it.

Whatever is done, at the moment when the truth, whether acknowledged or denied, suddenly becomes apparent, the dominant concern of the person in attendance must be for the patient's integrity and peace of mind. If denial of imminent death is, in fact, the only way the patient can handle the truth, then that may be the proper course. Truth sometimes can destroy, and in such cases it may have to be withheld.

Wherever the Scriptures speak of truth-telling, it is usually within the context of neighborly or loving concern. Truth is not merely fact, but fact of a particular moral quality. St. Paul's words are typical: "Speak the truth in love" (EPHESIANS 4:15). Many other instances could be given, where truth is coupled with qualities such as "kindness" (II SAMUEL 2:6), "mercy" (II SAMUEL 15:20; PSALMS 25:10; 57:3; 61:7; 85:10; 86:15; 89:14; 98:3; PROVERBS 3:3; 14:22; 16:6; 20:28; HOSEA 4:1), "peace" (II KINGS 20:19; ISAIAH 39:8; ESTHER 9:30; JEREMIAH 33:6; ZECHARIAH 8:16, 19), "faithfulness" (ISAIAH 25:1), "grace" (JOHN 1:14, 17).

In a relationship characterized by such deep concern, the question whether or not to tell the patient is answered not by any abstract principle but by the immediate realities of thought and feeling, as the patient and the person attending him deal together with the moment of truth.

Chapter 2

PAIN RELIEF, ADDICTION, AND THE DYING PATIENT

THOMAS A. GONDA

Pain is a phenomenon that is often related closely to death. The following brief account particularly concerns pain that is associated with death which is a result of subacute or chronic conditions rather than the short-lasting, albeit frequently severe, pain that is often related to more sudden death from acute illness or accident.

In attempting to understand management of a dying person's pain, it appears useful to distinguish between pain at (1) a personal level and (2) at an interpersonal level with full recognition that these divisions are interrelated. At a *personal level* pain is (a) a feeling (a subjective and highly individual experience of which the individual is aware), (b) an alerting signal of some sort, (c) closely related to a body part and (d) quantifiable by the individual. Once pain is communicated to someone the above definition is no longer applicable. Pain at the *interpersonal level* must now be considered within the context of an interaction of persons. Fundamentally, what can be observed now is the expression of pain; that is, pain behavior as contrasted with pain feeling. Pain behavior is a communication from one person to another. Most commonly the transmitted message has as a major component a plea for assistance. That is, pain behavior usually says, "I've got a signal that tells me something is wrong—now I'm telling you—help me!"

Most illnesses and accidents that result in death do involve destruction of tissue and concomitant irritation of the nerves that supply such tissue. This is usually the case whether the destruction is on the basis of an invading growth, a degenerative disease, a loss of blood supply or simply a direct injury. It is to be expected then, that in most instances of other than very sudden death, the dying person experiences pain at the personal level. Depending on many factors, including his background as well as current situation, an individual will deal with the pain feeling in a more or less predictable fashion.

All of us have seen pain behavior that we would characterize as "stoic" or as "exaggerated" or as "sympathy seeking" or as "masochistic." Pain behavior (the interpersonal communication) in terminal conditions is much colored by the individual's feelings concerning his impending death. Feelings of anxiety, for example, may greatly intensify pain feeling as well as tend to exaggerate pain complaint. On the other hand, the expression of pain may be the disguise or camouflage for feelings of depression occasioned by the real or threatened losses of function now, and of death not too remotely.

In our culture we tend to shy away from discussion with the dying about the sources of his anxiety and depression; even, in fact, frequently we avoid direct recognition of the anxiety and depression itself. Instead, the focus of interpersonal interaction is on the dying's complaints of pain. Through this route the expression of pain, more or less successfully, however indirectly, is a mask for the expression of, among other feelings, those of discomfort regarding helplessness and dependence and hopelessness as well as fear and avoidance of the dehumanizing effect of terminal illness, separation and abandonment.

In our culture the patient is quite dependent upon the physician to whom he has gone to seek help with his illness. Since pain is very frequently associated with terminal illness, it is not surprising then that in the patient's attempts to deal with the problem of death (whether or not he has been explicitly told that his condition is terminal) he will place much reliance upon his physician to directly "do something" to alleviate his "pain." However, in their communications with patients, physicians most often circumvent, or in other ways, avoid talking about dying. Instead, the physician's focus turns to the patient's complaint of pain in a literal way. This expression of pain, however, we know may well be a disguise of feelings of depression or anxiety concerning impending death. Even the physician who intellectually recognizes that the patient's complaint of pain may well be a camouflage for depression or anxiety, because of his training and background as well as unresolved feelings about death, would many times prefer to treat the pain complaint solely as he would treat what is commonly called "somatic pain." Pressures to do this come not only from within himself but also from the patient, and very frequently from the patient's family to whom the patient also expresses his feelings of pain rather than his other feelings as, for example, those of depression and anxiety.

Thus the physician frequently treats the dying patient solely with medications that are aimed at alleviating "somatic pain." The patient does indeed find that these analgesics (usually narcotics) are helpful by their pharmacological effects, at least for a time, in the alleviation of some of his distresses. From time to time this small degree of comfort brought about by the drug action is sufficient to help the patient reconstitute himself sufficiently to work at least partially through his feelings of depression and anxiety. On the other hand, as death comes closer and along with it the degree of debility and dependence and helplessness becomes greater, the patient may well, and frequently does, become increasingly demanding. Pain complaints intensify. The tendency of the physician is to further increase the dosages of medication and before long the patient shows both psychological and physiological dependence upon the drugs. He is addicted. It must be borne in mind that such a way of dealing with the patient's terminal illness might be quite reasonable and quite logical; and depending upon the personality of the individual and the nature of the illness which is leading to his death, such management is preferable to some others. After all, there is nothing inherently wrong with addiction in the course of management of the dying patient. In many instances, in fact, such management allows the patient to carry on reasonably—as well as to die in relative comfort.

In summary, then, while the complaint of pain is an important signal that something is wrong, it also often masks as well as substitutes for other uncomfortable feelings such as depression and anxiety. Frequently, the management of pain in terminal illnesses through the use of narcotic drugs may be preferable to other modes of dealing with the patient's pain complaints even though addiction may result.

Chapter 3

THE RIGHT TO DIE IN DIGNITY

FREDERIC P. HERTER

(n)y work is surgery, particularly in relation to cancer—I have, therefore, seen much death and witnessed much grief, and my own life has had its normal share of the latter.

PREPARATION FOR DEATH

It is not unnatural that many wish death to come quickly, without warning or deliberation. The specter of long lingering death so often associated with chronic diseases, and the fear of protracted suffering (that so often occurs with cancer), is universal. No one would choose to become an emotional or financial burden on his family. Moreover, most people are reluctant to face the reality of death; by choice, they live as though death did not exist, and they take any and all measures to avoid the self-examination inherent in the acceptance of certain death. Thus it is not unusual to hear people proclaim envy of those who die suddenly and without anticipation or suffering, as by accident, or a coronary thrombosis, or stroke.

More often than not, however, death follows a variable period of illness; for most there is an obligatory prelude to death, a period often consumed with physical suffering or mental anguish and, with few exceptions, marked by a tenacious clinging to life.

It is my experience that death seldom comes peacefully, without resistance in one form or another. The classical picture of the family patriarch on his death bed, surrounded by family and friends, issuing his final profundities before closing his eyes for the last time, occurs rarely. More often, death is "eased" into by slow and painful steps; the ill are occupied by symptoms or by

14

the rigors of treatment and have little or no opportunity for quiet contemplation. Preoccupation with physical comfort precludes serious examination of the meanings of death or of a life spent. Physicians are frequently responsible for this frenetic and fearful form of ending; bound by a misapplied duty as healers, they resist death often more vigorously than does the patient. Too seldom do they allow their charge the dignity of dying uncluttered by lies or half-truths or the paraphernalia of keeping life's flame flickering for a few moments more. Too seldom do they give the patient the credit of being able to accept the finality of his condition. This blame must be shared with the families of the dying, however. Almost invariably they exhort the responsible doctor to play games with the patient, to withhold the truth, to offer hope where hope does not exist—to do everything, in fact, to keep the patient ignorant of the realities. Although there is occasional justification for such an attitude in terms of patient response, and although this vicarious expression of fear is natural to almost everyone, the consequence is that the physician is effectively barred from entering into any meaningful relationship with the patient and the family itself is deprived of a basic and honest unity at a time of crisis.

I am impressed by the ability of most people to accept the truth, and, wherever possible, I believe it is the duty of the physician to be candid with the patient and family alike. Needless to say, there are rare instances in which the truth is brutal and should be withheld; nor should candor ever be absolute. A stated prognosis should be realistic without conferring complete hopelessness—this can be accomplished without dishonesty on the part of the physician, for in his experience, he has certainly seen extraordinary, if not miraculous, things happen in seemingly hopeless situations. The truth should never be thrust on anyone in arbitrary fashion.

There are those who for reasons of their own would rather not ask questions or receive explicit answers. Although perfectly aware of the truth themselves, they may feel that silence confers some mystical protection, and consequently are reluctant to come to verbal grips with reality. Others prefer to distort the truth to their own advantage, no matter how graphically the information is presented. If such patients prefer this form of ambiguity (i.e., referring to acknowledged bone metastases from breast cancer as arthritis), they should be permitted it. The physician should never violate these not uncommon patient reactions.

Wherever and whenever possible, however, and particularly when directly asked by the patient, a physician should be honest in his answers. This applies not only in relation to hopeless forms of cancer, but to all conditions in which the prognosis is grave. The truth, surprisingly enough, comes as a form of relief to many. Instead of living in a world of anxious and guarded uncertainty, they suddenly find themselves face to face with the enemy —the battle lines are drawn, and they are given the opportunity to bring into play reserves of courage and understanding which perhaps even they were unaware of. Recently, I operated on a twenty-year-old girl with a particularly vicious form of cancer. Her father, a physician, insisted not unnaturally that she know nothing of the nature of her disease; moreover, he asked that his wife be left ignorant of the diagnosis as well. I accepted his conditions under protest, and a complicated play-acting sequence ensued. An extensive operation was performed, and both the patient and her mother were ostensibly satisfied that a benign process was being treated. Two weeks after discharge, the girl returned to the office for a dressing. During a short interval in which I was called out of the room, the patient's chart was left unguarded; she quickly scanned it, learned her true diagnosis, and confronted me with her knowledge on my return. I readily confessed to the subterfuge and explained that her father had been trying to spare her and her mother the anguish which the truth might bring. Her reaction was interesting. Not only did she express relief at knowing the truth, which she had suspected all along, but *she* then wanted to spare her mother the truth, and her father the fact of her knowledge! On advice, however, she did tell her father and subsequently her mother, with gratifying results. The family was once again unified, the burden was shared, and my position as physician was consequently greatly simplified.

Although this story may be somewhat peripheral to the theme, it does reiterate the point that most individuals are better equipped to bear the truth, no matter how devastating, than we give them credit for, and that avoidance of candor can often lead to disastrous disruptions in important relationships. To those facing imminent death, this form of honesty is of even greater significance.

A period of preparation for death is clearly more a necessity for some than for others. The head of a family and its sole supporter must make provisions for the continued security of his dependents: wills must be made, legal advice sought, insurance policies brought up to date, personal property allocated, orderly business successions established, and guardians for the children named. In a thousand ways, the practical aspects of responsibility must be tidied up. It is extraordinary how few middle-aged men entering the period where coronary heart disease is common, have made suitable provisions of this sort; too often are estates disposed of under state law, after long and involved litigation, because of elementary practical omissions.

To others, a spiritual preparation for death is of far greater importance. Knowledge or premonition of impending death may give an opportunity for long deferred self-examination, and for bringing into focus a meaning to life and death. A reconciliation of conflicts in one's faith may be accomplished with or without the aid and comfort of the clergy. An attempt may be made to mend personal fences. Tenuous relationships may be cemented. Bonds between husband and wife, between parent and child, assume a poignancy and an importance never before fully realized. Each day may become, rather than an accepted passage of time, something precious and meaningful.

It is said that people die as they live. There is much truth in this. Those who have found a meaning to life are unafraid at its end; a person totally at peace with himself is fearful of nothing. For those to whom "success" in life has been measured by material standards alone (and there are many in this category), death is approached with anguish and bitterness. One may predict then, to a large degree, an individual's manner of dying against the background of the essential character of his life.

This is not necessarily a factor of conventional religious faith or affiliation. The agnostic or atheist may accept death with a tranquility equal to that of the true believer. And yet in general terms it is true that a person whose life has been spiritually oriented has less difficulty facing the reality of death. I have envy of the devout Catholic to whom death is but a transition from one life to another, and of the Orthodox Jew for whom death is an active and meaningful event, and, in fact, of all those who believe in a life beyond or are truly aware of the all-embracing "love" of God. To these faithful, death may come with regret, but also with quiet and equanimity.

Preparation, both of practical and emotional nature, is also of importance to the families of those dying.

Vicarious involvement with death may be as difficult to bear as death itself; it is also very much more complicated. Not only is the physical aspect of impending death a frightening, unpleasant and unaccustomed pain, often making the attentions at the bed-side a tortured task, but the imminent loss of a loved one brings into play a host of emotions, occasionally conflicting ones. Loss of security, loneliness, guilt in its many forms, are all intermixed in various proportions with the transmitted fear of death itself. There is also a frenetic urge to compensate for past inadequacies in a relationship. This takes the form of overattention, of a wild and senseless seeking for different or more sophisticated medical attention. "Tribal" forces are brought into play in an attempt to share responsibility for the vigil; the clan gathers, overwhelming in number and awesome in inference to the dying person. The sense of "being needed" may assume an importance out of pro-portion to the content of a past relationship. All these factors make the counsel of the physician, of the minister, of the unre-lated friend, a needed and comforting thing to the family of the dying. The sharing of confidence and responsibility must be accomplished. As expressed before, candor must mark the rela-tionship between doctor and family. Not only should the nature of the disease be discussed at length, but, more importantly, the probable manner of dying. "How will he die?" is the often asked question, and more pertinently, "Will he suffer?" Clearly the doctor can allay fears, insofar as is possible, with respect to suffering. He can also make clear the fact that everything con-ceivable is being done from a medical point of view, and will freely offer the opportunity for consultation with another physician if there is only a trace of apprehension on the part of the family in this regard. He will attempt to dispel guilt about previous omissions or mistakes in judgment or management by the family. How frequently and how naturally is the query ventured: "Would things be different now if I had done something else?" A certitude that everything *had* been done properly and intelligently by the family, and *was* being done medically at the moment, must be repeatedly stressed.

Practical matters attendant on death should also be discussed frankly with the family. Most people are unfamiliar with procedural matters, and this ignorance is manifested by unnecessary anxiety. The need for certification of death by a physician should be explained. The manner of disposition of the body should be detailed, along with the role of the undertaker. Prior contact with a reputable undertaker should be encouraged, and appropriate clergy should be informed. The responsible physician can explain to the family the importance of autopsy examination, so that the request for permission for such an examination after death will not appear arbitrary or in poor taste. Even apparently trivial details, such as how to make public announcement of death through the newspapers, can be of aid in dispelling fear and panic.

Chapter 4

THE CHILD FACES HIS OWN DEATH

GILBERT KLIMAN

*L*ittle systematic attention has been given to the emotional problems of dying children and their families. The emotions aroused by the anticipation and occurrence of a premature death are so painful that scientific inquiry has been hampered. The professional tendency to avoid these problems is exemplified in the writings of one author[6] who has advocated that

> Life but not death is children's business. [Therefore] when a child who may conceivably die during hospitalization brings up the possibility of his own death, we reassure him with great conviction and help him deny the possibility. We would not reconcile a child with thoughts of his own death or feel the need to prepare him for it.

This approach, while humane in its intention, is in our opinion one which must be modified greatly with pediatric doses of truthfulness. There is some evidence that children and their families are generally able to deal better with the reality of fatal illness than with socially enforced avoidance of that reality.

As a background for this approach to the problems of the dying child and his family, it is helpful to focus upon what has been learned about adult attitudes toward children in regard to death. It seems clear to many investigators that adults who used to consider children innocent of sexual knowledge are now undergoing a change of attitude. But the theory once held of a child's innocence about sexual matters, is now being applied to knowledge about death. Gorer has commented incisively upon the increasing development of a social custom in England to avoid and deny death.[1] Such avoidance and denial are most strenuous when there is a death in a young child's family, even to the extent of lying to the child[2] about the death of a parent. Adults often

20

believe that small children are unaware of events taking place around them. Delays of twenty-four to ninety-six hours have been noted in telling children that a parent has died. The ill effects of this knowledge are compounded by the children's ability to understand that great turmoil is taking place for which no explanation is given. As a result they suffer in dire isolation, their anxiety unrelieved by any reliable structure of shared reality.

In defense of those who would shield children from painful realities, we should make it clear that children up to the age of ten cannot very well understand the concept of death. And the idea of the permanence of death may be as incomprehensible as the idea of infinity. A preschool child is likely to believe that death is reversible, or that it involves travel to another country or a long vacation. His understanding of the facts of death is just as fantasy-ridden as his understanding of the facts of sex. It is now generally considered an adult responsibility to help children cope with their childish sexual observations and questions. But this is not the case with childish observations and questions about death, especially when the child perceives the deterioration of his own body.

A bolder note of adult responsibility has been sounded, however. The National Cancer Institute has begun to report upon its experiences with dying children who have been fortified by facts about their condition. Vernick and Karon[7] have been studying 150 children, suffering for the most part from leukemia, and ranging in age from three to twenty years. According to their findings, even a three-year-old child "knows" he has a serious problem as soon as the physician gives the family the diagnosis of leukemia. The child keenly observes changed behavior among those whom he has previously trusted and who now seem to be keeping something from him.

The National Cancer Institute investigators have lately been adopting a regular procedure of informing child patients of their diagnosis and answering questions which then are liberated. It appears that without the adult initiative in offering comment and giving information, many children accept the emotional and intellectual isolation enforced upon them. Some children are able to report upon this condition after they have been liberated from it. A nine-year-old girl remarked, "I knew it was leukemia. I knew I had something serious, and leukemia is serious." An eleven-year-old commented, "I know there is no cure for leukemia. But at least I'm glad you told me what I have." A more poignant comment was made by a sixteen-year-old boy whose mother could not bring herself to talk to him about his leukemia until a half-day before his death: "Mother, I knew I had it all along." The boy and his family had lost six months of what could have been a positive, meaningful sharing of their mutual burdens. He had carried it alone, out of touch with the sympathetic struggles of his parents.

A rare opportunity was provided the author to help a leukemic boy, who was participating in a psychoanalytic project at the Center for Preventive Psychiatry. At the center, a new technique is being used to help children who suffer from various emotional stresses. A small digression is needed at this point in order to orient the reader to what follows. In order to multiply the effective time of a child analyst, a nursery and kindergarten program has been so arranged that the analyst can be in the classroom with a group of his patients. During the past few years, two analysts have used this method in working with children from three to six years old. Eighteen children have participated in the preschool classroom groups. The children meet for regular nursery or kindergarten classes, four days a week, in groups of up to seven. There are two teachers for each group, and one analyst. The analyst comes into the classroom for ninety minutes, four times a week. During that time, the children talk and play with him intermittently. They act in much the same way that other children act with an analyst, communicating in spontaneous, appropriately childish ways, but with certain advantages. The analyst can talk to them not only about symptoms, dreams, history, or current events, but also about their interactions with the other children (often very revealing of problems with brothers and sisters at home) and about their interactions with the teachers (often very revealing of problems with their mothers). To date, the method has been highly encouraging. It appears to be fulfilling its goals of carrying out psychoanalytic treatment and multiplying the effectiveness of the scarce supply of analytic time for children.[3,4]

A leukemia child, whom we shall call Charles, was four years and seven months old when he was brought to the center for psychological help. His illness had been discovered not long after his fourth birthday. During his initial hospitalization, Charles underwent a number of painful and puzzling treatments and procedures, including blood transfusion, sternal marrow puncture, and various punctures of the arm veins. After leaving the hospital at the end of two weeks, he had to continue taking medicine daily. He emerged in a temporarily excellent state of health, with his blood picture returned to normal. But a sad change had occurred in his emotional health. This previously cheerful and reasonably well-adjusted child had had only one definite sign of emotional stress in the past—wetting his bed at night. This was not serious or even abnormal behavior for a boy of four. Yet now Charles was beginning to cling to his mother. For several weeks, he would not sleep without her. He wet himself in the daytime as well as at night. And he could not attend nursery school because of his inability to leave his mother. Furthermore, an ominous change in his personality began to appear. Charles had decided it was better to be a girl. Shortly after emerging from the hospital he began to imitate his mother's and sister's voice and style of walking. He began to insist on female roles in games and he would persistently dress up as a girl. The frequency and intensity of this behavior suggested that his mother's concern was correct. Charles was on his way to surrendering his masculine identity.

The psychoanalyst, in taking a history of Charles's life, quickly learned that another serious burden had preceded his leukemia. He had lost his father through marital discord, separation, and geographic move. Furthermore, his father was never as close to Charles emotionally as he was to Charles' sisters, who were older and who had established relationships with the father prior to the marital break. What was particularly clear was that the marital discord and the weakness of tie to the male parent had disposed Charles to an emotional collapse. Yet the emotional collapse had not occurred until after the leukemia was diagnosed.

As part of the history it was also learned that there had been no specific communication with Charles concerning the value of the numerous painful procedures he experienced in the hospital. He was ignorant of the adult views of the seriousness of his illness, and although he was a very bright boy, he had no information about leukemia or the medical program on which he was embarked. There was a special barrier between the child and the other members of his family. Charles had already been lost to his family; they were no longer in touch with him about these vital issues. His desperate clinging to his mother and his inability to separate from her may be understood partly as an effort to compensate for his feeling of isolation from others, and to compensate for the empty, lonely aspects of coping with his inner and outer perceptions of drastic, perplexing, and unspeakable bodily and environmental changes.

A number of psychoanalytic and guidance procedures were followed in helping Charles and his mother. (They are described in detail in *Psychological Emergencies of Childhood.*[5]) Those which will be of special interest to parents are touched upon here.

The analyst found Charles to be an exceptionally intelligent youngster. He was eager to talk, play and paint. And he had a good capacity to participate in psychoanalytic treatment. But some of the measures used, and indeed those which were the most important, might have been performed by a parent rather than by an analyst. In particular, it was necessary to inform Charles that the analyst did not accept his bright, falsely cheerful view of his first hospitalization. When Charles spoke of having "a wonderful time," the notion was gently challenged. Deep interpretation was not necessary on this issue. What happened may be understood as making Charles aware that here was an adult who could talk realistically to him; therefore, Charles did not have to shield that adult.

Charles gradually discussed his worries—and his ideas about what was happening to his body. Ideas about needing extra parts for his body were quickly communicated to the analyst, understood as the sort of need a child has when he believes his body is in serious trouble.

Charles' mother began to realize that her son was capable of benefiting from greater communication of realistic facts. Although she had shielded him from the knowledge of a pet's death, she reconsidered this maneuver. After a week she told him the truth. The analyst was deeply impressed that once Charles' mother was able to show him she could talk to him about death, he felt free to share his own fear with her. Until then he had been silent with her on that subject, which we can infer was partly because he felt she was neither available nor willing to enter into discussions about death.

Within five minutes of being informed of his pet's death, Charles came into the nursery classroom, where he met the analyst. As his mother stood in the doorway, gripped by Charles' glance and his obvious desire to include her in the conversation, Charles began to talk to the analyst about his pet's death. But he did not stop there.

As his mother listened, Charles said with calm sadness, "You know, Spot was sick and he died." Then he added, "You know, I'm sick and I'm going to die."

Neither his mother nor the analyst had told Charles of his possible death. But he anticipated it. He could not tell us, however, until he had tested out the ability of his mother to hear painful truths. Until then he had to suffer alone, as if to spare his mother agony.

Once the relationship with his mother had improved to a point where both could speak truthfully, a great deal more could be done for Charles. It was now possible to give him some transfusions of adult strength and support by means of answering his questions and learning his childish theories about his illness and about death. It was possible to give him hope with simple medical facts explained in ways appropriate to his intellectual and developmental status.

The analyst and teachers found themselves trying to deny, repress, and avoid certain aspects of Charles' illness, and thus learned to respect the difficulties of Charles' mother. There was a mutual process of emotional growth, and, with it, Charles overcame each of the neurotic symptoms with which he had entered the psychoanalytic project. He became free of his effeminate voice and gait, his transvestist play, bed-wetting, and clinging to his mother. He was able to attend school regularly without separation panics.

Most of the improvement and work described took place within a two-month period. It gives hope for other children and other families that much may be accomplished with simple measures. These measures are principally to help the patient's family share with the child their own emotional resources in dealing with realistic dangers. In addition, the doctor must offer himself as an object with whom the patient can share his fears frankly, and discuss realistically the dangers to his life and the fantasies related to those dangers.

A child often has an emotional and psychological maturity far beyond that expected from one of his years which enables him to face death—even his own—with acceptance and serenity.

It should be pointed out that a child is most perceptive of what is happening in his environment, and often knows long before he is told (or even if he is not told) of an impending death in the family, including his own. If *he* is ill, he is likely to sense that his illness is incurable; but the need to shield those close to him often prevents him from revealing his knowledge, and he carries his burden alone.

In those instances in which one sibling is dying, if parents are made aware of this situation and discuss such an event freely and frankly with their children in terms that the children can understand, it will draw the family closer together and give them greater strength with which to face their bereavement. It will also avert future emotional difficulties for the surviving children by providing an atmosphere of trust and love which will make it possible for them to meet and solve the problems of later life.

Finally, and most important in the context of this book, when a child is dying, a positive awareness by the family of the equanimity and courage which dying children can and do bring to facing their own death should lighten meaningfully the burden of grief which they carry when the event comes to pass.

REFERENCES

1. GORER, G.: *Death, Grief and Mourning* (A Study in Contemporary Society). New York, Doubleday, 1965.
2. KLIMAN, A.: Eighteen Untreated Orphans. In *Psychological Emergencies of Childhood*. New York, Grune, 1968.
3. KLIMAN, G.: *Progress Report on The Cornerstone Project.* Foundation for Research in Preventive Psychiatry, Port Chester, New York, 1967.
4. KLIMAN, G.: *Bulletin of The Foundation for Research in Preventive Psychiatry,* Port Chester, New York. 1967.
5. KLIMAN, G.: *Psychological Emergencies of Childhood,* New York, Grune, 1968.
6. PLANK, E.: Death on a Children's Ward. *Medical Times,* pp. 638–644. 1964.
7. VERNICK, J., and KARON, M.: Who's Afraid of Death on a Leukemia Ward? *Amer J Dis Child, 109:*393–397, 1965.

Chapter 5

DEATH AND BEREAVEMENT IN LATER LIFE

ROBERT KASTENBAUM

A death. We mourn. Why? Is it always for the same reason? Here we encounter the death of a youth. We grieve for the kind of person he was. But we grieve also for the loss of what he might have become. We mourn for the blotting-out of an expected future.

Here we encounter the death of a person who was in the prime of his adult life. Again we mourn for what he was and what he might yet have become. This time, however, there might well be a different quality to our sense of bereavement. We grieve for the premature termination of a promising existence.

And now we encounter the death of an elder. Whom do we mourn? Do we grieve for the person he might have become had his life not terminated at this point? Do we sorrow over the loss of the person as he was in his later years? Or are we moved only by memories of what he once had been? Yet again—could it be that we do not actually feel grief? Perhaps it is another sort of sentiment that rises within us.

Our relationship to death and bereavement is neither simple nor static. At any moment in time, our orientation toward nonbeing is a complex of thoughts, feelings, and behavior that almost defies description, let alone explanation. Furthermore, this orientation shifts from situation to situation. The prospect of death has a rather different character when we are musing philosophically before the fireplace as compared with bumping through stormy skies thirty thousand feet above the ground. The sense of bereavement is not identical when we learn of the death of a friend as compared with that of a stranger.

28

The manner of death, the age of the deceased, and our own previous experiences with bereavement are among the many factors which influence our response. And as we ourselves grow up and grow older, we are likely to place different interpretations upon intimations of mortality either in ourselves or in others. Death may be an ultimate and universal fact, but our psychological relationship to this fact undergoes a complex developmental process as we ourselves develop throughout our life span.

It is not reasonable to expect that the orientation toward death and bereavement will be constant for all people who are at a given chronological age. Life experiences particularize us. Psychoanalytic contributions have made it clear that lifelong patterns of thought and feeling are influenced strongly by our situation in early childhood. More recently, a renewed appreciation has been evidenced for the ways in which life experiences can alter our behavior even when we are well along in our adult years.[4] It is also fairly obvious that orientation toward nonbeing cannot be separated easily from our ethnic and socioeconomic backgrounds.[10]

To insist that generalizations are precarious is not to conclude that we have nothing to learn by focusing upon death and bereavement in the later years of life. We simply must continue to recognize that every elderly person is a unique being, not an anonymous deduction from some abstract, quasi-scientific proposition.

Let us explore death and bereavement in later life from two vantage points: the elderly person as viewed by others, and the elderly person as viewed by himself. Some of the statements which follow derive from well-documented research, other statements from clinical experiences and pilot studies, and still other statements from personal observations and opinions that do not claim scientific verification. We will attempt to keep these statements sorted out.

FROM THE OUTSIDE

Value of Life

What does the death of an elderly person mean to us? This question is best approached by considering what his *life* means to us. There is an abundance of evidence to indicate that elderly people, in general, are regarded as less valuable than the young. This devaluation is widespread. Specialists do not care to treat the elderly. Sudnow[49] reports that elderly people admitted to the emergency service of a county hospital often receive delayed and perfunctory treatment. Even the ambulance driver seems to have made up his mind as to the level of medical care that should be offered. Personnel whose full-time responsibility is the care of elderly in-patients report themselves to be much less willing to invest time and energy in the treatment of the elderly* as compared with the young and middle-aged.[26] This orientation is even more pronounced in the personnel who serve all age groups.[31] Psychotherapists tend to avoid clients who are of advanced years just as they do clients who have a limited life-span no matter what their age.[38] Privately, several dentists have confided to me that many of their colleagues are derelict in their services to the elderly. The same story can probably be repeated for most if not all of the helping professions.

Other studies have shown a prevailingly negative attitude toward the elderly on the part of young and middle-aged people from a variety of backgrounds.[8,32,36,50] There is an occasional bright spot. Children seem to have some affection and understanding in addition to occasional dislike for the elderly,[19] and young adults, if their elders meet certain conditions, seem willing to accept them.[13,32]

If the lives of elderly people are held to be relatively less important or precious than the lives of the young, then we might expect their deaths also to have less impact. This is precisely the point that has been made by Dr. Barney G. Glaser, a research sociologist.[18] After studying the management of the terminal patient in several hospitals, Glaser reports that the death of an elder usually involves less "social loss" than the death of a young or middle-aged person.

At this point, then, our conclusion is that the death of an

---

* The author's personal experience at the all-geriatric hospital where this study was conducted suggests that the staff members (mostly nursing personnel) devote much more effort and sympathy in caring for aged patients than their own self-reported attitudes would suggest.

elderly person is likely to be perceived by society as a relatively small loss because it terminates a life that had come to be regarded as reduced in value.

Social Death

Is it stretching the point too far to suggest that elderly people often are treated as half-dead while they are still physically alive? The concept of "social death" has been described more than once.[23,30] Reference is made to our tendency to sever our relationships with some people so completely that they are "as good as dead" to us. A person may become socially dead to his family or peers if he violates a crucial tenet in their code of honor (e.g., marries outside his group, commits a particular kind of crime, contracts a certain disease, etc.). We no longer honor his existence. We do not speak of him or make him welcome in our home.

There are degrees of social death. Imagine that you are standing by the bedside of a person whose medical condition is known to be very poor. He appears unresponsive, comatose. It is tempting, is it not, to behave as though he were not really there *as a person*. You might find yourself getting involved in a conversation about his condition without speaking directly to him. He is a mere shell. This perception may also be accompanied by a mechanistic approach to his physical care. He is adjusted and tended the way one services a disabled machine. The assumption is that there is no phenomenological life within. Therefore, it is appropriate to regard and treat him as a non-person, *i.e.*, socially dead. It is a sobering thought that even in such an extreme instance we can be mistaken.[30] The object we are treating as socially dead may be a sensitive human being who hears and understands all that is said and done in his presence.

The elderly person who is critically ill may be regarded as socially dead in the extreme sense we have described. But even when he is in good health, he is likely to experience subtle forms of this treatment. The elder who does not have spending money is socially dead to the merchant—of what use is he? Fortunately, perhaps, the same elder retains some vestige of social import if the local or Federal Government sees fit to spend money on him. Consuming is a social function. The more that an elder spends or has spent on him, the more "alive" he remains in the economic sphere of the community. In so-called primitive societies, elders often enjoyed certain privileges and powers.[47,48] The old woman whose position gives her a decisive voice in family arrangements remains very much alive. The same may be said of the old man who controls the land or wields the tribal mysteries. But in our own nation, in our own times, these powers and privileges have become eroded. We have been under less and less compulsion to make arrangements with powerful elders. And so it is that elders have started to slip among us as disenfranchised spirits.

You may continue to hold your elders dear to you. This is because you are a kind and loving person, or because your elders are especially attractive or admirable people. Again, it may be that you learned respect for your elders when at an impressionable age and have not been able to throw them over even when the opportunity presents itself. It is possible that fewer people in the coming generations will go through the motions of honoring their elders because of strong guilt-socialization. Every elder may have to fight for his social existence on his own merits ("Yes, Dad: But what have you done for me lately?"). The shock waves of one series of technological and social changes following hard upon another tend to widen the psychological gap between generations. The current advice, "Don't trust any one over thirty" suggests that we are in some danger of becoming socially dead to each other even when the actual difference in age is relatively small.

Orientation Toward Dying and Death

How do elderly people orient themselves toward the prospects of dying and death? It is likely that our response to the impending or actual death of an elder will be influenced by our own notions of what he thinks about death. Immediately, the problems begin to close in around us.

1. Social commentators keep telling us that we are reluctant to communicate with each other on the topic of death.[15,37] If these observations are correct, then we would have to conclude that most of us know very little of what other people think and feel about death.

2. It has already been suggested that we tend to devalue the lives of the elderly and to regard them as though they were half-dead. If these propositions have some truth to them, then we would not expect much in the way of dialogue between the young and the old in general. And if young and old are not exchanging confidences on a variety of topics, then it is probably also true that communications on the topic of death are especially meager. A recent study by Kalish tends to bear out this latter point.[22]

3. The scientific literature on what young people think that elderly people think about death is slim. Not much help is to be found here.

We begin, then, with the impression that most of us have little basis for understanding how the elderly person orients himself toward dying and death. Reinforcing this impression is the fact that relatively few of us are privy to the thoughts and feelings of elders as they proceed through the preterminal and terminal phases of life. The medical and paramedical caretakers who are most frequently on the scene seldom enlighten us with their observations (perhaps because we seldom ask them). Furthermore, we have no criteria for judging how we will feel when we ourselves are old and thinking of death. This perspective is unavailable to us. We have difficulty enough in attempting to reconstruct how we interpreted death when we were children— or even in clarifying our ideas and feelings right at the present moment.

Yet younger people do have opinions regarding the death-orientations of the elderly. Three opinions have most frequently come to my attention; I have no evidence for determining which of these opinions is the most prevalent one in the general population. Let us consider these opinions briefly.

1. *Most elderly people are quite fearful of death.* This opinion seems to be based upon various combinations of the following

factors: (a) It has been shown that young people tend to avoid the topic of personal death and to express strong fears when it is brought squarely to their attention.[2,9] Therefore, it is natural for young people to assume that elders also fear death. (b) It is also natural to assume that elders will be even more fearful of death because of their relatively limited life-expectancy. (c) It has been suggested that one of the reasons that young people sometimes shun the elderly is that the latter remind us of death.[16,24] If it makes us uncomfortable to be in the presence of a person whose appointment with death is presumed to be closer than ours, then it is easy to attribute our discomfort to the elder as well. He makes us uncomfortable by reminding us of death: it must follow that he himself is fearful.

2. *Most elderly people are ready for death.* This opinion seems to be based upon (a) the observation that many elders have slowed down their pace of life and withdrawn into a smaller sphere of activity; this looks like a gradual movement from life to death; (b) the logic that elders should be ready for death because they have already put so many years behind them—they have had their lives; and (c) the sentiment that death would be less disturbing both to the elder and to society *if* it were welcome.

3. *Most elderly people are oblivious to their fate.* This opinion seems to be focused on the death-bed scene itself. It is reasoned that the combination of advanced age and major illness deprives the dying person of his orientation. He does not really appreciate what is happening to him. The person has already succumbed, although the body lingers for a while longer.

We will comment further upon these opinions after reviewing what is known about the elders' own orientation toward dying and death. It is worth keeping in mind that our various opinions about the meaning of death to elders have practical consequences. How often do we visit an elderly person who may be close to death? What do we say and do when we are with him? The answer to these questions probably depends to some extent upon our interpretation of his state of mind. Similarly, our relationship with a healthy elder is likely to be affected in one direction if we assume that he is preoccupied with negative feelings about death, and in another direction if we assume that he is ready for death.

HOW DO WE RESPOND TO THE DEATH OF AN ELDER?

Two answers to this question have already been implied:

1. We probably respond less to the death of an elderly person than to the death of a younger person.

2. There are great individual differences in our response.

It is plain to see that these answers are insufficient. Once again we must grope toward an understanding without much in the way of scientific knowledge to rely upon. You will appreciate that the impressions which follow here are simply my personal observations, which may or may not resonate with your own.

Let us first reconsider the statement (which does have some research support) to the effect that the death of an elder is a relatively small social loss. This observation usually is interpreted in the way we described earlier, namely, as one manifestation of the elder's reduced social value. But there is a simpler explanation. Many of the people who would deeply mourn the death of an elder have themselves preceded him to the grave. His community of peers is reduced. The unyielding statistics inform us that he is likely to have fewer surviving brothers, sisters, and age-peer friends. The elderly woman very often has outlived her husband, and the reverse situation also occurs. Furthermore—and forgive me for introducing so obvious a fact—the elder rarely is survived by his parents and others of the preceding generation. The situation is quite different in the death of a young person. The youth will be mourned by those younger than himself, those of his own age, and those who are one or more generations advanced in age.

We might say that the elder dies to a different society from the one in which he has lived most of his days. If his former social world were to miraculously return to the scene, then it is highly probable that we would witness widespread and heartfelt bereavement for the deceased elder. He meant something to his age-mates and elders that we younger people cannot quite appreciate. But we do not have to speak of miracles to appreciate this situation; it already exists to a lesser degree. There is a subtle bias that insinuates itself into the observations and interpretations made by even the most sophisticated social scientists. In particular, when we read that *society* experiences the death of an elder as a minor loss, it is appropriate to ask, *Who* is this society? I suspect that reference is being made to society minus the elderly. Studies of social loss generally have focused upon the reactions of younger members of the community. If equal attention were given to the reactions of the elderly, then there might be evidence for revising the basic proposition. We would now have to say: Elders are mourned by their age-mates in much the same way as a person of any age is mourned by those who were close to him.

It would still be true that society in general might feel less bereaved. But this difference could be regarded as quantitative rather than qualitative. It is not so much that a man's life and death are regarded as intrinsically of less significance because of his advanced years. It is simply that relatively few of us were in the position to know and appreciate him in his full worth and individuality. Is this a petty distinction? I think not. And if the difference in bereavement has to do mostly with the number of available mourners, then we should anticipate a steady increase in the social significance of an elder's death. This prediction is again based upon a simple consideration, namely, a longer life expectancy. The percentage of elders in our society has increased greatly within recent years and probably will remain high for some time to come. We will be having more company in our journey through the later ·ears of life. We will be able to share each other's joys and sorrows to an extent that was not possible when few of us reached advanced age.

The death of an elderly person may affect younger elements of society more than is appreciated at the time. I am thinking now of *what dies with an aged man or woman*. A way of life dies. Each generation of elders experienced and coped with life in a manner that will never be duplicated. Their special skills, their ways of viewing the world, their special memories—all these will disappear. Many people who are now in their later years of life, for example, were immigrants to this country. They did not have easy lives. What did they learn as they tried to bridge the psychological distance between the "old country" and the United States? What resources did they develop as they struggled to establish themselves financially and socially, as they performed hard work under conditions to which most of their children and grandchildren would never submit? The answers to questions such as these are slipping away from us with every death of an immigrant.

Today there seems to be a renewed appreciation for "Americana." Silent films are in demand, once-discarded objects have become "camp," private collectors and museums have begun to treasure relics of the recent past. Perhaps there is more than nostalgia at work. Perhaps we sense that it is important to our own sense of identity to remind ourselves where we came from, who were the people and what were the circumstances of yesterday. It would certainly be a step in the direction of greater maturity for a society to be able to look backward with curiosity and empathy, as well as to look ahead with hopes and plans.

Unfortunately, we do not seem to have realized as fully as we might that the elderly comprise our most valuable link with yesterday. But eventually we may learn to bestow our attention upon the living examples as well as the objects and records of the past. When we do so, we will have a keener sense of loss upon the death of an elder, and a keener sense of appreciation for him while he lives. Public interest in the elderly seems to be developing rather quickly after many years of neglect. It could well be, that in coming generations the younger people in society will be better prepared to appreciate their elders as representatives of an unique way of life as well as individuals. Faint indications that we are starting to appreciate what we soon will be missing can be heard already: "They don't make these things the way they used to." "I don't know how she kept house and raised a family without electricity and running water." "How did he manage to get so far without schooling?"

There is also a sense in which we may be *reassured* by the death of an elder. It does not seem polite to admit that the death of a human being who had done us no harm can soothe our spirits. Nevertheless, I have observed some responses to death that suggest this phenomenon does occur—although it tends to operate backstage rather than in the center of our consciousness.

We all recognize the obvious fact that death can occur at any age. Furthermore, we are aware that sudden death is an ever-present possibility. Yet I believe that many of us have an implicit death-schedule in mind. We are inclined to feel that some of the people we know will die before others. Great-grandfather's turn will come before great-grandson's. A relative who has been in poor health for years will die before another relative of the same age who has always enjoyed excellent health. We may compute probability judgments such as these without clearly recognizing that we have done so. The death of an elder and the death of a sick person surprise us less than the death of a young person and a healthy person because of these implicit computations.

A few more steps in psychological logic are required to see how the death of an elder can be reassuring to the survivors. In effect, some of us say to ourselves: "My turn to die will come one of these days. I would prefer to think that this event is still a long way off. How can I convince myself? Well, suppose that I credited death with being a rational, sensible agency. Death follows a certain logical plan, just as I attempt to apply logic to my own life. Sometimes death makes a mistake, coming too soon or too late. Basically, however, I can depend upon death to do the right thing."

Starting out with this line of reasoning we may then continue as follows: "Death, reasonable agency that it is, will not reach for me until it has worked its way through higher priorities on the list. Now, let me see . . . how many people do I know who are higher on the list? Well, there are seven people in my life who are either a good deal older or a good deal sicker than myself. This means that I am number eight. I have a certain amount of insulation: there are seven lives between death and myself."

This inner monologue leads each of us to develop our own "pecking order" of death. When the person with the highest death priority in our own pecking order does expire, then we experience a mixed reaction. We sorrow for his death according to the nature of our feelings toward him. But we also feel reassured. Death *is* behaving as it ought. We can depend upon death to ignore us for a while longer. By contrast, what happens when death reaches past the high priority entries? We are genuinely surprised, perhaps shocked, to learn that death has come to a person whose turn should have been remote. The death of a person who is as young and healthy as ourselves (or even younger) is likely to fill us with apprehension. The facade of rationality has been pierced, and we are brought up against the realization that our insulation from death is illusory.

If there is some truth in what I have been suggesting about the "pecking order of death," then we have another partial explanation for the relatively small social disruption that is occasioned by the death of an elder: we express fewer signs of bereavement because the death exerts something of a tranquilizing influence on our anxieties. We are protected in our (not quite conscious) belief that Death operates according to a rational plan.

Finally, we should consider, if briefly, the quality of the emotional response engendered in younger people by the death of an elder. Sometimes we do mourn the death of an elder in much the same way as we mourn the death of a younger person. And there are occasions when we mourn the death of an elder with the same kind of feeling, but with a lesser degree of intensity. Yet a question remains: Is there a more or less distinct *quality* to our sense of bereavement when its object is the death of an elder?

I would suggest that the death of an elder does arouse a special sentiment within us under the appropriate circumstances. By this I mean that (a) we knew the deceased fairly well, (b) we admired and respected him, and (c) he continued to live in a way that we admired and respected until his personality dissolved with the dissolution of his body. In other words, he taught us something not only by his life but also by the way he met death. Under these circumstances, our sentiment is not given over exclusively to the sense of loss. Nor do we find it meaningful to mourn deeply for the future experiences that are now denied him. Instead, we may sense that we have *gained* something. The nature of this enrichment, this parting gift, is difficult to describe or define. Perhaps the feeling has something in common with our experience in witnessing a beautiful sunset. If the day must end, then this is a lovely and appropriate way. And the ending also illuminates all that went before it. I think that we learn something valuable about what a life means when we have an intimate relationship to a death that terminates a long, eventful, and complete existence. Such an experience may, in fact, help us in our gradual, beneath-the-surface preparation for our own eventual encounter with death.

FROM THE INSIDE

But how does the elderly person himself view death and bereavement? This question will be examined in terms of what is known about the elder's attitude toward his own life, his orientation toward the prospect of his death, and his response to the death of others.

Value of Life

Rosenfelt has described a certain combination of thoughts and feelings that she terms *the elderly mystique.* Her research, personal experiences and review of the scientific literature led Rosenfelt to conclude that many elders regard themselves in a negative manner.[46]

> We know that many a person at some point late in life comes to consider himself old, and this implies he views himself as different in important respects from what he considered himself to have been earlier. According to the mystique, this point marks an unmitigated misfortune, which a series of lugubrious losses, deficits and declines has forced upon his attention. Despite his grim determination to "think young," destiny has had the last laugh and has forced him to the mat for the final countdown [p. 38]. Health and vigor, it is assumed, are gone forever. The senses have lost their acuity. The memory is kaput. Education and new learning are out of the question, as one expects to lose his mental faculties with age. Adventure

and creativity are for the young and courageous. They are ruled out for the old, who are, *ipso facto,* timid and lacking in moral stamina. As for the pleasures of sexual relationships—the very thought of the old person in such a context brings smiles. Some people are even prone to associate the sex life of the aged with senile delinquency.

While the old person is taking stock of himself, he might as well become resigned to being "behind the times," for it is inconceivable he should have kept abreast of them. As a worker, he has become a liability. His rigidity, his out-of-date training, his proneness to disabling illness, not to mention his irritability, lowered efficiency and arrogant manner, all militate against the likelihood of his being hired or promoted. Fussduddiness is his special quality [p. 39].

The list goes on, but the point has been made. In agreement with Rosenfelt, let us add some further points as follows:

1. The elderly mystique derives in large part from the older person's incorporation of youth-oriented values into his own self-image. He has come to believe the popular stereotypes about aging.

2. Yet these stereotypes are seldom on the mark. Scientific research and new action programs involving the elderly are subjecting many of the assumptions about aging to critical reappraisal. What seems to be happening, then, is that many elders are taking an unrealistically dim view of their own worth and potential.

3. Although many elders may be mistaken in the negative views they have accepted, these views may operate in such a manner as to confirm the worst expectations. Sociologists refer to this situation as a "self-fulfilling prophecy"—believe it, and that's the way it will turn out. As Rosenfelt puts it,[46]

acceptance of so limited and limiting a view ends by not only blinding its holders to the full range of possibilities available to them but also by so deforming them in conformity with its warped image that they have become as restricted as the mystique would have them. A vicious circle is set in motion [p. 41].

It is fairly clear that many elders do regard their lives as being less valuable now than when they were younger. There is also some evidence to suggest that those elders who maintain themselves in high spirits tend to deny that they are "old."[7,35] But the reasons why a particular individual of advanced years

classifies himself or declines to classify himself as "old" are somewhat complicated and not entirely understood at present.[32] We
should not lose sight of the fact that some elderly people accept
their years without hesitation and without any noticeable decline
in morale and happiness.[7,32]

If a general conclusion is possible on this subject, then it
probably can be said that both young and elderly members of
our society tend to regard the later years of life as less valuable
than the earlier years. There are probably more exceptions to this
generalization among the elders themselves; but there are also
many elders who take what seems to be an unnecessarily dim
view of their lives.

Orientation Toward Dying and Death

It was reported earlier that young people seem to ascribe
three different orientations toward the elderly: (1) Most elderly
people are quite fearful of death; (2) most elderly people are
ready for death; (3) most elderly people are oblivious to their
fate. Let us compare these opinions with what has been learned
about the ways in which elders actually do orient themselves
toward dying and death.

The available research findings suggest that elderly people
in general are *not* extremely fearful of death.[20,44] In fact, they
express fewer death fears than do most younger people.[9] Furthermore, those elderly people who express strong fears of death are
likely to be suffering from acute emotional or psychiatric disturbance.[11] This finding implies that extreme fear of death when it
does occur among the elderly is not a normal reaction. One is
reminded of an earlier investigation which found that death
fear is higher among those young and middle-aged adults who
are psychiatrically disturbed.[6]

Does fear of death increase as an elder's health deteriorates?
Our research suggests that there is no increase in the number
of elders who express death fears as they begin to enter the
preterminal phase of life.[29] On the contrary, some geriatric
patients who had characteristically expressed the premonition
that their death was at hand now made no reference to death

as the event became ever more visible on the horizon. Independent research with a different population of elders also has indicated that preoccupation with death does *not* increase as the prospect of death increases.[42]

But the book is not closed on this subject. A person may keep his fears to himself (or even *from* himself), or the fears may be expressed in such an indirect manner that we do not comprehend their meaning.[17] It is possible that as we become more sophisticated in our research strategies, more death fears will disclose themselves to us. Even today there are some psychiatrists who believe that *all* elderly people have a strong fear of death.[52] This proposition cannot be absolutely denied, but we must remember that the available evidence runs counter to such a claim. Granted that our knowledge concerning fear of death is far from adequate,[28,40] it appears justified to conclude that elders have *not* exhibited stronger or more frequent fears than younger adults.

The opinion that elders are quite fearful of death may involve a confusion between fear and attention. Grandmother is likely to speak about death more often than the younger people around her. She has more deaths to remember than we do. She may also be concerned that her funeral arrangements be made in a certain manner, and that the disposition of her belongings also be clearly understood in advance. We are apt to regard all these concerns as "morbid." Why does she have to go on that way about death? It probably isn't good for her, and it makes us feel uncomfortable.

My suggestion is that conversation about death need not be interpreted invariably as morbid or fearful. When a person is so preoccupied with death that he cannot attend to any other subject (especially if his own death does not seem to be in immediate prospect), then it is reasonable to speak of a morbid concern. Similarly, we can speak of "death fear" when a person's thought and behavior has been paralyzed or disorganized by the prospect of death. Grandmother might indeed become morbid or fearful if she felt herself to be unprepared for death. But her understandable interest in making arrangements serves to protect her from such disorganization or paralysis. She can continue to live her sort of life precisely because death has been recognized and "put in its place." Naturally, her orientation toward death can be developed with greater ease and security if those around her also face the topic with equanimity.

If elderly people are not often overwhelmed by fear of death, then we are left with two alternative views: that they are ready for death, or that they are oblivious to their fate. Let us begin with the latter alternative, for it is the simpler one. It is true that mental efficiency sometimes declines with advanced age. Some intellectual functions seem to decline more rapidly than others, and some individuals show more loss than others.[5,21] It also appears to be the case that certain types of mental functioning become impaired as the elder begins to enter his preterminal phase of life.[41] But these alterations do not necessarily cloud the elder's mind. He still knows very well what is happening to him. Even if his memory is not quite so trustworthy as it once had been, and even if he cannot solve new problems easily, he remains able to appreciate his own situation in the world. The most direct evidence for this statement comes from a recent study of aged patients who died in an all-geriatric hospital.[29,51] Despite the fact that the average age at death was eighty-two years, and despite the fact that many of the patients were receiving a variety of drugs, it was found that only two of the fifty-nine elders were consistently disoriented during their final phase of life. Almost all these patients, then, retained enough mental functioning to appreciate that death might be in close prospect.

This finding has an important practical implication. If it is likely that elderly people are aware of their condition even when critically ill, then it is incumbent upon us to be sensitive to their psychological comfort up to the very last moment. We cannot simply provide medical or custodial care. The person is still there. We should not take the risk of mistaking his feeble or passive condition for an absence of comprehension.

We have one more view to consider: that the elderly person is ready for death. This opinion does seem to coincide more closely with the facts than do either of the alternatives. But we must be cautious in accepting this view. The following considerations should be kept in mind:

1. As Cicero pointed out centuries ago,[12] having many years to look back upon does not guarantee that one is the slightest bit more ready to accept death. The crucial problem concerns the absence of *future* time, and this is the same problem whether one has had a long or a short past.

2. Most studies have indicated that elderly people face death in a number of different ways.[14,34,45] We cannot say that all elders are ready for death if we mean that there is one way and one way only to prepare. In our studies of elderly patients, for example, we found that two patterns of orienting oneself to death occurred with almost equal frequency.[33] Some patients accepted the prospect of death quite explicitly. These people tended to withdraw from social activities and eventually to refuse medical assistance. Other patients remained involved in daily life right up to the end. They also recognized that death might come at any moment. In a meaningful sense, these patients also were ready, but they demanded that death catch them in motion. Both of these styles of life involved an acceptance of death. Neither type of elder tried to deny the reality of death or to pro-long his struggle. But one patient would try "to put my house in order" and then wait calmly for the end, whereas another patient would "live until I die." Which style of death-orientation is more appropriate? I do not know.

3. Readiness to accept death may occur too soon. By this I mean that an elder may lose his will to live when, in fact, there is still reason to believe that he might have months or years of good living yet in prospect.[27,38] This over-readiness sometimes derives from a state of poor health or physical depletion which is reversible. The elder feels that he is beyond help. He may even resist efforts to restore his health, believing them to be useless. We have seen numerous instances in which an elder who was ready for death abruptly put this notion aside when good medical treatment restored his health. It would have been a mistake to regard his readiness for death as a permanent orien-tation. There are also occasions when an elder loses the desire to continue living. He may, for example, interpret his placement in a hospital or other institution as a sign of rejection by his family. Again, this is a state of mind that can sometimes be reversed.

4. Certain physical conditions make it difficult for a person to achieve a sense of psychological readiness for death. Emphysema is a striking example. How can one develop a serene orientation toward death when one is struggling to draw sufficient air into the lungs? There are circumstances, then, in which it is not reasonable to expect an elder or any other person to face death with equanimity. We should avoid increasing the sufferer's discomfort by blaming or embarrassing him because he is agitated at times.

5. Readiness for death often depends upon the satisfactory working through of psychological and social problems. It is difficult to develop an accepting orientation toward death while one is still wrestling with unsolved life problems. Often we can help the dying elder to resolve some of these problems (which might include old guilt feelings that have returned to haunt him, or an unfinished piece of business). His mind now at greater rest, he is more likely to come to terms with death in a comfortable manner.

In general, I am suggesting that most of us have the psychological resources to develop an appropriate orientation to the prospect of our own death, especially if this event is to occur in our advanced years. But individuals are likely to differ in the specific way they relate themselves to the prospect of death, just as they have differed in their style of life. Sometimes the readiness for death comes sooner than necessary; at other times, readiness is thwarted by unsolved problems that in themselves may have nothing to do with death. It is possible in many instances to intervene sensitively to help the dying individual achieve the orientation that is most appropriate for him at this particular time in his life.

Bereavement in Later Life

Many descriptions and explanations have been offered regarding bereavement at other age levels. Some of these observations are quite applicable to bereavement in later life. Lindemann, for example, has pointed out that an acute grief reaction may show itself in a concealed form, namely, in an increase in physical symptomatology.[43] Exhaustion and digestive disturbances are among the most frequent somatic outlets for grief. The bereaved reaction can also take the form of disturbed behavior. The individual behaves in a restless, somewhat inappropriate manner. He cannot stay at a task; he does not know what to do with himself. These and other general characteristics of bereavement are too well known to belabor here.

Let us concentrate upon aspects of bereavement which are found more often among elders. Perhaps the most obvious point is that the older person is likely to have experienced multiple losses. He has outlived many friends and relatives. Furthermore, many of his remaining intimates may also be in precarious health, so that he is in constant apprehension about their well-being.

Can a person experience multiple bereavements without showing some cumulative effect? It is highly doubtful. The elder is particularly vulnerable to the psychological effects of loss because he has fewer opportunities to find substitutes. One does not replace a life-long friend. The middle-aged son or daughter who dies cannot be replaced. Moreover, bereavement may follow so closely upon bereavement that the elder is never able to complete his "grief work." It is often estimated that normal mourning requires approximately a year to run its course. It is possible that even more time is required when one is an octogenarian who is mourning for the spouse whose life had been shared for thirty, forty, fifty or more years. But other deaths may intervene before the mourning is completed. The elder can reach a point at which he feels he no longer can respond fully to a new death; he is still so closely involved with the old deaths.

Furthermore, bereavement may follow as a result of other losses. The old house has been sold. The old neighborhood has been so transformed that it is unrecognizable. Prized possessions have disappeared. It is not uncommon for a person to grieve over this kind of loss. One's own body may become a source of grief rather than pleasure. Some elders experience a loss in motility. Others may suffer marked impairments in vision or hearing. A stroke may leave the victim with a serious impairment in speech or reading. It is understandable if some elders begin to mourn for the piecemeal loss of themselves.

Some elders also carry a special burden of bereavement. I am thinking of the person who represents the last survivor of his family line. This "death of a family" may be only symbolic, as in the case where there are surviving children or grandchildren, for example, whose names have been changed by marriage. But the termination of a family line may be actual, as in the case of the aged bachelor or spinster who represents the only remaining family member. Under such circumstances, the survivor might well feel a particularly heavy sense of loss. He cannot obtain solace from the prospect that his family line will continue after his own death. Instead, he may even trouble himself with recriminations or regrets that he did not manage to continue the line. Whatever the particular dynamics involved in a given individual, it is likely that "the last leaf" will experience some form of mourning for the deceased family tree as his own death approaches. We would not be surprised to find that ideas or dreams of reunion with loved ones occur frequently to such people. The hope of reunion would certainly soften the burden of being the last of the line. We are not acquainted with any systematic research into the thoughts and feelings of people who represent the last of their line; this could be a most informative topic for study.

Perhaps enough has been said to make it clear that bereavement experiences, in many forms, often make a strong impresssion upon the life of the elderly person. Unless he has unusually strong psychological resources or unusually strong and sensitive confidants, then he is likely to absorb more losses than he can accommodate. One might go so far as to suggest that *many of the negative behavior patterns we tend to associate with old age are the result of a bereavement overload.*

What changes would we expect in a person (of any age) who has been forced to contend with too many losses in too short a period of time? He might attempt to reconstitute his personal world by replacing the losses. This process often requires a great deal of time even under the best of circumstances. And if there were *no* appropriate replacements available (as in the death of a life-long friend), then his response would have to take another form. One might lose himself in work or other engrossing activities, at least until the burden has lightened. But this alternative often is closed to the elderly. What now? The person may simply take these emotional blows "on the chin." I am referring here to the process of developing bodily symptoms when grief cannot be handled adequately by the psychological structure. The person becomes increasingly preoccupied with bodily functions, often is in a state of discomfort, seldom has free energy to invest in new activities or relationships. Furthermore, the experience of multiple losses may lead to a sense of extreme caution. "I had better not care about anybody or anything else. Sooner or later I will lose these people and things as well. And I just cannot bear to lose and mourn again." With such a sentiment in effect, the overly bereaved person may pass up opportunities to become reinvolved with life.

The reaction to multiple bereavement can take even more extreme forms. Suicidal attempts are possible. It is well known that the suicide rate increases during the later years of life.[31] The person may also collaborate in bringing about his own death without committing a suicidal act *per se*. Neglect of health and nutrition and involvement in subintentional accidents are among the ways in which the bereaved person can increase his likelihood of death. He may give up when stricken by a relatively minor ailment and thus allow his condition to worsen. He may reduce his activities so drastically that both body and mind are in poor tone to respond to any kind of stress.

The reaction may also take the form of increased irritability or bitterness. If the individual cannot bear to keep the overload of negative thoughts and feelings within himself, then he may begin to attribute hostile impulses to others. He becomes paranoid, distrustful, unpleasant company.

All of the negative reactions that have been catalogued above are observed in those elderly people whom we usually consider to be suffering from the general effects of old age. But we now have an alternative explanation, namely, that the adverse changes exist in consequence of multiple bereavements, not because of some mysterious and immutable transformation that occurs as a direct consequence of aging. One line of support for this alternative explanation can be found in the similarity between the behavior of normal adults who have just experienced a massive loss through a natural disaster and the behavior of geriatric patients.[25] Another line of support is in the well-known fact that many elders do retain good morale and effective functioning. This would be unlikely if aging necessarily and intrinsically results in the psychobiological changes noted above. Finally, we call attention to the many studies which have demonstrated that bereavements at younger age levels can produce negative effects on mind and body at a later time.[1,3,31]

IN SUMMARY

It was recognized that no simple description or explanation is possible of death and bereavement in later life. Individual differences are numerous and our scientific knowledge is scant. Nevertheless, a few propositions were advanced. These propositions take into account the existing scientific knowledge, but contain much that has no basis other than the author's opinions and speculations.

Among the interpretations made were the following:

1. There is a strong tendency in our society to consider older people as less important than younger people.

2. This attitude sometimes influences the behavior of both young and old in such a manner that the feared, undesired state of affairs is brought into being. We may force elders into a reduced style of life and the elders themselves may behave as though they had no alternative.

3. It is sometimes assumed that most elders are either preoccupied with fear of death or are oblivious to their fate. These opinions are *not* well supported by the available evidence.

4. In a general sense, it is probably true that many elders are ready for death. But the specific nature of this readiness varies from person to person and also depends upon the total circumstances in which he finds himself.

5. Apart from the personal loss associated with the death of an elder, there may also be (a) a sense of reassurance to the survivors, based upon the implicit concept of a "pecking order" of death; (b) a sense that a way of life is perishing, as well as

an individual; and (c) a sense of enrichment when an admired elder ends his life in an admirable way.

6. Many elders suffer from a succession of bereavements. They are affected not only by the death of loved ones, but also by losses of many kinds. It is not uncommon to develop a *bereavement overload.*

7. When a bereavement overload exists, the elder is likely to show a variety of adverse changes in mind and body. These changes often are mistakenly attributed to "growing old." Such an error in interpretation may deter us from offering the assistance that could ameliorate or reverse the reactions.

One more word. Honest communication on the topic of death and bereavement is probably the most useful single prophylactic measure to avoid unnecessary suffering. It is obvious that by *honest* communication we are not referring to blunt and tactless behavior. It is also obvious that honest communication should not be postponed until the later years of life. What we tell our young children about death, the examples we set for them in our own behavior, how we relate to the elderly, the sick, and the dying throughout our entire life-span will be important determinants of the way in which we ourselves meet death and bereavement in later life.

ACKNOWLEDGMENT

Many of the observations which are included in this paper were made during the course of USPHS mental health research projects MHO-4818 and MHO-1520 at Cushing Hospital, Framingham, Mass.

REFERENCES

1. ALMY, T. P.: Experimental studies on the irritable colon. *Amer J Med,* 10:60–67, 1951.
2. ALEXANDER, I., and ADLERSTEIN, A. M.: Affective responses to the concept of death in a population of children and early adolescents. *J Genet Psychol,* 93:167–177, 1959.

3. BARRY, H.; BARRY, H. III, and LINDEMANN, E.: Dependency in adult patients following early maternal bereavement. *J Nerv Ment Dis, 140*:196–206, 1965.
4. BETTELHEIM, B.: *The Informed Heart.* Glencoe (Ill.), Free Press, 1963.
5. BOTWINICK, J.: *Cognitive Processes in Maturity and Old Age.* New York, Springer, 1967.
6. BROMBERG, W., and SCHILDER, P.: Death and dying. *Psychoanal Rev, 20*:133–185, 1933.
7. BUTLER, R. N., and PERLIN, S.: Psychiatric aspects of adaptation to the aging experience. In J. E. Birren, *et al.: Human Aging:* A *Biological and Behavioral Study.* Bethesda (Md.), USPHS, 1963, pp. 143–158.
8. CALHOUN, M., and GOTTESMAN, L. E.: Stereotypes of old age in two samples. Division of Gerontology, Univ. of Michigan, 1963 (mimeo).
9. CAUTELA, J. R., and KASTENBAUM, R.: Assessment procedures for behavior modification with the aged. Presented at 20th annual scientific meetings, The Gerontological Society, Nov. 1967 (St. Petersburg, Fla.).
10. CHORON, J.: *Death and Western Thought.* New York, Colliers, 1963.
11. CHRIST, A. E.: Attitudes toward death among a group of acute geriatric psychiatric patients. *J Geront, 16*:56–59, 1961.
12. CICERO: *On the Art of Growing Old.* Providence (R. I.), Brown UP, 1959, (tr. by H. N. Couch).
13. EISDORFER, C., and WILKIE, F.: Attitudes toward older persons: A semantic analysis. Presented at 20th annual scientific meetings, The Gerontological Society, Nov., 1967 (St. Petersburg, Fla.).
14. FEIFEL, H.: Older persons look at death. *Geriatrics, 11*:127–130, 1956.
15. FEIFEL, H.: *The Meaning of Death.* New York, McGraw-Hill, 1959.
16. FEIFEL, H.: Introductory remarks for death symposium. 72nd annual scientific meetings, American Psychological Assoc., Sept., 1964 (Los Angeles, Calif.).
17. FEIFEL, H.: Contributions to the symposium: Death as a research variable in social gerontology. Eighteenth annual scientific meetings, The Gerontological Society, Nov., 1965 (Minneapolis, Minn.).
18. GLASER, B. G.: The social loss of aged dying patients. *Gerontologist, 6*:71–73, 1966.
19. HICKEY, T., and KALISH, R. A.: The attitudes of young people and children toward adults and the elderly. Presented at 20th annual scientific meetings, The Gerontological Society, Nov. 1967 (St. Petersburg, Fla.).
20. JEFFERS, F. C.; NICHOLAS, C. R., and EISDORFER, C.: Attitudes of older persons toward death: A preliminary study. *J Geront, 16*:53–56, 1961.
21. JONES, H. E.: Intelligence and problem-solving. In J. E. Birren (Ed.):

Handbook of Aging and the Individual. Chicago, U Chicago Press, 1959, pp. 700–738.

22. KALISH, R. A.: The aged and the dying process: The inevitable decisions. *J Soc Issues, 21*:87–96, 1965.

23. KALISH, R. A.: Life and death: Dividing the indivisible. Presented at 74th annual meetings, The American Psychological Association, Sept. 1966, (New York. NY).

24. KASTENBAUM, R.: The reluctant therapist. *Geriatrics, 18*:296–301, 1963.

25. KASTENBAUM, R.: The crisis of explanation. In R. Kastenbaum (Ed.): *New Thoughts on Old Age.* New York, Springer, 1964, 316–323.

26. KASTENBAUM, R.: The interpersonal context of death in a geriatric institution. Presented at 17th annual scientific meetings, The Gerontological Society, Nov. 1964 (Minneapolis).

27. KASTENBAUM, R.: The realm of death: An emerging area in psychological research. *J Human Relations, 13*:538–552, 1965.

28. KASTENBAUM, R.: Death as a research problem in social gerontology: An overview. *Gerontologist, 6*:67–70, 1966.

29. KASTENBAUM, R.: The mental life of dying geriatric patients. *Gerontologist, 7*:97–100, 1967.

30. KASTENBAUM, R.: Psychological death. In L. Pearson (Ed.): *Dying, Death and Rehabilitation.* Cleveland, Western Reserve UP, in press.

31. KASTENBAUM, R., and AISENBERG, R. B.: *The Psychology of Death.* New York, Springer, in press.

32. KASTENBAUM, R., and DURKEE, N.: Young people view old age. In R. Kastenbaum (Ed.): *New Thoughts on Old Age.* New York, Springer, 1964, 237–249.

33. KASTENBAUM, R., and WEISMAN, A. D.: The psychological autopsy as a research procedure in gerontology. In D. P. Kent; R. Kastenbaum, and S. Sherwood (Eds.): *Research Action and Planning for the Aged: The Power and Potential of the Social Sciences.* New York, Behavioral Publications, Inc., in press.

34. KLOPFER, W. G.: Attitudes toward death in the aged. Unpub. M. A. thesis. College of City of New York, 1947.

35. KOGAN, N. and SHELTON, F. C.: Beliefs about "old people": A comparative study of older and younger samples. *J Genet Psychol, 100*:93–11, 1962.

36. LANE, B.: Attitudes of youth toward the aged. *J Marriage and Family, 26*:229–231, 1964.

37. LERNER, M.: *America as a Civilization.* New York: Simon and Schuster, 1961.

38. LESHAN, L., and LESHAN, E.: Psychotherapy and the patient with a limited lifespan. *Psychiatry, 24*:318–323, 1961.

39. LESHAN, L.: Mobilizing the life force: An approach to arousing the sick patient's will to live. In *Third International Psychosomatic Cancer Studies,* in press.

40. LESTER, D.: Experimental and correlational studies of the fear of death. *Psychol Bull*, 67:27–36, 1967.
41. LIEBERMAN, M. A.: Psychological correlates of impending death: Some preliminary observations. *J Geront*, 20:181–190, 1965.
42. LIEBERMAN, M. A.: Vulnerability to stress and the processes of dying. *Proc 7th Internat Congress on Gerontology*, 1966, v. 8, 513–519.
43. LINDEMANN, E.: Symptomatology and management of acute grief. *Amer J Psychiatry*, 101:141–148, 1944.
44. MUNNICHS J.: *Old Age and Finitude*. Basel (Switzerland), Karger, 1966.
45. RHUDICK, P., and DIBNER, A.: Age, personality, and health correlates of death concerns in normal aged individuals. *J Geront*, 16:44–49, 1961.
46. ROSENFELT, R.: The elderly mystique. *J Soc Issues*, 21:37–43, 1965.
47. Rosow, I.: *Social Integration of the Aged*. New York, Free Press, 1967.
48. SIMMONS, L.: The role of the aged in primitive societies. New Haven, Yale UP, 1945.
49. SUDOW, D.: *Passing On*. Englewood Cliffs (N. J.), Prentice Hall, 1967.
50. TUCKMAN, J. and LORGE, I.: Attitudes toward old people. *J Soc Psychol*, 37:249–260, 1953.
51. WEISMAN, A. D., and KASTENBAUM, R.: *The Psychological Autopsy: A Study of the Terminal Phase of Life*. Monograph of Community Mental Health J. New York, Behavioral Publications, Inc., in press.
52. WOLFF, K.: Personality type and reaction toward aging and death: A clinical study. *Geriatrics*, 21:189–192, 1966.

Chapter 6

THE NURSE'S EDUCATION FOR DEATH

BERNARD SCHOENBERG

A s we ponder over the events preceding and following the death of a loved one, we may recall a host of situations in which the nurse was the central figure. The nurse serves as the physician's delegate to whom the daily task of recounting to the bereaved-to-be the grave details of the patient's illness is assigned. Not infrequently, it is the nurse who makes known to the family the personal fears and wishes of the patient.

She sets the mood of the sick room, guides the conversation within it, and by her presence, controls the intimate final words between the patient and the family. One may remember the importance attached to the nurse's words, the inflection of her voice, or the inferences of her smile or frown. For the bereaved-to-be it may imply that he had not been considerate, understanding, tender or loving enough; or that perhaps he had spoken inappropriately or had not interpreted the nurse's "signals" correctly.

These and innumerable other examples illustrate how important it is for the bereaved to understand the nurse's reactions to death and the dying patient. This is particularly true because her approach to death may strongly influence the mental images which the bereaved carries away with him.

The following chapter is devoted to the factors, during training and during years of practice, which, to a significant degree, determine how the nurse copes with the patient, the bereaved and the hospital personnel. From this essay, the bereaved will gain a deep appreciation of the value of the nurse's presence as well as a more complete understanding of the professional nurse's reaction to death and grief; in so doing, he will achieve a deeper insight into his own feelings which have, in many ways, been shaped by association with her. Moreover, from all of this, he may well obtain a measure of relief from a number of perplexing recollections and mixed emotions that continue to disturb him.

A full realization of the crucial concepts described in this essay is essential to the understanding of the nurse's behavioral pattern

towards the dying patient and his family. This understanding
may afford significant assistance in the recovery from bereavement.

A.H.K.

The term *patient care,* rarely heard before World War II, has
become increasingly popular as medicine has once again become
concerned with the patient as well as his disease. Although
increasing interest has been expressed in the practice of a more
comprehensive form of patient care, recent developments in
medicine have resulted in a separation of the physician and nurse
from the patient. Since current practice involves a strict division
of labor in caring for the patient, many traditional functions of
the nurse and physician have been transferred to others, resulting
in a further dilution of the traditional one-to-one relationship of
patient and nurse (or patient and physician) and the division of
responsibility for patient care among numerous individuals.

The nurse has undertaken more of the physician's tasks and at
the same time remained responsible for the bedside care of the
patient. Much of the responsibility for the emotional care of
patients has been delegated to her, but accompanied by only
minimal authority and frequently inadequate preparation. In
addition, the nurse has been burdened with increasing super-
visory and administrative duties, and as a result is forced to
relinquish some of her traditional functions in the field of patient
care to others who have no formal preparation. Many nurses are
unprepared for the sensitive task of recognizing and meeting the
emotional needs of patients in a variety of settings. Reports from
many areas of nursing illustrate the inadequacies of current
efforts to train students to fulfill this difficult task.

This report is based on the author's experience over the past
ten years as a consultant psychiatrist in a program supported by
the National Institute of Mental Health and established to
improve patient care by integrating the concepts of behavioral
science into the nursing student's curriculum. At first, much
effort is expended by the nursing student in learning a new
technical language and in acquiring skills which make little
creative or intellectual demand. Many students state that they
experience a shift in emphasis from the "creativeness and per-

sonal initiative" advocated in college to an attitude of "compliance and conformity" in nursing school, with great emphasis on the acquisition of technical skills. The student must wear a uniform in class as well as on the ward and is constantly reminded of her student position in a highly organized hospital with its strictly defined hierarchy. She becomes aware of her "loss of identity" and frequently complains that she feels "like part of a herd of girls."

During her second week at nursing school, the student enters the clinical field, where her time is gradually increased from eight to twenty-four hours per week. More than 75 per cent of the students express feelings of anxiety, tension, and strangeness as the initial reaction to the clinical experience. Although the feelings of strangeness disappear after one month many of the students continue to show evidence of anxiety and helplessness.

The student is reminded that errors in medication or practice may result in a patient's death, and almost immediately she is confronted with patients facing terminal illness and mutilative surgery. She learns how to administer bed baths and injections by practicing on classmates, and she is exposed to the nudity of both men and women in a ward population of minority groups with whom she has had minimal or no prior contact. She feels unprepared to deal with patients usually many years older, who turn to her for solace and gratification of dependency needs.

The flood of new experiences in the clinical setting result in feelings of anxiety, guilt, and depression. Even under ordinary circumstances, the period of late adolescence is for many students a time of crisis during which they undergo a marked variation in their tolerance for conflict and anxiety. When conflict and anxiety cannot be mastered, the result may be a failure to resolve the process of adolescence. Some reports have emphasized that no sense of adult functional identity can be completed until after adolescence is well past and its changes assimilated. The demands made on the nursing student by her initiation into professional life are overwhelming at a time when she is also struggling with problems related to establishment of her own personal identity.

When students are unduly anxious, they move from a position

of interest in the patient to one of task orientation. One of the defensive attitudes of the student is isolation from intimate contact with others, despite the occupational demands for closeness. She attempts to avoid the anxiety-provoking relationship which emotionally supportive care will stimulate. Patient care induces so much anxiety for some nurses that the hospital may, to the patients' detriment, unknowingly develop a particular kind of social system to protect the nurse against anxiety, guilt, and uncertainty. The system protects the nurse by preventing an intense relationship with patients and requiring concentration on developing skills. The student struggles to hide her feelings of anxiety, dependency, and helplessness, for she is expected to appear competent and independent in the clinical setting. The disillusionment, cynicism, and rigid defenses which tend to develop under these circumstances are a natural reinforcement for a social system which protects the nurse from the major source of anxiety—intimate contact with patients.

Assisting the student in the difficult process of socialization and in gaining an integrated approach to patient care is a formidable task for the educator, and requires bringing together specialists from a number of different disciplines. The teaching project referred to earlier in this report utilizes a multidisciplinary group approach in which twenty students meet weekly in a two-hour conference with a teaching unit composed of a nursing instructor, psychiatrist, social scientist and nursing supervisor. The faculty, interested primarily in developing attitudes and only secondarily in teaching facts, tries to provide an environment in which the student can explore her own feelings and attitudes towards patients, physicians, the hospital, and the profession of nursing. The student is supported in an exploration of her preprofessional attitudes, stereotyped ideas, idealized expectations, prejudices, and a host of other subjects which cause conflict and anxiety. She is encouraged to discuss any of the elements contributing to the emotional turmoil stimulated by her clinical experiences and the radically changed character of her social life. Through the medium of interviewing and discussing patients in the group conference, it is possible to initiate a dialogue with students about their own anxiety and attitudes.

It is in this context that the faculty became aware of the intense anxiety generated by the student's confrontation with terminal illness and death. Surprising to the older faculty members is the realization that few students have encountered death before entering nursing school. One reason for this is that people no longer die at home but are institutionalized in the general hospital, specialized hospital (cancer), or nursing home. The American traditional funeral described by Jessica Mitford in *The American Way of Death* is now rarely seen—"simplicity to the point of starkness, the plain pine box, the laying out of the dead by friends and families who also bore the coffin to the grave." Life is prolonged in the modern well-equipped hospital, so that, although a patient would prefer it so, he no longer dies in the familiar comfort of his own home. Our modern society, unlike death-oriented cultures, is preoccupied with youth, beauty, vitality and strength. Death itself is essentially a taboo topic and has become a subject of scientific interest and investigation only during the last decade.

During late adolescence, and even beyond it, anxiety related to feelings of uncertainty is displaced onto death, the most uncertain of all things. The anxiety related to death is ordinarily soon repressed, so that most college students report only very rare or occasional thoughts about it. But at a time when most college students are coping with anxiety related to death by repression and denial, the nursing student is confronted with death as a fact in her daily life and is asked to deal with it effectively, and remain accessible to her emotions. Many students find this is a formidable task and some can only cope with the problem by becoming inaccessible to the dying patient and shutting out their own emotions. Emotional withdrawal, avoidance, and isolation with emphasis on tasks and nursing rituals, become the means of maintaining stability. Unfortunately, the student's early experiences become the prototype for her later relationships with patients. The major problem for the educator at this time is to maintain the student's openness. Openness describes a way of reacting to the environment by permitting maximum contact and feelings and allowing a high degree of involvement with the environment.

During the first years of the program it appeared that the faculty were as unprepared as the student to delve into the problems related to death. The health professions in general have a system of values which emphasizes the preservation of life, and death is therefore regarded as an indication of failure. The nurse, unlike the physician and hospital chaplain, has intimate physical and emotional contact with the patient during his entire hospitalization. Although much of the responsibility for the psychosocial care of the dying patient has been delegated to the nurse, it is the physician who decides what the patient and family should be told about the patient's condition and prognosis. In the modern general hospital, the nurse has to provide emotional support for the patient, his family, ancillary personnel, and at times the physician. The student soon realizes that the social system offers many opportunities to escape from this difficult burden by avoidance, denial, and emotional withdrawal. In group discussion, the student, with her great need for intimacy and fostering the welfare of the patient, is soon aware that the consequences of withdrawal from the patient are guilt and shame. She becomes peripherally aware that a defense which enables her to avoid reality is costly to her in that it removes her from many sources of professional gratification.

At first, the nursing student may be angry with the physician who fails to fulfill her magical expectations of his ability to prolong life. Guilt that she may feel over the patient's death is easily projected onto him and his shortcomings. She may assume rigid attitudes about allowing the patient to know his diagnosis and prognosis and assume a position that every patient *should* be told or every patient *should not* be told. As she gradually becomes aware that some patients want to know while others will not accept the truth even when told, her attitudes become more flexible. She may realize in time that the "good" nurse individualizes and has very few rigid rules. The student becomes less harsh in her judgment of the physician when she recognizes that her behavior with the patient should be related to the patient's individual personality and character traits. She may realize before long that her interaction with the patient also should change as his illness progresses.

The faculty emphasizes the need to become aware of patient's behavior and needs. When the student recognizes some of the patient's needs even when they are unspoken, she feels less helpless and ineffectual. For example, she realizes that giving the patient the opportunity to vent his feelings, or spending time with him to relieve his feeling of loneliness, can be very reassuring. Often, in their lack of experience, students fail to realize that the starched white uniform is symbolic of authority to the patient in a helpless, dependent state. But when they recognize that the patient's anger and irritation is not directed toward them personally, they feel capable of dealing with it. They are surprised to learn that simple explanations and clarifications are supportive measures for the patient. Normal, routine procedures become challenges that require careful thought if the student is to avoid placing the patient in a dependent, child-like position.

When patients are interviewed in the group conference, the students are usually impressed with the supportive and, at the same time, honest attitudes of the faculty members. Emphasis is placed on allowing the patient to maintain his dignity by dealing with him in a dignified manner. Many students find acute conditions resulting in death less difficult to manage than caring for the terminal patient. The acute situation requires activity such as preparation for surgery, infusions, numerous diagnostic procedures and life-saving measures. The chronic conditions, on the other hand, require day-to-day contact with the patient and his family while the student is essentially in a passive position. The relationship of the patient with other patients and ancillary personnel presents numerous problems. The student may experience some relief when the patient complains of pain, since efforts to control pain require activity such as injections. During the conferences, emphasis is placed on *all* interactions with patients as an active process requiring tact and careful thought. For example, students are surprised when they find they can gain factual information from the patient which can be helpful to the physician or social worker. Also, they find that defining limits or boundaries for patients by enforcing rules or hospital regulations can, in some situations, offer reassurance.

In group conferences, some students become aware that they entered nursing to alleviate fears of death. As children, they usually regarded the nurse and physician as magical, omnipotent figures who could save them from death. These students show a tendency to work assiduously with the dying patient, encourage hope, support the patient's unrealistic expectations, and regard the patient's death as a personal failure more than a personal loss.

Other students may come to realize they have entered nursing with a conscious fear of death. They attempt to avoid assignments to dying patients and tend to remain emotionally inaccessible to the patient. The patient's death stimulates fear, anxiety, and depression and results in further withdrawal from patients. Some students readily accept assignments to dying patients but live in dread of being assigned the physical care for the final disposition of the dead person. One student expressed her guilt openly to the group when she experienced relief that "her patient" had died during a shift when she was not on duty. While the patient was alive, she had functioned very effectively. Almost all nursing students find it exceedingly difficult to care for dying children or adolescents. In group conferences, the strong identification with these patients is soon uncovered and discussed.

Another source of guilt for the student is the anger she may feel toward the dying patient who makes her feel helpless and ineffectual. Other patients make numerous trivial demands in order to maintain contact. When the student realizes what underlies the patient's requests, her anger is diminished and consequently her sense of guilt. Many students, as a consequence of emotional attachment or identification with the patient or the patient's family, regard the patient's death as a personal loss and suffer grief reactions, although they recognize that they are expected to exercise restraint and maintain their composure in the clinical setting. It is not unusual for these students to become tearful when discussing their emotional reactions during the group conference. Some students return to religion and its assurance of immortality despite a period in college of doubt, intellectualization and agnosticism.

In their identification with the patient, some students feel the patient could not tolerate awareness of his prognosis. They show excessive sympathy for the patient and feel childlike and helpless. They realize that the patient also wants to maintain his composure and dignity. Assisting the patient in maintaining his dignity, composure and hope by responding appropriately, showing empathy, consistency, reliability, and maintaining emotional availability, produce a sense of accomplishment in the student. At other times, the student's personal views may be in conflict with the patient's attitudes. In one group, the students and faculty members alike were having difficulty discussing the dying patient. A member of the teaching unit volunteered to take the role of a dying patient. The group became involved as the nursing instructor presented the case history. A student who offered to play the part of the nurse described her role as trying to assist the patient in "finding peace with the Lord so that he may find eventual salvation." Knowing from previous discussions that the instructor was an atheist, the group members were angry with the student for trying to impose her views on the "patient."

By the end of the first year of training, some students begin to see dying as a "normal crisis" in the family much as they would illness, divorce, and birth.

The studies which follow, written by nursing students, illustrate how they learn to cope effectively with the dying patient. Both reports indicate a high degree of psychological awareness, sensitivity, dedication and courage.

Illustration 1

I wish to focus on and limit this paper to a qualitative case study of the nursing care of a sixteen-year-old boy, five months prior to his death. Its purpose is to show that the nurse can favorably intervene in the course of a patient's dying.

"Good morning, Bob. How are you feeling?" He turned his swollen, sullen face to the wall and muttered angrily, "Typical question. You don't *really* care, so why do you ask?" Had I not read this boy's chart before beginning the morning care, I probably would have spent the next few minutes assuring him that I did care.

I had taken time that first morning in Physical Rehabilitation to read the charts of my assigned patients. In addition to the medical workup, there were extensive social service and psychiatric notes on Bob's chart. The social service worker described Bob as highly intelligent, manipulative, and emotionally developed beyond his years. She noted that he considered all nurses stupid, basing his judgment on his observations that they were all inappropriately and unrealistically optimistic and unwilling to be honest with patients. Thus, slightly defensive and girded with insight, I replied to Bob, "You're right. It was a stupid thing to say. I've never talked with you before and therefore I couldn't possibly 'really' care." He turned and looked at me through swollen lids and I added, "However, it's not every patient who really cares whether or not I really care." I recognized him for the individual he was and began a candid relationship that was to challenge me and require careful experimentation with the limits of my role as a nurse.

In a week my rotation through the Rehabilitation Service was completed, but the care of this patient for me had just begun. I was not assigned directly to Bob while working on the wards but had spoken to him several times. The conversation included a few facts about his illness, hostility towards the staff that had "failed him," and his frank opinion of nurses. His illness is a rare disease of unknown etiology and, like most patients, he is subject to the extensive complications of his disease as well as to the side effects of the high doses of drugs necessary to maintain his life. Bob first developed signs about one and a half years preceding his admission. The diagnosis was made within two weeks after he came to the clinic and in a short time he was able to return to school. His major problem was weakness and gastrointestinal bleeding. He had several severe bleeding episodes which required multiple transfusions and long periods of hospitalization. I learned from Bob's hospital chart that during one episode of bleeding, while he was on the "danger list," he took the State Regents Examinations and scored in the nineties.

When he was admitted to Rehabilitation, he had hopes of recovering his strength but soon became discouraged and withdrawn. He intellectualized his disease, talking about his illness and the likelihood of further remissions. From all he had read "it will most likely progress and everyone knows what will happen then. I will die from one complication or another." By making the listener feel uncomfortable and totally ineffectual, he places himself in complete control of the situation. Following his detailed and knowledgeable description of his disease and prognosis, he discussed his progress since entering the hospital's Rehabilitation Unit. He recognized that he wasn't improving and said it was "disgusting" to hear staff members babble about the progress he was making. As I listened, I occasionally nodded and asked several questions, none of them particularly leading. He looked at me closely and suddenly said, "You don't seem stupid. Why do you want to be a nurse?" I asked in return, "What makes you think nurses have to be stupid?" He quickly replied, "Anyone who could be satisfied with taking temperatures, blood pressures, urine specimens and rubbing backs has to be stupid." "Do you really think that's all nurses do?" I asked, realizing he wanted to know what I felt the nurse had to offer. I told him that illness imposes many adjustments on a person and that a "good" nurse can perceive what adjustments have to be made and can help the patient make them to the best of his ability. Again he turned towards the wall, but this time without anger, and asked, "Do you think you could help someone die?" I told Bob that I didn't know but I would be willing to try. There was a long silence, broken by the charge nurse, who assumed that I wasn't doing anything important and she called me to assist her. I was about to refuse but decided it was a good time to leave. I interpreted his question about death as a "feeler" and realized that Bob had two questions to consider: (1) could he trust me with such important matters? and (2) did he want to? With this in mind, I returned to talk with Bob the following day. He talked at length about his parents, who had been divorced fourteen years ago. He was very angry with both of them because he had spent his life going from one home to another. His mother was described by him as emotionally unstable. She was always apologizing for having given him up as a small child and he felt unable to talk with her. However, he considered her very intelligent and realized that regardless of her motives she had in the past few years sacrificed a great deal for him. His mother had fallen through a window when Bob was two years old and had sustained a concussion which left her in a comatosed state for a considerable period. During her hospitalization, she became hysterical and required physical restraints, which caused partial contractures of her hands. The deformities impaired her ability to find employment but she did hold several jobs.

After the accident, Bob was sent to live with his father, who had remarried. He was never accepted as a member of that family and was sent to his paternal grandparents, where he lived until five years ago, when his mother regained custody of him through lengthy, involved court proceedings. Although he recalled wanting to go with his mother, he resented leaving familiar surroundings. He hated his mother for taking him and for ever having left him. His mother went to a quack doctor for treatment of her hands and suffered third degree burns with further contractures of her fingers. This incident preceded the onset of Bob's illness, and since his mother was unable to work, she was forced to go on welfare. When her hands had healed sufficiently, trying desperately to gain his affection, she insisted on caring for him. Later, on seeing her deformed hands, I marveled that she was able to do any work, let alone care for a bedridden sixteen-year-old boy. Bob's explanation was that his mother did all of this not because she loved him but to appease her own guilt.

When Bob told me all of this I tried to focus on the "feeler" he had thrown out the previous day. "Bob, yesterday you asked me if I could help someone die. Do you think you are dying?" Following a long silence he shrugged his shoulders and said, "I'm not dying right now, but I guess it won't be long." I asked, "Is that why you refuse to participate in your treatment, withdraw from other patients and reject your mother's love?" Perhaps the statement was too strong—he didn't answer and tried to change the topic. He made one last attempt to intellectualize and said, "Perhaps, I would mind dying more if I hadn't spent most of my life doing things alone. It won't seem like I'm leaving so much behind, this way." Suddenly he began to weep.

We talked once more before I left the ward and he expressed a wish to talk with me again. I promised to return and added that meanwhile he should be careful not to cheat himself. I learned later from classmates that his attitude towards other patients changed markedly and his physical therapist told me that he had renewed enthusiasm for his exercises. One week before he was to leave the hospital, I arranged with his doctor to take him out for a car ride. Bob was quite blasé about the venture until I told him we were going to Jones Beach. He was not strong enough to leave the car, so we sat eating hot dogs, watching the sea gulls, and enjoying the "life" that was everywhere. Bob seemed to live at that moment from the energy generated by the environment. He talked a great deal of his hobbies and activities at school. The highlight of his day was when I made the wrong turn on the Cross Bronx Expressway and ended up on a one-way street in the Botanical Gardens. When we stopped laughing, he said, "Maybe I was wrong about you. Perhaps you are stupid." When the attendant moved him from the car to the wheelchair, he choked up and whispered to me, "Thank you, Miss Larson."

He went home as scheduled, and when I returned from vacation in the fall, I visited him at home. His mother answered the door and I found her to be an effusive and articulate woman. She led the way to Bob's room, apologizing for the apartment, which appeared to be immaculate. Bob was lying in bed reading, his long bent legs resting limply to one side. He had lost more weight and his face was swollen. There was a clean bedpan at his side and I learned that he was having severe diarrhea.

Bob greeted me and dismissed his mother as if she were a maid. I made myself comfortable and we exchanged a few remarks about the intervening period. Then I accused him, "You have quit, haven't you?" He looked directly at me and said, calmly, "Look, we both know I'm going to die soon anyway. What difference does it make what I do now?" I replied, "If you quit, you have a 100 per cent guarantee that you will be unhappy until the day you die. On the other hand, if you try—try to do some of the things you find enjoyable—there is a chance that some of that time will be enjoyable." It wasn't cheery, but it was honest. If there was one thing lacking in Bob's life right then, it was a person who would be honest with him.

During my visit, his mother entered the room a number of times and on several occasions used the word guilty. Bob apologized for his mother, but his voice was tender and betrayed the love he felt for her. I said, "It's no wonder you don't like the hospital. You couldn't pay anyone to care for you in the way your mother does. You discount her efforts by saying she is merely trying to relieve her guilt, but from what I've seen in the past half-hour, it's clear that she loves you very much." A few minutes later, he answered, "I would like very much to believe that." I continued, "Then quit rejecting her. Accept her love and return it." I realized that I was being authoritarian but there wasn't time for an indirect approach. We said goodbye and I chatted with his mother for a while on the stoop. She discussed her guilt and went on to talk of her unsuccessful marriage, her accident, and the irony of Bob's disease after her bitter struggle to get him back. Feeling the need to verbalize some of the major issues and clear the air, I said, "You know his time is quite limited, but it is not the result of something you did or did not do. He doesn't need a mother who feels guilty and allows herself to be ordered about like a servant. More than physical care, he needs your love. He is still a boy and needs discipline and must come to know that you take care of him because of love, not because of guilt. *Talk* with him and *tell* him you love him! You may not believe this, but he does love you very much."

I returned the following week, wondering if my direct approach had been of help. Bob's mother remained in the room. She sat calmly beside him and several times she reached out to touch him. When she left the room to get something, Bob turned to me and said, "What did you say to my mother last week?" Stalling, I said, "When?" As he tinkered with a gadget on his bedside table, he said, "I don't know why, but this has been the best week we've ever spent together. We talked for many hours and even when I was very sick with diarrhea, I felt close to her and unafraid." His mother returned shortly and after several minutes, as I was about to leave, I turned and said, "I see you are working on your radio again." He smiled and turned to look at his mother, who was watching him.

The following weekend I was away, and on my return I found a message to call Bob immediately. I tried, but the phone was busy, and instead of waiting I went immediately to his home. He had received a notice from the Haverstraw Rehabilitation Center that, if he wished, he could come the following day. It was difficult to get into such a hospital and the chance might not present itself again—at least that was the aspect he chose to dwell on. He had thought about it all week and had decided, as he put it, "not to quit." His lungs sounded as if he were full of fluid and he was still troubled with diarrhea. I asked when he had seen a doctor and suggested that he return to the medical center until he regained his appetite and could control his diarrhea. He had discussed it with his mother and his doctor and decided that he would enter the Rehabilitation Center. After making this decision, he and his mother had felt closer than before. He described the past week as the most spiritual of his life. When they weren't talking, they prayed and cried together. They were both content, and Bob wanted to see me so he could say "goodbye." He thanked me for not letting him quit, because the last two weeks had been the best he could remember.

As Bob's mother walked to the door with me, she held my arm and said, "Bobby knows he is dying and he wants it this way." Nodding, I asked, "How are you doing?" She looked down and said, "Two weeks ago I would have been in hysterics at this point, but now" (she looked up), "I feel at peace with Bob and myself."

Bob died at noon on Tuesday at the Haverstraw Rehabilitation Center. When his mother phoned me, I was very shaken, but the job was not yet finished. I went to see her and listened as she recounted Bob's role in her life and where the holes were going to be. She talked a great deal about the last two weeks and how this period had prepared her for the end. She described the last week as a period of mourning preceding death and said how comforting it was to let Bob see her grief and share it. It had been an opportunity to dissolve some of the barriers that existed between them. We talked of her future plans and she expressed concern for her "people" (Negro). She felt she was rich in many ways—she had had three years of college and had a good mind.

Six months have passed since I saw her last but she writes to me. Her family and members of the hospital team predicted that she would be unable to tolerate Bob's death. I don't believe she will have the mental breakdown that was predicted for her.

This experience has been the most gratifying of my student career.

I realize that there were many aspects of this relationship of which I was unaware or too involved emotionally to cope with effectively. But, I am not a psychiatrist—I am a nurse, whose goal was to help Bob make the adjustments dictated by his illness. Increased verbal awareness of his needs allowed Bob to approach death with less fear and resentment. Recognizing Bob's fears allowed his mother and me to separate our fears from his.

One of the implications for me of this experience is the future need for a "nurse specialist" in caring for the dying patient. The specialist would be called in to evaluate the dying patient's needs and work with the staff to develop an awareness of the impact of their fears on the patient. If the patient returns home for terminal care, this nurse would make home visits and re-evaluate the problem with the visiting nurse in mind. She would work with the community agency in the same manner as the ward personnel. Furthermore, there is the burgeoning area of Community Health Programs which could be an ideal home base for a "nurse specialist" in this area. She would have psychiatric consultation available to improve the quality of her care.

Illustration 2

Mr. Grant, a fifty-one-year-old Negro longshoreman, entered the hospital following a history of three years of chronic illness. He was married and had two children, a boy and a girl, eleven and six years of age.

I was assigned to him on Thursday, the end of his second week of hospitalization. I was uninformed about the medical aspects of his disease, but in the next week I was to learn much. After he died, his chart was sent to the pathophysiology laboratory and was, therefore, not available for this report. Much of the following information is taken from notes and conversations with other students and staff members who cared for Mr. Grant during his three weeks of hospitalization.

That first morning, as I approached his beside, he appeared to be sleeping after a restless night. On the bedside stand was a small quantity of vomitus, which immediately made me anxious since I knew he had eaten that morning for the first time in three days. I waited for two hours until he awakened before approaching him for his morning bath. He looked annoyed and told me he had already had a bath. Then, with a smile, he added, "I guess you won't leave me alone until I have a bath." I assured him he would feel more comfortable when he was cleaned up and had fresh linens on his bed. I added that I would try to hurry but he wanted to do his own bath and politely asked me to leave him for awhile.

When he finished, I washed his back and assisted him with his robe as he moved into a chair so that I could change the bed linens. Again, there was a moment of resentment and annoyance, followed by a faint smile when he said he could manage without help.

When I returned after taking his urinal to the utility room, he was gone. He was not on the ward or in the solarium and I became concerned. I found him walking back from the visitors' room down the hall and took his arm. "You worry too much. Maybe I should be holding onto you!" With that he laughed and reversed his hold so that he was supporting me. I asked if he felt weak or dizzy, but he assured me that he was fine. When we returned to the ward, I explained he could sit up in his chair but should call for a wheelchair to visit down the hall or make a phone call. He thanked me but insisted he didn't want to be a bother. I reassured him and asked him to repeat the procedure for making a call. I then left him to rest.

The following morning, when I came onto the floor, I found him walking out of the telephone booth in the visitors' room. He didn't look well and stated that he felt shaky. I steered him back into the visitors' room as he leaned heavily on me. I placed him in a wheelchair and took him to his bed. Without mentioning yesterday's incident, I told him that he should have called for a wheelchair. He smiled sheepishly and said he had forgotten, and repeated that he didn't want to be any trouble. I could see the concern in his eyes and realized that he felt ill. I had tried to be gentle but firm and was surprised when suddenly he whined, "Why are you always hollering at me?" I thought he would start crying as he added, "Always hollering, like you was my mother or something." He rolled to the other side of the bed and remained silent. After a while I asked, "Are you angry?" When he didn't answer, I said, "I didn't mean it to sound like hollering." I was at a loss when he continued his silence so I prepared for his bath.

The night nurse reported that he was awake most of the night, sitting in the solarium, holding his head in his hands. Evidently, the nurse had made no attempt to get him back to bed or comfort him. I mentioned to him that I knew he had been awake but he was reluctant to discuss what was troubling him. He made remarks about his improvement—he had not vomited, his appetite had improved, and he was tolerating fluids. My encouragement seemed to comfort him and I didn't press him about his worries.

During his first week of hospitalization, Mr. Grant had been described by other student nurses as thoroughly "nice," but at the same time very independent, belligerent, and often forgetful. How many of his attitudes may be attributed to his disease or treatment is uncertain. He was very friendly with other patients, his family, and the numerous co-workers who visited him. With visitors he appeared to be well respected and was usually the dominant figure. He appeared more willing to accept the authority of doctors and male attendants than of nurses and students.

I soon learned that the day before I first cared for him, he dressed and prepared to leave the hospital insisting he was well. The doctor persuaded him to stay, but that evening he called his wife and pleaded like a child, imploring her to take him home. His wife refused, and following this, he became sullen and withdrawn. He insisted he was fine but had symptoms of headache, nosebleeds, weakness, dizziness, nausea, vomiting and diarrhea. He also had two episodes of prolonged and severe bleeding from incisions in his groin made several days after his hospital admission.

The following week was one of severe acceleration of his disease. He was placed on strict bedrest and restricted fluids. He was confused and became combative when restrained. Despite the severity of his illness, he would leave his bed whenever he was left alone. That Wednesday he was found sitting in his chair, and when the student nurse tried to get him into bed he said, "If I get into that bed, I'm going to die there. You just want me to get into that bed to die!"

When I walked onto the ward that Thursday, I could hardly believe he was the same person. He had been moved to a single room and was lying uncovered, wearing only a "johnny" coat, incontinent of urine and feces, arms and legs twitching, a look of absolute terror on his face. Mr. Grant reached out as I approached and grabbed my arm. My first question was, "Are you in pain?" He didn't answer but held onto me very tightly and then wrapped his arms around his legs to control the twitching. Clutching my arm he asked desperately for water. "Please, please, can I have some water?" I was able to give him a few sips of water and he continued to plead for more water throughout the morning. Each time I refused, he glared at me in anger and turned away. He continued to twitch incessantly and would grab out at my hand, arm, or apron. When I had to leave him, I told him. "I am going to leave for a few minutes, but I'll be right back." He would, nevertheless, hold onto me but I didn't struggle with him. When I reassured him sufficiently, he would hesitate for a while and then release his grip on me. He communicated to me his desperate need to have someone at his side. When I returned, he seemed unaware of my presence until I spoke or touched him. As I worked, I continued talking to him, telling him what I was doing.

Later that morning, although he asked for water and a bedpan, he became resentful when I tried to wash him or change the bed—to do anything other than be there for him to hold on to me. He would hold on desperately and then suddenly change his mood and push me away, asking me to leave him alone. I knew he was angry about not getting water, his inability to control his body movements and his incontinence. The look on his face was the same when he was pleading with me to help him or yelling at me to go away. He was desperately terrified. When I had to take his temperature, I told him what I was going to do and asked if he would turn on his side. He told me he couldn't do it and asked me to go away. After asking several times, I told him I would help him turn. He asked how I could do it. I explained how I would position him and turn him on his side. He looked terribly confused and said with great annoyance, "I can do that. Why don't you tell me what you want. I can do that!" Because of his twitching, I turned him only with great difficulty, giving him considerable support. It was a very frustrating experience for us both.

That night, Mr. Grant suffered his first *grand mal* convulsion, so I was very apprehensive about working with him on Friday morning. His condition had worsened, and he became less responsive to direct questions. He twitched incessantly and kept asking for water. When he complained that he was cold, I put extra blankets on him. He soon threw off the covers and clung to me desperately. The desperate expression of terror persisted when he pushed me away, beating me with his fist and arms. The next minute he grabbed me again without saying a word.

A medical student came in to listen to his heart and check his reflexes. The student described the heart "rub" and "squeak" he heard through his stethoscope. He then grabbed Mr. Grant by his shoulders to get his attention and speaking right into his face said, ever so brightly, "Old heart sounds just fine!" Mr. Grant immediately sat up and grabbed me around the neck and stared at me with the most frightened expression I had ever seen. He looked as if he were going to cry, and I moved to put my arms around him when he dropped back onto the pillow, shaking with tremors.

A moment later, a student nurse came in to give him his medications. "Can you take these?" she asked. He lifted his head and swallowed the medicines. At that instant, he shoved me away again and yelled, "Why are you always holding onto me? Always holding onto me!" When the other student left, he reached out again and grabbed for my hand. It continued that way throughout the morning, his alternately calling for help and rejecting it. He was very fatigued and began dozing off as I left his bedside that morning. He had two more seizures and died on Sunday.

It was evident during the last week that Mr. Grant's reactions were related primarily to his fear of impending death. He felt that he was dying, although he had not been told directly. His symptoms were becoming more severe and his family and the hospital staff were gravely concerned. Still, there was a persistent effort to maintain control, as well as a recognition of his desperate feelings of helplessness. Consequently, he expressed the concurrent need for and resentment of closeness and help. Throughout his hospitalization he showed a delicate balance between controlling and expressing his frustration and anger.

These case histories have been presented to illustrate that nursing students can be supported in effectively working with dying patients. To maintain intimate contact with patients and remain accessible to their own complex of feelings is a difficult task but the rewards for the students are numerous and gratifying.

Nursing faculties have, in recent years, tried to assist the student in coping with the emotional aspects of terminal care. As students are given the opportunity to explore and verbalize their experiences with patients in a supportive setting, they have less need to repress their feelings and withdraw from the patient. When students can establish intimate relationships with patients, they become aware of the "patient" as an individual with his own particular needs.

Many university and teaching hospitals hold "death conferences" when a patient dies in an effort to determine if anything more could have been accomplished to maintain the life of the individual patient. An appropriate parallel would be a "life conference" preceding death to determine what steps the health team should take to assist the patient, his family, and the hospital personnel responsible for his care, in dealing with the problems of dying so that there will be minimal pain and anxiety.

ACKNOWLEDGMENTS

Parts of the introductory portion of this paper have been presented at the Symposium and Workshop on Multidisciplinary Group Teaching of Psychosocial Aspects of Patient Care, Columbia University, March 31 and April 1, 1967.

The author is indebted to Miss Ylene Larson and Miss Dorothy Turek for allowing him to quote from their case studies, and to the large number of nursing students, patients, and faculty members who participated in the Mental Health Project, School of Nursing, Columbia University.

Chapter 7

THE NURSE REFLECTS

JEAN E. FOX

ᘜhe family, specifically those closest to a dying patient, need from a medical staff not only the very best that modern medical technology can offer but also a full measure of human feeling and compassion. With the expansion of medical knowledge, the foreknowledge of death and the predictability of its occurrence in a disease process become more of a certainty.

The problems of grief and bereavement begin the moment that full knowledge of the impending death of a loved one is learned, for how a patient dies and the degree of involvement of the family in the care of the dying have an effect on the final loss. Verbal exploration of the fears that must be faced, the uncertainties of the future, the sense of helplessness before eventual loss, all these open the hearts of one human being to another, and offer a bridge to recapturing the world of love and hope. Affirmation of life and the growing process by all persons involved in meeting the problem of dying far outweigh the morbid and pessimistic attitude of previous years.

Judging from the behavior of those who have undergone bereavement, one thing is certain. If there is love, then sorrow and pain will be present during, before, and after the moment of death. This is a reality as much as the fact of death itself. When faced and handled well, sorrow and pain add to understanding, compassion, and unity with one's fellow man. Sorrow, like joy, can and should be a binding force rather than a totally shattering emotion.

My first professional encounter with death came early in my student days on a busy floor where some twenty-five patients were exposed to one another in a large general hospital. To me, as a novice, the profound feeling aroused by my unaccustomed view of death was heightened by the nonchalance and apparent noninvolvement of the personnel on the floor. An old woman had died, and with the same casualness that he would show in starting administration of intravenous fluids, the intern made his pronouncement of the time of expiration, wrote a short note in the chart, and went about his business. The nurse followed along the same impersonal line, clearing the deceased's name from all the ward lists, jotting a note in the chart and directing an aide and an orderly to prepare the body for the morgue. Everything was done with great efficiency and in a perfunctory manner. The movement of the floor continued with no comment about the event that had taken place, no sign of reflection about the fact that one of the most awesome experiences in a person's life had just occurred. No one seemed to care.

The years of schooling passed, but at no time was there any form of discussion or exploration of the meaning of life or the meaning of death in relation to our work with patients. Here we were, men and women dealing intimately with life and death on a day-to-day basis, but our mental apparatus was geared only to the scientific, the social, and the psychological aspects of disease. We never quite concerned ourselves with the root question of what the essence or meaning of life was all about. It seemed as though we were meeting these situations only on a very practical level, never caring to examine the deeper philosophical significance.

Several years later, while caring for a terminal cancer patient in New York City, I encountered a second incident that made an indelible impression on me. The patient was a middle-aged school teacher with a husband, several grown children, and many brothers and sisters. One day I went to the patient's home to bathe her and to administer some medicine. In the course of the bath, the patient told me that she had cancer, knew she would die soon but did not want the family to know that she was aware of her condition for fear that it would heighten their anxiety. She then told me of the loneliness and frequent fear that she experienced during her illness. Although the physical discomfort was acute, it could be tolerated far better than her sense of loss and aloneness. In the other room were several members of the family, and on questioning them, I learned that they were "screening" the patient from knowledge of her terminal state under the delusion that she was not aware that she was dying. Both the patient and her family were suffering far more acutely than was necessary, because of the desire to protect one another.

Later on, I had the opportunity to work on a floor that was specially designed for the care of the terminal cancer patient. This meant that all known human means of restoring health were supposedly gone, so that only palliative measures could be offered. The reputation of the floor was such that no one would choose to go there if there was any possibility of working elsewhere. Odors, pain, hopelessness, and slow decay prevailed, with narcotics being the most heroic means of helping the patient. Fortunately, a happy blend of several factors within two years radically altered the complexion of the floor. Chemotherapists and radiologists began to work with even the most advanced cases. A most radical change was demanded of the nursing staff. Whereas the physician could come to the floor for a short period daily and go back to his laboratory or office, the nurses were left with the twenty-four-hour duty of caring for the dying. The phenomena of change in this care came primarily from listening and looking. We, the living, were forced to enter with the dying into their world, to see things through their eyes, to listen to all they could tell us of the experience that remains unique and singular to all of us. Death, we found, was in most instances kind, and often filled with a peace and serenity that escaped the living; for the fear that underlay our attitude to the dying came from the intense involvement we had with life, with growth, with doing, with curing, that animates the entire medical field and society in general. The moment that anyone working with the dying patient stops and begins to probe into the meaning of death (certainly never expecting to find an easy or ready answer to the questions that come), he will begin to move beyond the defeat that death seems to bring, into the arena of hope, joy, and growth.

But what does this have to do with the bereaved? It has

very much to do with the loved one left behind, for it is not possible to separate the person undergoing the dying process from the bereaved. They are interlocked in one of the most profound and awesome of experiences, and the depth of the relationship will be measured in sorrow in equal degree to the love that exists between the two people.

The reactions of bereavement are of course varied. A young woman, approximately twenty-five years old, whose husband died within a six-month period from a highly malignant tumor, was brought quickly to maturity through her husband's fatal illness and death. The husband, cognizant of his diagnosis, had been the one to make decisions, manage the family planning, and handle financial affairs. Knowing that his life-span was short, he had had the wisdom to assess the plight of his young wife in dealing with very real, practical problems that formerly he had assumed. She, in turn, voiced fear not only of his dying but of the ensuing responsibility for herself and their young son. With her openness in expressing the emotional dilemma in which she found herself came a positive increase in her growth, and we found that giving her the opportunity and encouragement to talk was of paramount importance. Coupled with this was a slow but steady involvement in the care of her husband. To teach not only this particular wife but countless others how to rub the back of the loved one, how to feed him when weakness sapped his limited energies, how to straighten bed linens, and how to offer a bedpan, gives the nurse a means of joining two persons as the dying process goes on. The ability to give support and physical comfort in an active fashion establishes a bridge of involvement through directly meeting the sick person's basic physical needs. In these tasks, this young wife gained in competency and confidence simultaneously. She began to learn that the world of responsibility that she was entering more fully was not as fearful as she had anticipated. Her greatest conflict came in the terminal month, when she was torn by her desire to stay with her husband all day long and yet not neglect her young son. It was felt by the husband and the nursing staff that some part of each day should be devoted to her home and child, so as to prepare her for the future time when the final

severance came, as well as to offer her relief from the hospital
atmosphere. This shuttling from the world of the living to that
of the dying avoided the problem of total preoccupation with
the sick. The husband still served as counselor and confidant,
but it was increasingly more obvious that the dominant force
of the family was now shifting to the wife. The husband's sense
of well-being in knowing that his wife was learning to cope
with finances, house repairs, insurance policies, etc., was reflected in his ability to meet death extremely well. For the man
of the family to know that his family will survive after his
death is important beyond description.

As time grew short for this couple, the wife asked to stay at
night with her husband. Night after night she could be found
curled up in a chair as close to the bed as possible. There she
could hold his hand, minister to any physical need or quietly
talk with him during the long, dark hours which can bring pain
and loneliness. Despite her fatigue and the physical strain their
being together was of vital importance to them both. The desire
to prolong these moments was clear from her need to be in his
physical presence. This desire became so strong during the last
week of his life that she could be persuaded to leave the hospital
for only an hour or two a day. His last day was a slow entry
into stupor, and then coma, with a hush of silence around his
bed as his wife sat dry-eyed with her hand in his. At the
moment of death, she sat momentarily stunned. Then suddenly
there was a wail of "Oh, Bob . . . oh, Bob," and a torrent of
tears came pouring out. Tears that had been checked for all the
months preceding, now came as though in an endless flood. I
sat with her, saying nothing, but with my arms around her. For
grief at this time is so deep and shattering that nothing seems
to penetrate but the sense of touch. To hold the grieved one in
your arms and console her like a child offers momentary protection. Those who, like this young girl, can openly express
their sorrow are most fortunate, for many others are caught in
an emotional vise which for days, weeks, and sometimes years
can keep them from expressing sorrow.

In the hospital, it is good to have some member of the nursing
staff present to encourage crying, to subdue hysteria which is

frequently present, to offer consolation, to extend an embrace, and to help guide the bereaved through those initial moments following death. The scale of reactions is wide. Many insist on seeing the dead person; they want to kiss the body; they talk to the corpse; they walk away and then return to the body as though not certain that what they have seen is true. This movement around the corpse should be permitted, intervention coming only when it proves to be an excessive ritual with morbid demonstrations. There seems to be a strong natural inclination to see and often to feel the dead person as though to experience the reality of the event that has taken place. Often there now comes a moment of relief, for up to this point there has been the foreknowledge of death during long days when hope and hopelessness could follow swiftly one upon the other. There has been a cessation of the normal flow of life, the dying process taking precedence over everything. Now that which had been anticipated and dreaded has happened. The act of death is over; it is finished. A new set of circumstances lies ahead, bearing the possibility that out of death, life in fuller measure may come.

If those who are left behind have been deeply involved, have been able to give expression to their sorrow at death, have grappled honestly with the anger and sometimes despair that comes with the death of a loved one, they are able to receive the verbal consolation and accept the spiritual energy that can come to them from many sources. It has been found to be helpful at this point, as a family is leaving the hospital, to talk for a few minutes about the positive aspects of the death. If the patient has had a painless, peaceful, and serene death, these facts should be brought to their attention. All the good things that had happened during this illness, remarks made by the loved one that had particular significance to the family, the personal factors that revealed strength and nobleness in his character, all these can be reviewed, so that the bereaved leave the hospital remembering that there was much in this experience to build upon. To have done everything possible to make the dying process a time of growth in love and understanding will make this moment, when the family must leave to build a new future, a time of hope despite the sorrow.

It is not uncommon for a husband, a wife, a mother, or a sister to come back to the hospital later. Some return to say thank you, a few to see patients they have come to regard as friends; but mostly, they return simply to talk about the deceased. The nurse must remember this has been one of the most exhausting emotional experiences that a person can have, and therefore he needs to have someone to talk to about his feelings and thoughts. There is always, whether it be sorrow or joy, the necessity to share a strong emotional experience with a friend who will understand. This has been found to be true, particularly after the funeral, when the day-to-day reality of living without the loved one leaves a void yet to be filled.

In the case of the young wife, her active grieving period was of short duration, since the pressure of having to find work forced her to move out of herself. The fear of supporting herself and her young son had been brought to light early in those first days of her husband's hospitalization. During the months to follow, she was put in contact with a hospital department where, after her husband's death, she was able to find a position. Although she could never return to the floor where her husband had died, she was eager to work in the same hospital, for it gave her a sense of contributing to the battle to overcome the disease that had taken her husband. This was her way of not only providing a livelihood but of continuing to feel a oneness with her mate.

There is a tendency, as technology grows, to become embarrassed by basic needs on an emotional and spiritual level and to view things from a purely intellectual plane, buttressed by the astonishing advances that our scientific achievements have brought. We who are building the earth are brought into the wonder and mystery of a world yet hardly explored when the phenomenon of death is simply expressed through a funeral. Such a funeral was witnessed when a patient died suddenly, leaving behind his wife and two daughters who had had no time to prepare for the loss of a loved one. In the congregation were perhaps sixty persons, comprised of church members, friends, family, and a few casual acquaintances. Seated on the side of the simple altar in a small choir stall were a group of five women; before the altar was the open coffin, with the immediate family sitting close by. As the minister began to talk, it became apparent that this was not to be a formal service. He had known and loved the deceased personally, and in his talk he drew from the deceased's life the main trends that had been of importance in the formation of his character. His schooling, his marriage, his contributions to his fellow man were all brought out.

As the minister talked, the choir began to intone a hymn and, as a pause ensued in the oration, the voices would rise in song. Gradually the entire congregation was drawn into the song; then they became awesomely quiet in listening to the voice of the minister continue with the story of the dead man's life. Outside, the leaves were splashed with fall colors, brilliant in splendor and caught by the gleam of the sun. Pointing to the trees, the minister made a parallel between the life of all men and the flow of nature reflected all around us. He spoke of how those leaves, now so brilliant, so kind in lending shade to the passerby on a summer day, so capable of arousing joy and wonder when the first spring shoots appeared, would soon lie dead on the pavement, dead like the man in the coffin, leaving behind a barren, naked tree. But despite death, there would, with time, be other leaves on the tree, since the life force in nature did not die any more than the love force in man dies. It was often hidden, dormant, quiet, but always ready to break out again in new patterns, in new relationships, with a greater depth and scope to its being. The eternal building force would never be overtaken by death; for out of death new life would come, and from sorrow would come eventual joy.

As his words ended, the entire room was filled with song, a song wherein the words were of sorrow, but the atmosphere was charged with a joy and hope that had sprung from the words of the minister to the congregation. That family left with the past goodness of their beloved echoing in their hearts, and they could feel the strength and love of the congregation stretching out to help them. This had been made possible for them by belief in a supreme law that had become a reality that permeated their lives. The power of life and love emanating from a supreme source cut through the fear, the ugliness, the hopelessness, the loneliness that comes with death, and joined that family to their dead on a level that would make this but a temporary separation.

As I reflect on families that have struggled through disease, death, and bereavement, I reach certain conclusions. Some have done well, others have faltered and been permanently scarred, but all have done the best they could in a situation that was changeless and timeless. When we face death, despite all our modern day wonders, we still must answer the basic questions of who and why we are. This was summed up by a Christian philosopher, who said

> The thought of death is an austere but beneficial and reliable companion, the first to occur whenever our mind attempts to live on a high plane. It lifts us above visible nature and, together with the concept of God, brings us a true sense of our destiny. It frees us from the spell of worldly possessions and from intellectual pride by reducing to their true worth the small pleasures of life, and, to their brevity, its small pains. It subdues hatred, awakens pity, shows all men to be equals and brothers, dispels selfishness, inspires heroism, endows the soul with a magnanimity and allows it to find sweetness in austerity. The day when we are capable of facing death squarely will mark the dawn of a new era of greatness, freedom and felicity.*

* Alphonse de Parvillez, S.J.: *Joy in the Face of Death*, translated by Pierre de Fontnouvelle. Desclee Co., New York, Paris, Rome, pg. 222.

Chapter 8

EXPERIENCES OF PERSONS REPRIEVED FROM DEATH

RICHARD KALISH

One can not possibly fall into the category of the bereaved or "bereaved-to-be" without deep and anguished concern over what agonizing thoughts troubled the now dead or dying beloved one as death relentlessly approached. Doubtless, also, because of the bereaved's love, this contemplation can become for him a major source of torment and disturbance. Only under most unusual circumstances can he have sure knowledge of the dying man's innermost thoughts.

The information which follows derives from a research investigation concerning this area. The conclusions supported by the data may give the bereaved some insight into the departed's thought processes.

A.H.K.

The behavioral and psychiatric scientist who wishes to study the relationship between man and the process of dying is confronted at the outset by a basic impasse: he cannot penetrate death itself. His investigation is of necessity founded on the experiences of observers, the surviving family and friends; rarely, on the testimony of the terminally ill themselves. However, one group of people, in relation to this subject, have not been accorded any systematic attention. They consist of those who at a certain time had strong reasons to anticipate an imminent death, but, who, after all, did not die.

It would seem that this study offers an optimistic note to those who have recently suffered bereavement. It is not that their loss becomes any lighter, but that the fears, the discomforts, and the anger of their deceased friends and relatives may well have been less than has been normally assumed. Our data lead

84

to the supposition that the actual process of dying and the fears of death may be much greater in long-range anticipation than in the actual encounter.

The impetus for the present study came from an earlier project in which respondents were asked whether they had ever faced what they believed to be their own inevitable death.[4] Of over 600 participants, approximately 15 percent had had such an experience. Later, informal discussions substantiated the point that a great many people have faced the probability of their own death, some more than once. Several important measurable variables emerged from these discussions. First, and to be anticipated, the experiences varied in terms of the precipitating circumstances. A near drowning, an automobile accident, a forest fire-fighting brigade encircled by flames, an airplane crash, and a medical misdiagnosis were but a few of the occurrences described.

Second, they differed as to initial reactions. Did the subject panic? Was he calm? Angry? Worried about others?

Third, the long-range impact was a major variable. How did the event affect the individual's relationship with others? With his God? How did it affect his day-to-day living and his planning for the future?

Fourth, what was the duration of the episode? Was the encounter momentary, as in being hit by an automobile, or lengthy, as in the recovery from a heart attack?

The fifth variable was the level of certainty regarding the imminence of death. This needed to be answered from both an objective and subjective point of view. Thus, being caught in an earthquake might have an objectively low possibility of resulting in death. Some people, however, would respond as though they knew they were about to die, whereas others—standing two feet away—might feel certain that nothing would happen. One victim of an automobile accident said he had always felt that nothing could kill him but illness or old age; thus, it never occurred to him that the accident might cause his death, as indeed an objective observer would have thought highly possible.

Other variables that obviously need to be considered include the age of the subject at the time the event occurred, his present age and the number of years intervening; the possibility of memory distortion and amnesia for certain events; the relationship between reported somatic changes and actual somatic changes; and many others.

Before describing this study we would like to discuss the importance of such information. It has often been stated that the dying patient is deprived of what this and other authors consider to be his fair share of emotional and social support during his final days and hours.[1,7] As a result, innumerable suggestions have been given as to what should be done for him, ranging from a more careful structuring of the roles of those who administer to the dying,[5] to the utilization of psychotherapy with the terminally ill,[6] to a suggestion that a community of the dying be established where LSD and other drugs might be freely dispensed. All of these ideas are highly controversial; all impress this writer as having at least some merit; all would be costly in terms of money and professional time; and all would encounter immense resistance from both the medical and the lay communities.

To evaluate the underlying problems sensibly, rather than being bound by past prejudices, it is necessary to know more about what the dying person actually experiences. Would psychotherapy or psychedelics provide a useful service to the dying? What are the inadequacies in the present roles of those administering to the dying? Does the dying person profit from knowledge of his imminent death or would he prefer to die without this awareness? Incidentally, it is interesting to mention a study which showed that "the overwhelming majority of physicians wanted to be informed" of their own incurable conditions, but fewer of them (statistically significant at the .01 level) were willing to inform others of theirs.[2] As a nonphysician, the author questions this double standard and wonders whether physicians consider themselves superior to laymen in their ability to deal with such problems, or whether the difficulty of the confrontation with the patient has led to a behavior born of anxiety which was subsequently justified.

Sir William Osler, some decades ago, informed us that only a small proportion of the dying express great fear or panic;[3]

more recently, psychological analyses have suggested that fear of death and dying is unusual in the terminal geriatric patient.[5] Nonetheless, the practitioner's approach to the dying usually assumes that the pending encounter is one that the patient wishes to avoid at all costs.

Improved care of the terminal patient and management of the dying process is only one application of improved knowledge regarding the feelings and experiences of those facing death. Many human beings face death as the result of a chronic medical condition, a dangerous job, or military combat. How can these people best be prepared? Is the best approach to avoid the subject and allow the realization to evolve from experience, or could the combat officer or person with a serious medical problem be helped by learning something of the feelings of others in similar circumstances?

Our improved understanding of those who have faced death will be of profit to others besides the near-victims. A great number of professional and vocational personnel deal directly and indirectly with death and the process of dying. Besides all those associated with hospitals and with funeral establishments, there are those who work with the very old, those who work in the fields of estate planning, pension administration, insurance, the ministry, psychotherapy, social work, the legal profession, and others. A misapprehension of the nature of dying can lead to innumerable inadequacies in working with the dying and the bereaved.

Up to this point, we have discussed the usefulness of being able to generalize from information gained from survivors of near-death as well as situations whose death is foreseeable. We must also consider the needs of those who have themselves survived the death encounter. The emotional problems of the arrested terminal cancer case, the near-victim of a bombing raid, or the mother who felt she was going to die in childbirth are important medical and psychiatric problems in and of themselves.

It would be nice to report that our research has already made considerable headway in solving those problems, but we must lay such optimism to rest immediately. Our study has made only a small scratch on a large surface. Perhaps its real value will be in laying the groundwork for further, more penetrating follow-ups.

To outline the research procedures briefly: 185 undergraduate students were given the assignment of interviewing one or more individuals who had at one time faced their own death. An optional, and easier assignment was given as an alternative to those who did not wish to do this, and students were explicitly told that even evidence of an unsuccessful attempt would fulfill the requirement. Student interviewers were given a brief outline to follow and some instruction in the techniques of interviewing.

A total of 170 students turned in adequate papers; nine others turned in papers that fulfilled the assignment but could not be used for analysis; the remaining six did not turn in a paper. The 170 papers submitted reported 323 analyzable interviews (191 males and 132 females). The class period during which the papers were returned was occupied with comments and experiences of the interviewers, who seemed to have found the assignment easy and interesting. No student indicated any difficulty in obtaining a qualified subject.

TABLE I
PRESENT AGE OF SUBJECT

Age	No.
10–19	24
20–29	94
30–39	42
40–49	80
50–59	50
60–69	16
70–79	10
80–89	3
Not stated	4
Total	323

There are obvious limitations to this methodology. The quality of the papers submitted was highly variable and the possibility of a few fictional subjects was high. In addition, even experienced interviewers would have found it difficult to evaluate the validity of recall of a highly emotional experience occurring anywhere from a few weeks to six decades earlier. Over and above everything, the sampling can only be termed accidental, and the data cannot be properly related in general to other populations.

Also open to criticism was the coding of the data. The author and an assistant independently coded the first 115 interviews, based on preestablished categories. Agreement was obtained on nearly eighty percent of the classifications. We then discussed points of difference and made a few changes in the categories. The remainder of the coding was done by the assistant. The high rate of rater-agreement may have occurred because the only variables coded were (1) the cause of the anticipated death, (2) the initial reaction (on 40% of the papers) and (3) the eventual impact. Since the protocols were usually brief and explicit, the author feels that the coding was adequate for an exploratory study of this nature.

Considering the uncontrolled variables, the results must be approached as suggestive rather than final, since this project was actually of only an exploratory nature.

Table II lists the circumstances under which the individuals believed they were going to die. It is most obvious that the largest proportion involve medical events that are relevant to physicians. This becomes more impressive when it is realized that all cases still facing imminent death were eliminated. The second largest category involves motor vehicles. The third, near-drownings. Then war-related incidents, guns (not in war), airplane occurrences, falls, and mental illness.

More relevant to the present discussion is the nature of the initial reactions and the long-range impact of these experiences. Table III indicates the initial reactions. Because the interview form did not specifically request this information, only 131 responses carried sufficient description to make a judgment. Since several cited more than one reaction, a total of 164 re-reactions are mentioned.

The most frequent initial reaction recalled is that of concern for the family and other survivors, with thirty—nearly 23 percent of all respondents—referring to such a concern. Panic or fear occurred in twenty-five instances, while sixteen individuals mentioned the experience of having past events "flash past."

TABLE II
CAUSES OF ANTICIPATED DEATH

Cause		
Physical illness		87 (13)*
Surgery	17 (4)	
Childbirth	12	
Heart condition	9 (3)	
Pneumonia	7	
Terminal diagnosis	6 (1)	
Cancer	5 (5)	
Allergic reaction	4	
Unspecified & other	27	
Motor Vehicle		78 (1)
Automobile (actual)	44 (1)	
Automobile (near)	24	
Pedestrian (actual)	4	
Pedestrian (near)	2	
Motorcycle (actual	3	
Motorcycle (near	1	
Drowning		55
War-related		31 (2)
Combat	12	
Lifeboat	2 (1)	
Bombing raid	1	
Captured	1	
Unspecified & other	15 (1)	
Airplane		13 (5)
Forced landing	4 (2)	
Parachute problems	4 (1)	
Turbulence	3	
Unspecified & other	2 (2)	
Firearms		13 (1)
Being shot at	7 (1)	
Being threatened	6	
Falls (incl. from tree and cliff)		7 (1)
Mental issness and suicide attempts		6
Wild animals and horses		5
Industrial accidents		4
Stabbed, fire (in home), clubbed, threatened with hanging, ship emergency, robber, choking, earthquake		2 (each)
Concentration camp, locked in freezer, pronounced dead, lightning		1 (each)

* The figures in parentheses refer to cases in which two causes were mentioned. When this occurs, the primary cause is listed under a different major heading. Thus, one of the four counted in the parentheses by surgery might also have been a pedestrian in an auto accident, but not a victim of a heart condition.

Prayer or other religious feeling was recalled by fourteen people; only eleven claimed to be calm and unafraid.

Table IV contains the recollections of long-range impact. Of the 323 respondents, 286 gave analyzable explanations, of whom forty-eight gave two responses. Slightly more than one in five stated that they incurred no long-range effect. Most common,

TABLE III
INITIAL REACTION TO ANTICIPATED DEATH

Reaction	
Panic, fear	24 (1)*
Concerned about family, friends, survivors	23 (7)
Helpless, fatalistic, resigned	13 (4)
Prayed, thought about God	11 (3)
Calm, unafraid, "warm, light, and happy"	10 (2)
Recalled past, life flashed by	9 (7)
Fighting death, wanted to live, escape	6 (2)
Somatic changes	6 (1)
Felt ridiculous way to die	5 (1)
Angry with cause of death	5
Worried about others dying	4
Felt unreal, dreamlike	3 (1)
Regretted wasted life, not being better person	2 (1)
Wanted to get it over with	2 (1)
Mind blank	2
Sad	1 (2)
Tense, anxious	1
Not stipulated	192

* See footnote, Table II.

however, was the remark that the event produced increased caution in the future, an attempt to avoid a similar situation (e.g., the nearly drowned person would avoid swimming or boating), or an explicit fear of the cause and related factors. Twenty-four became more religious or began attending church. Twenty became more concerned about others. Although no personal histories are available, it would be interesting to investigate whether the increased concern for other people is the non-religious (that is humanistic) counterpart of an increased religious feeling.

It strikes us as less remarkable that 23 percent were fearful or in a state of panic than that 77 percent did not mention fear. Slightly less than 25 percent stated that they were unafraid, resigned, anxious to die and get it over with, fatalistic, or "warm, light, and happy." Another thirty-four focused upon other people in some fashion. Nineteen either fought death, were angry, or felt "this is a ridiculous way to die." Although sixteen mentioned the classic "my-life-flashed-before-me," only three recalled feelings of regret that they had not lived a better life or been a better person.

Our data are not inconsistent with other data drawn from

TABLE IV
IMPACT OF ANTICIPATED DEATH

Impact		
None		61
Avoiding response		82 (14)*
Subsequently more careful	46 (7)	
Stops activity or avoids some aspect	33 (6)	
New learning or tries harder	3 (1)	
Fear of cause		31 (8)
Meaning of life		25 (10)
Happy, lucky to be alive	8 (2)	
New look at life, more optimistic, desires better life	6 (2)	
Lives each day as it comes, as if it were last	5 (2)	
Lives life to fullest, meaningfully	3 (4)	
Anxious to live	2	
Questioned meaning of life	1	
Humanistic		24 (1)
Increased concern for others, closer to people	20	
Wishes to alleviate problem	3	
Desires make up past wrongs	1 (1)	
Religious		22 (8)
Becomes more religious, faithful	19 (5)	
More fatalistic, God's will	3 (3)	
Hostile reactions		15 (2)
Anger toward responsible person (thing)	6 (2)	
Distrust of experts	5	
Nightmares	3	
Overcompensates	1	
Death-related		10 (2)
More aware of death	7 (2)	
Ready to die	2	
Health deteriorated	1	
Personality changes		8 (1)
More self-confident	4	
Matured—wiser	3	
Less responsible	1	
Self-critical	(1)	
Miscellaneous		8 (1)
Stopped drinking or smoking	4 (1)	
Unhappy when thinking of it	3	
Made resolutions (unfulfilled)	1	
No response		37

* See footnote, Table II.

research and observations of the elderly and the terminally ill. The older person and the dying person often express much more concern about disrupting the lives of those around them than with their own future. The common expression "I don't want to be a burden to anyone" seems repeated in our data through the extensive concern for the impact of the death upon the survivors.

Kastenbaum[5] describes two basic responses to dying in hospitalized geriatric patients: (1) the feeling that death is welcome, and (2) the feeling that death is an interruption. The former group may be compared to our calm and resigned people; the latter to those who were angry and fighting death. It may also be relevant to point out that, whereas eighty-seven (or 27%) of the subjects mentioned physical illness as a major precipitating cause of anticipated death, only three of twenty-five (or 12%) who mentioned fear or panic were physically ill. Near-drowning accounted for nearly half of the panic reactions.

Of potentially major interest to the practicing physician is the breakdown of these initial reactions of those with medical problems: were concerned for family and other survivors, fourteen out of forty-five; prayer and religious feelings, seven of forty-five; feelings of calmness or resignation, seven of forty-five. Interestingly enough, the physician in medical practice usually refrains from discussing with a terminal patient the subject of his imminent death because of the desire to spare the patient's feelings, but he often does confide in the family; the patient, on the other hand, declares that his greatest concern is for the family's feelings—that is the very individuals whom the physician is involving most deeply.

Fear and panic are apparently produced by the helplessness that occurs in such events as nearly drowning, experiencing a forced landing in an airplane, being lost, being in a bombing raid, or being locked in a freezer (1 each). Only two of the persons involved in seventy-nine automobile accidents mentioned fear or panic. The only war-related occurrence was that of being caught in a bombing raid. Both of those involved in airplane accidents mentioned the fear caused by forced landing, rather than fear of fire or turbulence. We may speculate that fear and panic arise out of situations in which the person facing death feels helpless, and has time, albeit often fairly little time, to dwell upon his circumstances.

Of incidental interest, 75 percent of the sixteen people who mentioned that their life flashed before them were either near drowning or in an automobile accident. These are sudden events, but—in most cases—they lasted from a few seconds to a couple of minutes. The possible meaning of this experience is rarely mentioned in the professional literature of either those studying

memory or those concerned with the psychodynamics of behavior.

Analysis of Table III showed that the most common long-
term impact was increased caution, fear, or withdrawal; about
two thirds of all responses either involved these reactions or
claimed no impact whatsoever. However, some events did produce what might be termed self-actualizing responses. Fourteen
people stated that they now lived life to the fullest or "lived
each day as it comes." Five stopped drinking or smoking or
both, while seven claimed that they had become wiser or more
self-confident. Seven were interested either in alleviating the
problem that threatened their lives or have learned how to avoid
a recurrence (e.g., a nonswimmer who almost drowned has
learned to swim). Ten were happy to be alive and eight re-
evaluated their lives and now wish to live a better life. Greater
concern for other people and increased religious involvement
are also likely to be considered positive outcomes of this experience.

Only a few mentioned unpleasant long-range effects. These
included nightmares, 3; unhappiness in recalling the event, 3;
deteriorated health, 1; and overcompensating by overeating, 1.
Of course, many of those citing increased fear, caution, or withdrawal from activities related to the anticipated death have
restricted certain aspects of their behavior. However, considering
the nature of the events, we feel that the reported negative
impact was slight. There was no mention of long-range emotional
problems, major somatic changes, or a permanently increased
anxiety level.

Thus, although what might be termed "defensive" behavior
is most common following an anticipated death, a substantial
proportion of individuals do mention some positive outcome,
whereas very few indicate any continuation of negative effects
other than the fear and avoidance of the specific death-producing
circumstances.

What practical applications can be drawn from these data?
We have already referred to two, assuming our data can be
taken at face value. First, fear and panic are rarely initial reactions to people who assume they face a terminal medical

condition, but concern for their family is paramount. Therefore, physicians and other hospital personnel might do more for terminal patients by informing them of their own physical condition, but not telling the family.

Second, people who once anticipated dying, but no longer do so, are not likely to report any strongly unpleasant long-range after effects. They may, however, require help in dealing effectively with the cause of their near death, such as by water, airplane travel, and so forth. Moreover, a small number (5) came out of their experience with a distrust of experts—usually of physicians who allegedly gave an incorrect diagnosis.

Other applications also come to mind. For example, since the remembered experiences of near death were frequently of a medical nature, the physician is intimately bound up in working with patients who have had such experiences. Also, many of the other circumstances would lead the individual directly to receive medical attention, i.e., being stabbed, being in an accident, nearly being drowned, being shot, and so forth.

Of course, the physician who has personally observed these patients, particularly those in a state of shock following the onset of strong fear or panic, or the overt anxiety accompanying participation in combat or getting out of an overturned car, might question the accuracy of the respondents' memories. The significant factor would thus be not the degree to which such memory is accurate, but the bases for inaccuracy. Information of this kind would shed light on the topic of perceptual and memory distortions.

And finally, since the death encounter can lead to an improved self-image, it may even be possible to utilize such experiences beneficially. In summary, it is again emphasized that the fear and discomfort which the lost loved one experienced may well have been far less than the bereaved assumes. This thought may be of some solace to those who have recently encountered the death of someone close.

REFERENCES

1. Bowers, M. K.; Jackson, E. N.; Knight, J. A., and LeShan, L.: *Counseling the Dying.* New York, Nelson, 1964.

2. FEIFEL, H.; HANSON, S.; JONES, R., and EDWARDS, L.: Physicians consider death. Proceedings, 75th Annual Convention, American Psychological Assn., 1967, pp. 201–202.
3. HUTSCHNECKER, A. A.: Personality factors in dying patients. In H. Feifel (Ed.): *The Meaning of Death.* New York, McGraw-Hill, 1959, pp. 237.
4. KALISH, R. A.: An approach to death attitudes. *Amer Behav Scient,* 6:68, 1963.
5. KASTENBAUM, R.: The mental life of dying geriatric patients. *Gerontologist,* 7:97, 1967.
6. LeSHAN, L., and LeSHAN, E.: Psychotherapy and the patient with a limited life span. *Psychiatry,* 24:318, 1961.
7. WORCESTER, A.: *The Care of the Aged, the Dying and the Dead,* 2nd ed. Springfield, (Ill.), Thomas, 1940.

PART II

PHILOSOPHY—RELIGION—SURVIVAL

It is time that our materialistic belittling of the meaning of death be replaced by the sense of humility and the acknowledgment of higher powers which, I think, is the only means of finding solace in a world which otherwise may appear senseless.

J. T. FRAZER

Chapter 9

DEATH AND THE PLOWMAN

By
Johannes von Saaz

A disputation and a consolation from the
year 1400 . . . adapted* into English

JACOB NEEDLEMAN

*D*eath and the Plowman, or *The Bohemian Plowman,* was written in the early 15th century by a certain Johannes von Saaz,
about whom we know practically nothing.† There may be no
other work in Western literature that expresses man's hatred of
death with more force and understanding.

The form of the work is that of a legal dispute between plaintiff (the Plowman—his "plow" being the quill pen of a writer)
and defendant (Lord Death). The Plowman's complaint concerns the death of his young wife, a complaint which he unremit-
tingly hurls in the face of all the arguments that Death can
muster. Much of the work's power comes from the Plowman's
constant repetition that he is in pain. No matter what Death
says, the agony and the reality of his loss remain the Plowman's
heaviest counter arguments.

Lord Death's defense is that he is part of the natural order
of God's creation: in this consists his "reasonableness" and "justice." The man, therefore, who violently laments Death's sover-

---

* Those familiar with the German texts will immediately see why this version
is termed an adaptation, rather than a translation. I have tried, however, to take
only those liberties with the text which may help to convey some of the force of
the original. A fine scholarly English translation, to which I am greatly indebted,
is that by Ernest N. Kirrmann: *Death and the Plowman.* Chapel Hill, The University of North Carolina Press, 1958.

† See Kirrmann's translation, pages XII-XIV for a complete summary of the
meager biographical information that is available to us.

eignty is, in fact, refusing to understand reality. Such a man is a fool. Indeed, it is foolishness itself which has brought the Plowman's pain in the first place, in the form of his inability to love wisely. Ultimately, Death's counsel to the Plowman is that he must acquire wisdom. He must learn that everything he sees, loves, desires, or hates, including himself, will soon be destroyed by death. Contained in this counsel is Death's devaluation of all the Plowman holds dear: man, woman, marriage, love, "holiness" —all the primary emotions and beliefs and relationships of human life.

The Plowman is neither willing nor able to accept this. Nothing can lessen his pain. No recompense for his loss is possible. He cannot believe that God created a world in which wisdom lies along the lines that Death draws. No argument, however telling, can persuade him that death is not evil. He unyieldingly asserts his own sense of values and finds unacceptable what in the light of these values is surely an injustice: his young wife's death and the pain now weighing upon him. He has, in this sense, eaten of the tree of the knowledge of good and evil; thus death becomes his destroyer.

The final judgment of God reveals the perspective in which both the Plowman and Death are in error: death and life serve higher purposes than either the Plowman or Death is aware of. Yet such is the supremacy of the Divine rule that even this error makes relative sense and serves its function, as we see in the concluding Plowman's Prayer to God. This prayer expresses the Plowman's turning to God, not for the consolation and recompense he had hitherto sought, but for a newly understood *help* from God's created reality (which now *includes* death), a prayer for the tranquillity of heart without which it is impossible truly to mean "amen": so be it.

J. N.

1. *The Plowman*

Grim undoer of the world, baleful outlaw unto all mankind, fearful murderer of the good, Death, be you accursed! God, your maker, hate you; endless affliction dwell upon you, fierce disaster rule within your house, be forever scourged to the inners of your being! Dread, want and grievance never leave your side; sorrow, misery and anguish plague your ways; lacerations, presentiments of deep disgrace and crippling punishments all, in all their power, everywhere oppress you! Heaven, earth, sun, moon, stars, ocean, river, mountain, field, valley, meadow, the deepest pits of Hell, and everything that has a life or being, hold you as its bitter, loathsome enemy, maledicted unto all eternity! Be consumed by evil, disappear into the sorest grief, and dwell beyond recall for now and all the time to come within the heaviest contempt of God, man, and God's creation! Shameless miscreant, may the evil that you are turn and endlessly prevail upon you; may terror and fear never let you free; may there be ever wringing of the hands and cries of murder shrieked at you by all men and by myself!

2. *Death*

Listen! Listen! Listen! What new wonder be this now!!
Terrible and most unprecedented curses do assail Us.
And whence they come we do not know.
Surely, We have long and everywhere withstood
Threats, laments, cries of murder, wringings of the hands,
And abuse of every sort. Therefore, man,
Declare thyself; announce thy name and let Us hear
What sorrow We have let thee know that thou with such
Unseemly words dost now address Us. To such a thing
We are not as yet accustomed,
Though many be the stalks that we have reaped,
Those rich in knowledge, noble, beautiful and powerful,
Whereby widows and orphans, nations and entire races have also
Known their share of pain. Thou dost comport thyself
As though an earnest need gives thee much oppress,
Thy lament has no rhyme,
Whereby We gather that thou wouldst not sacrifice
Thy understanding to the excellence of sound or rhythm.
But if a raging fury hath the better of thy sense, then
Hold thy tongue, and wait; be not rash and quick to level
Heavy maledictions that in better time shall plague thee
With remorse. Suffer not to think that thou canst
To any small degree divide Us from Our mastery and thorough might.
So name thyself and if thy need be speech, tell Us
Of the matter that thou hast from Us so strongly suffered.
We shall soon acquit Ourself; thou shalt mark Our honesty.
But We do not know as yet whyfore thou dost so fervently
Assail Us.

3. *The Plowman*

I'm called a plowman, my plow the sharpened feather of a bird, and I live in the country of Bohemia. I will never cease hating you. You have most fearfully ripped away the thirteenth letter of my alphabet and with it my entire store of happiness. As though they were but weeds, you pitilessly tore the gentle summer flowers from the meadow in my heart; and with the cunning of a thief you kidnapped my greatest and my only gladness, my chosen bird of joy; you have plundered from me what is not to be replaced. Judge for yourself if it is for nothing that I bring forth such anger, fury and lament, now to face a joyless life because you robbed me of it, a life deprived of its only source of rapture. Until now every hour was for me one full of happiness and cheer; the days and nights were short and never anything but pleasant; every year was for me a year of grace. Now suddenly I'm told: forget. I'm told to spend my days now crying and ceaselessly lamenting, full of misery and sadness, drinking muddy wine, clinging to a brittle, withered bough! So now you see me blown by every wind, straining in a wild, angry flood, ever at the mercy of the waves, vainly weighing anchor. Therefore will I shriek without end: Death, be you accursed!

4. *Death*

Wonder seizes Us at such unprecedented hate, the likes of which
We have never yet encountered. Now if thou be a plowman
Who maketh home there in Bohemia,
Then we think thou doest Us unjustly. The time is long
Since We have there worked anything essential,
Save for our recent lying in the hilly confines
Of a charming village there, wherein
Four letters of the alphabet, the nineteenth, first, third
And twenty-sixth twined themselves into a wreath. There
We administered Our graces to an honest, cheerful lady
Who bore, indeed, the thirteenth letter. She was
Completely virtuous, immaculate. Let none dispute Our right
To say "immaculate," for We were present at her birth.
And at that time Dame Honor sent to her a cloak and wreath of honor,
Both of which Dame Happiness dispatched to her. Now to her grave
She took that cloak untattered and unblemished, that wreath
Unviolated. May He who knoweth all things bear witness to Our part
And hers. She was above all others in the goodness
Of her conscience, her honesty, fidelity, and most especially
In charity of heart. Truly, it is seldom that we meet so excellent

A woman. If it be not this of whom thou speakest, then who it is
We know not.

5. *The Plowman*

My Lord, I was her husband, she was my wife. You took her
from me, my eyes' delight; she is gone, my shield of peace; gone is
my oracle, my seer. Dead is dead! Here I stand, poor plowman,
alone; gone is my gently guiding star; the sun of my well-being
has set, never again to rise! Never will the star of all my mornings
rise, its light has paled; gone is the soother of pain, night veils my
eyes, my eyes are veiled by darkest night. Truly, I do not think
there is anything that can ever bring me proper joy again; for the
proud banner of my joy is broken. Murder! To arms! Be this ever the
unending cry, shrieked from the heart's own source into the empty
anxious days to come as my own adamantine luster dims, as my
guiding staff is torn unmercifully from my hands, and as the way
is barred that leads me to the fountain of my health. Oh, endless,
endless, eternally unburdened grief, ruin, desolation and eternal
downfall be your proper legacy, oh Death! Die without honor,
gnashing your teeth while you rot in Hell and while the sickening
bile of degradation fills your mouth! God revoke your power and
scatter you like powder in the wind! Oh, be yours an unending
devilish existence!

6. *Death*

A fox struck a sleeping lion on the cheek;
For that his skin was flayed.
A rabbit bit a wolf;
Today he is still without a tail.
A cat scratched a dog;
From that time on she had the dog's infernal enmity to bear.
Thou seekest now to vex Us in like manner.
Still, We do believe a vassal is a vassal,
But a lord remaineth a lord. We would give thee proof
That we weigh justly, judge justly, and justly do proceed
Within the world; that we do not heed estate of birth,
Nor honor deeds, nor even look upon such things as beauty,
Talent, love, sorrow, age or youth when We approach the scales.
We do as doth the sun who shineth on both good and evil.
We take both good and evil in our fold.
The genius who is able to compel the muses
Must, at Our command, surrender up to Us his muses;

And neither whores nor temptresses withstand Us, nor
Doth it serve them if they ride on crutches or on goats.
Physicians who prolong the lives of other men
Also are compelled to give Us part; roots, herbs, salves,
Nor any number of apothecary measures will assist them.
Had We the interest to prolong a life because of sacrifices,
Gifts, love or sorrow, then might We today be king of all the world;
All sovereigns would have gladly set their crowns upon Our head,
Placed in Our hands their scepters;
We would own the papal seat and its triune mitre.
Indeed, were we now to give a reckoning of every butterfly
Or grasshopper—there'd be no end to it!
Leave off thy cursing and enumerate no babbling romances.
Do not beat the air above thee and splinters will not fall
Into thine eyes.

7. *The Plowman*

Could I but curse you, could I but castigate you, could I but
damn you until a power more evil than evil itself destroyed you,
it would be no more than you have earned from me. For great pain
brings forth great lament and I would be less than human did I
not bewail the passing of my gift from God, this gift which God
alone could give. These tears can never leave me, the falcon of
pride has escaped. And in this I am right so to lament her death,
for she was noble of birth, rich in honor, beautiful, singular among
her friends in wisdom and excellence of form, fine and true in
words, modest in body, and with others ever of good cheer. I say
no more, for I have not the strength to number all those virtues with
which God Himself provided her. Lord Death, you know this yourself. With such sorrow in my heart I have no choice but to come
to you with lamentation. Truly, if there were any good in you, you
too would be moved to pity. I will turn my back on you, I will
speak no good of you, I will forever be your enemy. May all God's
creation stand by me in opposing you. May you be condemned and
hated by all that is in Heaven, Earth and Hell!

8. *Death*

The heavenly throne was willed by God unto the angels;
Unto evil spirits fell the abysmal domains of Hell;
And unto Us, this realm of Earth.
God commanded that the virtuous shall earn the endless peace
Of Heaven,
And that the pains of Hell shall be the punishment for sin;

Just so, the earth, the air, the seas and all that dwell therein
Were set within Our sovereignty
That We might stand between abundance and plethora.
Now, foolish man, just think
And with thy thinking plow the fields of Reason;
Thou wilt see: since that time when God first formed man out of clay
Had We not started rooting out amid the vast increase
Of men upon the earth,
Animals and worms in deserts and in wild fields,
Scaly and slimy fish within the seas and waters,
Then for the very multitude of flying bugs
No one could exist;
For the very fear of wolves no one would venture from his house.
Men would seek to eat each other, as would each animal
And every living thing; for they would all of them
Lack nourishment. The Earth would be too small.
He is a fool who laments a mortal's death.
Let go! The living to the living, the dead to the dead,
As it hath always been.
Foolish man, be wiser in thy purposes or cease lament.

9. *The Plowman*

My stores are gone beyond recalling; shall I not despair? Condemned as I am to fill my life with pain, shall I not cry out? Oh merciful God, oh mighty Lord, grant that vengeance be mine against this evil gardener of despair! You have divided me from every rapture of my life, disappropriated me of honor. For I would have had great honor were my noble, august queen still playing with her children in their righteous place of birth. But those little chicks have lost their mother hen. Oh God, mighty Lord, how dear it was to see her ply her gentle corrections so that all who saw her blessed her, saying: "Praise and honor to this fine woman; may God grant her and her children all good." If my power had been equal to the gratitude I owed to God, then gladly would I have thanked Him in full measure. What poor man ever owned such great treasure? Say what you will, he to whom God gives a noble, pure and beautiful wife has a gift beyond all earthy gifts. Oh Almighty Lord of Heaven, how happy he is, blessed with a faultless wife! Rejoice, honorable husband, over your virtuous wife; rejoice, God gives you both great joy! What does he know of this, that foolish man who has never drunk from this fountain of youth? Although bitter sorrow overwhelms me, I thank you, God, inwardly, that I have known such a wife. As for you, evil Death, enemy of all men, may God hate you unto all eternity!

10. *Death*

We mark, however, from thy words
That thou hast not drunk from wisdom's fountain.
Thou hast not seen into nature's workings,
Nor looked into the contexts of worldly things,
Nor at all perceived the necessary changes in the Earth;
Thou art, in truth, a witless dolt.
Mark how the gorgeous roses and the aromatic lilies in the garden,
How the robust weeds and comely flowers of the meadows,
How the sturdy rocks and towering trees in the wild fields,
How the mighty bears and powerful lions
In the woods and fearful jungles,
How the valiant warriors,
How the nimble, the exceptional, the learned,
And masters and all-powerful men,
And how all earthly creatures,
No matter how intelligent, how clever, how strong they are,
And how long they hold themselves erect, and carry out their will:
Mark how every one of them, how each of them,
Doth come to nothing and falls and is destroyed.
And now
If all men
And all kinds of men, who ever were or are or shall be,
Must pass from being into nothingness, how, then, shall it be
That she whom thou dost praise and endlessly lament
Shall not deserve the fate of every other and all others like her?
Though now thou hast it not in mind, thou also wilt not escape Us.
All in their turn: each of you must come to terms.
Thy lament is vain; it shall not help thee;
It falleth on fallow ground.

11. *The Plowman*

I trust in God whose power holds us both in sway to shelter me
from you and mightily to avenge the heinous wrong you have
brought to bear on me. Like a conjurer you come before me, veiling
what is true with falsehood and vainly seeking to remove from me
the enormous sorrow of my senses, my mind and my heart. You
cannot; I remain in agony upon my bitter loss. Day and night she
never wearied. She was my restorative against all sorrow and adversity, my holy servant, guardian of my will and caretaker of my body,
sentinel of her renown and mine. Whatever was entrusted to her
was ever rendered back whole, pure—aye and increased. God was
her never-failing counsel. And God, for her sake, was ever gracious

and favorful to me; for her sake God gave me health, joy, and
success in all my undertakings. This she earned and deserved for
the purity of our house. Reward and gracious meed give unto her,
oh benevolent Disburser, Almoner of faithfulness, most bountiful
God! Be merciful to her beyond my own wishes! Oh! Oh! Oh!
Shameless murderer, Lord Death, evil iniquitor! The hangman be
your judge to bind you, by your speech, upon the torture-rack!

12. *Death*

Couldst thou but rightly weigh, measure or determine,
Thou wouldst prevent such talk from spilling from thy shallow head.
Thy cursing and thy vengeful summonings want insight and excuse.
Wherefore this braying, ass? Must We recite again?
All things noble, brave, good, or excellent in any fashion—
All things which live must perish by our hand.
And yet thou whinest and dost maintain
That all thy happiness depended on thy chaste and
Noble wife.
If, truly, thou dost believe that happiness depends on woman,
We would offer thee ripe counsel on the matter.
Tell Us: when thou tookst the renowned woman
As thy wife—
Didst find her excellent?
Or hast made her so?
When the one, then cast about with circumspection;
Thou shalt even better, purer women find upon the earth,
One of which would matrimonially suit thee.
But if the other, if thou hast *made* her all-excelling,
Then rejoice! Thou art the living master craftsman
Who full well dost know the means to fashion
And upbring still one more excelling wife.
And now one final confidence:
The more of love thou hast, the greater sorrow will be thy part.
Hadst withheld thyself from love,
Wouldst now be free of pain.
Great love for what one hath, great pain to be bereft of it.
Wife, child, riches and all that is good on earth
Must yield more sorrow at its end than joy at its beginning;
All earthly things and love must turn to pain.
Pain is the end of love;
Sadness is the end of joy;
Revulsion is the end of pleasure;
Ill-will the end of willing.

Such is life's course; learn it better
If thou wouldst put wit in thy braying!

13. *The Plowman*

Insult follows injury: a law well known to all who are oppressed. Just so, you heap abuse on me. You have weaned me from love to pain and I must suffer this from you as long as God so wills. But though I may seem stupid, and though I have garnered little wisdom from learned masters, I know one thing: you have robbed me of honor, thieved my joy, stolen the goodness of my days, murdered my ecstasy and are the destroyer of all that assured me joyous life. Now what shall I celebrate? Where seek consolation? Where refuge? Where shall I find asylum and cure? Where find true counsel? Dead is dead. Dead before its time is all my happiness. Dead too soon. All too soon you have torn away the dear and lovely one and have mercilessly made me to a widower and my children to orphans. Helpless, alone, and filled with sorrow, I remain unrequited by you; no amends could ever come from you. How is that, Sir Death, adulterer of all men's marriage bed? No one can expect a good from you; after foul crimes you would give to no one satisfaction, to no one recompense. I mark that in you there is no mercy to be found; your way is but to curse, to inflict. Such kindness as you show men, the mercies men receive from you, the recompense you give, the ends that you prepare for men, let all these in like measure be sent to you by Him who has power over life and death. O, Ruler of the heavenly legions, reimburse me for my loss, my harm, my affliction, my desolation! Avenge me thereof on Death, Oh God, Avenger of all evildoing!

14. *Death*

Better not to say it than to say it stupidly.
For foolish talk must lead to quarrel;
Quarrel to enmity;
Enmity to unrest;
Unrest to outrage
Outrage to pain,
And after pain, remorse must come to every muddled man.
Wouldst quarrel with Us;
Wouldst lament that We have done thee ill
In the person of thy much-beloved wife.
Thou canst not see how gracious her share of Us hath been.
We received her youth, her proud body,

The best of her life, the best of her dignity, the best of her time,
And honor.
That was Our kindness,
Which hath been praised and desired by all philosophers
Who say: Best to die when one seeketh most to live.
He hath not died well who desired death;
To call for Us is the sorrow of a life too long.
Woe and privation to those doubled with age;
Amid all riches, that is still their poverty.
In this six-thousand-five-hundred-and-ninety-ninth year of the world,
One thousand, four hundred years of the Christ,
We let thy blessed mortal die from thee
And from the tinseled miseries of Earth,
To come, in good reward, to the joy,
The life,
And the peace of God.
Though thou dost spite Us, We would wish thee well,
Thy soul with hers in its heavenly mansion,
Thy bodies limb to limb in this grave of earth.
We would be thy bondsman,
And her good works would stand thee in good stead.
And therefore hold thy tongue!
Thou canst as little separate light from the sun,
Coldness from the moon, heat from fire,
Or wetness from water,
As thou canst divide from Us
Our power.

15. *The Plowman*

The guilty have always had their rhetoric, and so do you. To
those you would defraud you show yourself as sweet and bitter,
gentle and hard, kind and severe. That I now know. But no matter
how you ornament yourself I know that because of your grim
enmity I have lost my good and beautiful wife. And I also know
that none but God and you have such power. But this torment
comes not from God. For had I gone against God—as, to my shame,
I have often done—then He would have taken vengeance on me, or
my immaculate wife would have righted it for me. No, you have
done this evil. Therefore, I would know: who are you? what are
you? whence are you? what is your excellence that you are granted
such power to bring me such evil so suddenly? To have withered
my joyous green. To have undermined my tower of strength and
brought it to its fall. Oh God, Comforter of all troubled hearts,
comfort me and recompense me, poor, anguished, miserable, lonely

man! Oh Lord, bring torment and lay payment upon grim Death, grasp and destroy him who is enemy to You and all Your beings! Truly, Lord, in all Your creation there is nothing more dreadful, nothing more abominable, nothing more terrible, nothing more bitter, nothing more unjust than Death! His work is to defile and confuse all Your earthly lordship; he'd take away the good before the bad; he'd leave the malignant, old, sick and useless while raking in the worthy and the useful. Judge, O Lord, judge the false judge!

16. *Death*

Men who do not think name evil good and good evil,
As thou dost.
Thou dost accuse Us of judging falsely,
And doest Us injustice, as We shall prove:
Wouldst ask who We be?
We are Lord Death, God's implement,
And honest working reaper.
Our scythe precedeth Us, leveling white, red,
Green, blue, gray, yellow and every color of bloom
And grass, unmindful of its brilliance, its strength,
Or its value. Its beautiful color does not serve the violet,
Nor its rich fragrances, nor its delicious juices.
Behold, that is justice.
Romans and poets have known Us well and understood Our honesty.
Wouldst ask what We be?
We are nothing, and yet are something.
Being neither life, nor essence,
Neither form, nor quality, nor spirit,
We are nothing;
Being the end of life, the end of being, the beginning of non-being,
The region between them;
We are something; We are a fate;
We befall everyone.
Great giants must topple before Us;
Everything that liveth must suffer Our transfiguration.
Our victory is therefore just.
Wouldst ask how We be?
We are not to be described,
Save that a painted wall in a Roman temple
Showeth a blindfolded man astride an ox,
Carrying in his right hand a cleaver,
And in his left a shovel. These weapons
Against a great swarm of people, shooting, throwing,

Fighting him. All sorts of people, each carrying the tool of his trade—
Even a nun with the Psalter—
Attack the man upon the ox, pelt him, strike at him.
We understand this picture:
This embattled legion will be conquered, all,
And buried. It is the picture of a man with basilisk eyes,
Before whom all living creatures must die.
Wouldst ask whence We come?
From everywhere, and yet from nowhere.
We dwell in every corner of the world,
But are composed of what is not.
We are sourced in the earthly paradise;
There God created Us and rightly named Us, saying:
"On the day that thou eatest of the fruit of this tree
Thou shalt die of Death."
Therefore We sign Our name thus:
"We, Death, on Earth, in the air, and on the waters of the sea,
Lord and Ruler."
Wouldst ask what use We be?
Thou hast already heard We bring the world more benefit than harm.
Desist, then, and be content;
Thank us that We have been kind to thee.

17. *The Plowman*

Old men tell strange tales, learned men speak of the unknown,
and travelers to distant lands prevaricate. If you be one of these,
your fictions are nothing ill. But if as a reaper you claim your
descent from paradise, and if you aim at right, then your scythe
cuts all unevenly. It roots out vigorous flowers and leaves the thistle
standing; weeds remain and good herbs must perish. You say your
scythe precedes you. How is it then that more thistles than good
flowers, more rodents than tame animals, more evil men than good
are left intact? With your mouth tell me, with your fingers show me:
where are the capable, upright men of other times? I think you
have them. And my love is with them; only dust is left to me. Where
are they gone who dwelled on Earth and spoke with God and earned
His grace and mercy? Where are they gone who lived on Earth
under Heaven and computed the planets and the stars? Where are
they gone, those rich in knowledge, the masterly, just, gifted men
so spoken of in our chronicles? You have murdered them all, and
with them my beloved; but the despicable still exist. Who is guilty?
Sir Death, if you dared acknowledge the truth, you would name
yourself. You boast of your justice, sparing no one, all in their turn

falling before your scythe. But I was present and saw with my own
eyes two mighty armies—each numbered over three thousand men—
warring in a green field. They waded in blood up to their calves.
You were whirling and buzzing among them from one end to the
other. You killed many in these armies and many you left standing.
Yet I saw more masters lying dead than servants. I saw you claw
particular men from the midst of their fellows like rotten fruit
plucked from a basket. Is that your honest reaping? Your justice?
Is that the straight path of your blade? Well, then, dear children,
come! come! come here and let us ride out together to meet him
and offer him honor and speak praise to Death who judges so
rightly. The justice of God is hardly as fair!

18. *Death*

He who doth not understand a thing cannot speak of it.
Thus it is with Us.
We did not know thou wert so capable a man.
We have known thee long, but we had forgotten it.
For were we not there when Dame Sybil gave thee wisdom?
When King Solomon, dying, gave thee his wisdom?
When God assigned to thee the power given Moses in Egypt
As thou slew'st the lion in the mountain of Timnah?
We saw thee number the stars,
Compute the sands of the sea and its fish,
Count the drops of rain.
With pleasure We watched thee outrace Asahel,
Taste in Babylon the meat and wine of honor.
And when thou didst bear against Darius
The pennant of King Alexander,
We looked on and wished thee well.
Our special joy was thy cleverness in Athens
When thou bested in debate the wisest heads of the academies,
Men who also understood many high matters.
And when thou imparted morals and patience to Nero.
We marvelled when thou didst navigate the wooden ship of Julius
   Caesar
Over the wild sea, through the stormy blast.
In thy workshop we watched thee fashion a glorious garment
From the rainbow,
Wherein thou didst weave forms of angels,
Beasts, birds, fishes—even the owl and the ape.
But we laughed aloud and boasted of thee at Paris,
Seated on the fortune-wheel, capering upon the cowhide,

Working black magic and banishing the devil into a grotesque glass.
And finally, when God summoned thy counsel over the fall of Eve,
We knew, truly, thy great wisdom.
Had We but recognized thee earlier, We would have bowed before
   Thee;
We would have left thy wife and all mankind to live forever—
Solely in thy honor.
For thou art verily a most clever jackass!

19. *The Plowman*

For the sake of truth, men often must endure mockery and vile
abuse. So must I. You praise me for impossible things and fantastic
deeds. Your anger seeks to cut me. Yet it is I who have been treated
basely, and I who howl with grief. May I then not even speak of it
without suffering as well your resentment and scorn? He who does
evil and will not bend his pleasure to listen to reproofs, let him
beware lest great enmity be his own reward. Pray, follow my example: you have been sharp with me, contemptuous, irate, unjust,
but I have tolerated it and take no revenge, no matter how warranted. And even now if I have wronged you or if my manner has
been unseemly, pray tell me and I will gladly make amends. But if
not, then it is you who must make amends for the harm done me,
or teach me how my heart may be made whole. Truly, no man has
ever been so hurt! Yet I would have you take note of my forbearance. Either undo the wrong done me, my children, and my wife,
or stand with me before Almighty God to be judged. You could
easily entreat me, for I would gladly leave the matter with you. I
have trusted that you yourself would see the injustice you have done
and yourself would give me satisfaction. Act with insight, or otherwise the hammer shall strike the anvil, iron upon iron, come what
may!

20. *Death*

Kind words do soothe a man;
Understanding bringeth peace,
And forbearance, honor.
An angry man doth take no heed of justice.
Hadst thou before been gracious with Us,
Then Our part were also gentle
In showing thee the error of thy grief and lamentation.
Hast not heard of Seneca?
A philosopher who wanted to die in his bath.
Hast not read in his books

That none should lament the death of mortals?
If thou dost not know it, then know it now:
As soon as a man is born he hath begun to die.
The end is the twin of all beginning.
He who was sent out is required to return.
Strive not against what is ordained to happen,
Nor quarrel with what each must suffer.
What is borrowed must be given back.
All men live upon the Earth as in a foreign land,
Proceeding from being to nothingness. A man's life
Is a swift runner. Now alive, done
At the flip of a hand.
In short,
Every man oweth Us a dying
And his inheritance is death.
Thy wife's youth?
But the moment a man is born he is old enough to die.
Thou dost perhaps deem age to be a precious good?
Not so; it is a burden, a sickness, ugly, cold,
And bringeth no pleasure to any man. It is useless;
It is good for nothing.
The over-ripe apple falleth in dung;
The rotted pear falleth into the slough.
Her beauty? Thou wouldst be a child to shed tears for that.
For all beauty must be ruined by age or death,
All rosy lips drained of their color;
Red cheeks must turn pale,
Brilliant eyes, dull.
Hast not read the philosopher Hieronymous
Who teacheth men to beware of a woman's beauty,
Saying: Beauty, even with all carefulness
Is difficult to hold because so coveted;
Ugliness, however, is an easy thing to hold,
For it bringeth no pleasure to any one.
Let go, Plowman!
Lament no loss thou canst not undo.

21. *The Plowman*

I have heard that a wise man ought graciously to accept good admonition. I will bear this reprimand of yours. But if he who censures well ought counsel well, then, pray, help me and teach me how I may expunge from heart, mind and sense this unspeakable pain, this grief, this immeasurable sorrow. My God, my heart is

broken beyond saying now that the true and constant honor of my
house is torn away. O Lord Death, the whole world cries out against
you as I do, that there could never be one so evil that in him not
any good existed. So counsel me, help me by showing how I can
tear such sorrow from my heart, and how my children are to be
repaid for the loss of their unblemished mother. Else I'll be forever
without spirit and they will despair forever. And this you cannot
hold against me for I have seen unreasoning animals, out of instinct,
mourn the death of a mate. Help, counsel and restitution are what
you owe me, for you alone have done me injury. Should this not be
given, then even if vengeance were beyond the reach of Almighty
God, vengeance would still be done—even if once again the shovel
and the cleaver must be used.

22. *Death*

Quack, quack, quack! cackles the goose,
Preach to him what one may.
Hast thou not already heard from Us
That one must not lament the death of men who die?
Why dost thou persist in setting thyself against
Things that are. We *are*
The appointed taker of the toll,
Whom all men must pay by yielding Us their life.
Verily, he doth outwit himself who undertaketh to deceive Us.
Let it sink into thy brain:
Life is made for dying;
Were there no life, We too would not be,
Our handiwork would not be,
Nor with it would there be the very order of the world.
Now, either thy pain is great,
Or thy stupidity.
If the latter, then pray thou to God for understanding.
But if it be thy grief, then have done with it,
Let go, and consider that man's life on Earth
Is wind. Wouldst seek counsel how to purge thy heart of sorrow?
But Aristotle long ago hath taught thee that joy,
Sorrow, fear and hope, these four,
Bring all the world to grief,
And those, especially, who know not how to fend them off.
Time is compressed by joy and fear,
Spun out by sorrow and hope.
Who doth not drive these four completely from his heart
Must be evermore enmeshed by care. Unhappiness

Must follow joy, and love must always come to grief, here,
On Earth.
Love and sorrow are linked. The end of one
Is ever the beginning of the other.
They are naught else than when a man doth clench
A thing in his mind he will not release—
Just as the contented man cannot be poor
Nor the discontented rich,
For peace lieth not in the having of things,
But dwelleth in the heart.
Who will not drive an old love from his heart
Must ever endure a present grief.
Drive from thy heart, thy mind, and thy sense
The very memory of love,
And thou shalt in one stroke defeat all sadness.
The moment thou hast lost a thing
And canst not win it back,
Act as though it never were thine own:
Thy sadness will leave thee forthwith.
And if thou wilt not do this thing,
Much grief lies yet before thee;
Each child's death will break thy heart anew,
And thy death theirs, and every parting will lay new sorrows
In all and for all.
Thou wouldst that the mother's loss be rectified.
Canst thou bring back years that have passed,
Words spoken, maidenhood deflowered?
Then canst thou bring back the mother to thy children.
We have counseled thee enough.
Canst comprehend it, thou dull pickaxe?

23. *The Plowman*

They say that to study long is to learn a little; in due time one
understands the truth of this. Your homely sayings are sweetly
agreeable—*Pfui!* Cast love, happiness, rapture and pleasure from the
world and leave it a sickly remnant? Now *I* will cite the ancient
Romans. They practiced it themselves and taught their children to
esteem pleasure and spend their leisure time in gymnastics, jousting,
dancing, wagering, games of running and jumping so that they
would not fall prey to evil. For the soul of man can never run
idle. Either the good or the bad must ever engage it, even in the
dreams of sleep. Deprive the mind of its worthy thought, and
corruption will rush in to take its place. Out the good, in the bad;

out the bad, in the good: this interchange must last as long as the
world. Ever since joy, modesty, propriety and other good manners
have been driven from the world, it has been full of meanness,
treachery, faithlessness and infamy. Were I therefore to drive
thoughts of the beloved out of my mind, my soul would be cor-
rupted. All the more, then, will I think of her. When a great love of
the heart is suddenly transformed to heartbreak, who can forget it
in the blinking of an eye? Only an evil man can do that; good
friends are always rooted in each other's thoughts. Great distances,
long years are no obstacles to those who love. If, then, she is physically dead to me, she will continue to live in my thoughts. Sir Death,
your counsel must ring truer if it is to help me. Otherwise, fluttering
bat, you must further endure the enmity of birds.

24. *Death*

Love that is not too dear,
Pain that is not in excess
Shall be the wise man's loss and gain,
But, alas, not thine.
Who seeketh counsel and will not heed it
Cannot well be guided. Our well-meant counsel
Fails to thrive with thee. Well,
Be it pleasing to thee or not, we would bring truth
Into the light of day,
And let him attend to it who may.
Thy dwarfed understanding, thy chopped-off thoughts,
Thy insubstantial heart yearn to make of men
More than they can be. But make of him what thou wilt,
Man, We say—begging leave of all chaste women—
Is this:
He is conceived in sin,
Nourished in the body of his mother
With unclean, unspeakable filth.
He is born into the world naked, and grimy as a beehive;
An abomination is man, a pocket of dung, a meal for worms,
A stinkhouse, a fifthy swill tub, a flyblown carcass,
A mildewed cannister, a sack without bottom,
A bag full of holes, a windy bellows,
A voracious gullet, a stinking sewer,
A fraudulent pinchbeck,
A birdlimed twig,
A paper anchor,
And a garishly painted graveyard.

Let him hear it who may: every roundly made man
Hath nine holes in his body, all of which exude
Such abominable filth the likes of which can scarce be found,
Were never so beautiful a man to come before thee.
And hadst thou the eyes of a lynx,
And couldst thou espy what lay within
Pale Shuddering would seize thee.
Tear away the arts of the tailor from even the fairest woman,
And thou seest a wretched puppet,
A fast-fading flower of momentary luster,
A clod of earth rushing to its decay.
Show Us a handful of beauty
—not painted on a wall—
In all the women who lived but a hundred years ago,
And take the Emperor's crown for thine own!
Therefore, let go of love,
Let go of sorrow,
Let the Rhine flow as do the other waters,
Thou wise blockhead of donkeytown!

25. *The Plowman*

I spit on you, vile slanderbag! That you degrade and besmirch the best beloved of God's creatures, and with it cast your filth upon the very Godhead Itself! I know now that you lied and were not, as you maintained, created in paradise. Else you would know that God created man and all things in their perfection, and gave to man dominion over all, and placed all creation at his feet that he should rule over the animals on the land, the birds in the air, the fish in the waters, and the abundance of all the fruits of the earth, as, in truth, he does. Were man as miserable, evil and unclean as you say, then would God have made a useless and a vile thing; He would be a Creator to be scorned instead of praised. And then the given Word would be false that God made the world and saw that it was good. Lord Death, make an end to your senseless braying. You defile God's sublimest works. Angels, devils, hobgoblins, wraiths— these are spirits under God's compulsion; but man is the greatest of God's works, the most perfect, the most free. It was said on the day of creation: In His own image hath He made him. When has ever a workman made so deft and rich a thing as that small and marvelous sphere that is the head of man—wherein such powers operate that reflect the processes of God Himself? There in the apple of the eye resides the most faithful of instruments masterfully formed as to a mirror, reaching to the clear circles of Heaven. There in the ear the sense of hearing, perfectly concealed behind a thin membrane, proves and determines from afar sweet sounds of every kind. There in the nose the sense of smell going in and coming out through two openings artfully adapted for the pleasures of all delicate and voluptuous fragrances. There in the mouth the teeth day after day grind the body's nourishments; there, too, the thin leaf of the tongue makes known the thoughts of men to men; and there, too, are the pleasures of the taste and test of food. Further: in man's head come thoughts from the very depths of the heart, thoughts that reach to the infinite, to the very Godhead Itself and beyond. Man alone possesses Reason, the noblest of treasures. His alone that fair configuration which none but God could have made, in which all meaning and art is quickened with wisdom. Let it be, Sir Death. You are the enemy of man and therefore speak no good of him.

26. *Death*

Scolding, cursing, extravagant dreams,
However much of them there be,
Can fill no sack,
No matter how small. Words are useless
Against a blabberer. However it be, Plowman,
With your claim that man is the epitome
Of Beauty, Truth and Good,
He will still fall into Our net,
Be caught up in Our snare.

Grammar, the basis of all good speech,
Cannot help him with clear and well-set words.
Rhetoric, the florid ground of splendid style,
Cannot help him with the colors and the tones of language.
Logic, the arbiter of truth and falsity,
Cannot help him with her hidden turns and labyrinthine paths to
 Truth.
Geometry, surveyor and appraiser of the Earth,
Cannot help him with her faultless measures and unerring weights.
Arithmetic, the queen of numbers,
Cannot help him with her calculations and her clever integers.
Astronomy, the mistress of the firmament,
Cannot help him with the influence of planets or the strength of stars.
Music, cordial deliverer of melody and song,
Cannot help him with her sweet sounds and high-wrought voices.
Philosophy, the acre of wisdom plowed crosswise and seeded
With the natural light of Reason and the will to goodness,

Cannot help him; nor can
Physics, with her many helpful droughts;
Geomancy, stipulator of the zodiac;
Pyromancy, reader of the fire;
Hydromancy, seer of the water;
Astrology, keeper of the supernatural lens;
Chiromancy, comely oracle of the hand;
Necromancy, wielder of the spirits of the dead;
Alchemy, strange transfigurer of metals;
Neither availeth the *Augur's*
Understanding of the voice of birds and his vision of the future;
Nor the *Haruspex's*
Consultations of the smoke that issueth from sacrificial altars;
Nor the *Paedomant* who from the innards of calves,
Nor the *Ornomant* who from the innards of partridges,
Ply their conjurations.
Nor the inconstant and ambiguous judgments of
The *Jurist,* that unconscionable Christian
Who doth braid together right and wrong along the crooked lines
Of his stunted articles of law.
Neither these nor any other;
Neither any nor all together with their arts and powers
Have help to offer. Each man must someday be toppled by Us,
Thrashed in Our fulling-mill,
And scoured in Our whirling barrel.
Thou mayst well believe it, thou blustering bumpkin!

27. *The Plowman*

One ought not repay evil with evil; a man must be patient. Such is the path of virtue, which I will follow—and perhaps you, too, will become patient after your impatience. I take it from your speech that you mean well and would advise me truly. Then if there is truth in you, give me true counsel as one bound by an oath. In what manner shall I now pursue my life? Till now I have lived within the joy of marriage; what shall I do now? Shall I remain a worldly man or enter the holy order? Both stand open to me now. In my mind I have examined all kinds of lives, weighed them and judged them carefully, and I have found they are all imperfect, frail and tainted with sin. I am in despair as to where to turn, for all human paths seem laden with flaws. Lord Death, give me counsel! I stand in need of counsel! In my heart I find, and I believe it to be true, that I shall never again have such a home as the one her existence made for me. By my soul I tell you: If I knew that once again I would find such a wife then I would live a married man for all my days. Happy and blessed no matter where he be is the man who has found a good wife. To such a man it is a joy to strive for the necessities of life and to vie for honor. And to such a man it is as well a joy to repay honor with honor, faith with faith, blessing with blessing. He need not watch over her, for the best watch is that which a virtuous wife keeps upon herself. The man who cannot trust in his wife will be constantly beset with care. Lord of the heavens, Lord of every dwelling place, happy is he whose bed is blessed with so pure a companion! He should look to Heaven every day and raise his hands in thanks. Do your best, Lord Death, most capable lord!

28. *Death*

To praise without end; to revile without purpose;
This is the habit of the mass of men in all their undertakings.
But praise and blame must be fitly measured
That one may have them at one's hand when they are truly needed.
Thou dost now sing extravagant praises
Of the joys of marriage; yet
—begging leave of all virtuous women—
We would tell thee something:
The moment a man taketh a wife,
The two of them are in Our prison.
At once he hath obligation and care,
A drag-sled, a yoke, a horse-collar,
A burden, a heavy load, an incisored devil,
A daily rasp of which he cannot be free
'Til We bestow Our graces on him.
Day upon day a married man hath thunder in his house,
And hailstones, and foxes and serpents.
A wife always straineth to be master; if he draw up,
She draweth down; will he this,
She would that; will he hither,
She would thither. Of this game he'll have his fill,
And end each day without a victory.
She can deceive,
And at the same time flatter,
And at the same time cajole,
And cheat, with it all, while smiling as well,
And also weeping,
While all the while she is most heavily obstructing;
All this is inborn in her.

Too ill to work,
But well enough for lust,
She is tame or wild when it doth fit her purposes.
In the art of rebuttal she hath scant need of lawyers;
Her practise is ever to do what is forbidden,
While resisting what is asked of her.
That is too sweet for her,
That is too sour;
That is too much for her,
That is too little;
And if it be not too late for her,
It is surely too early.
If she should praise a thing,
It must first be warped upon a turner's lathe,
And even then her praise is spotted with derision.
For the married man help cometh never:
Be he too kind or be he too stern,
He receiveth equal portions of abuse—
Equal, indeed, to that which he doth earn by being then
Half-kindly and half-stern; help there is none.
Each day bringeth another imposition
—or a scolding;
Each week bringeth outlandish demands
—growling;
Each month bringeth novel sorts of obnoxious filth
—or crimson wrath;
Each year bringeth new apparel
—or a daily recipe of rancor and contention;
And there is no help.
Of the vexations of the night, We will say nothing,
For at Our age we are ashamed of them.
And were We not minded now to spare the women who are virtuous,
We could sing thee still other songs of the dishonest ones.
Therefore, Plowman, know what thou dost praise;
Thou canst not tell gold from lead!

29. *The Plowman*

Revilers of women must be themselves reviled, say the masters of
truth. What then shall be done with you, Lord Death? This unreasoning slander, even if permitted you by women, is most con-
temptible and a great offense to women. In the books of many a
wise man it is said that without the guidance of a woman no man
finds his way to happiness, for having wife and child is not the

meanest part of earthly happiness. With this truth, Mistress Philosophy brought peace of mind to the Roman Boethius, himself the artist of consolations. Every thoughtful and wise man will bear me witness: no man is schooled save in the schools of women. Say what you will: a well-bred, beautiful and chaste wife surpasses all earthly goods that one may ever behold. Never have I seen a true man and a brave man who did not find his strength in the help of a woman. Wherever the worthiest assemble one may see it every day: in the market place, in the courts, in tournaments, in every summons to arms it is always women who bring about the best. He who is truly committed to a woman will not do evil. In the school of an upright woman one learns propriety and honor. It is women who have power over all earthly pleasures; they bring it about that everything festive and delightful is done in their honor. A brave man is threatened more by the wag of a woman's finger than by all force of arms. In short and clear: good women are the sustenance, the mainstay and the increase of every man. Of course, with gold there will be lead, with wheat weeds, with true coin counterfeit, and there will be vixens among women. But the good ought not suffer for the bad. How to that, Captain of Inverted Hills!

30. *Death*

A lump of dirt for a nugget of gold,
A turd for a topaze,
A pebble for a ruby—so taketh the fool—
A haystack is a castle,
The Danube is the sea,
A buzzard is the peregrine; thus nameth the fool.
And thou, as well, praiseth the raptures of the eye,
But seest not the root of things,
And knoweth not that everything there is
Is desire of the flesh,
The covetousness of eyes,
Or the aspirings of pride.
Flesh seeketh lust; the eye, possession; pride, honors.
Possession bringeth avarice; lust maketh wanton; honors breed
    vanity.
Couldst thou but know this,
Thou wouldst encounter suffering and joy with greater grace,
And wouldst leave Us in peace.
But sooner will the jackass comprehend the harpist's art
Than thou wilt recognize the truth.
For this reason We are so much troubled for thy sake.

When We tore young Pyramus from the maiden Thisbe,
Who were one heart and soul,
When We took away the world from Alexander,
When We destroyed young Paris of Troy and Helena of Greece,
We were never so sorely plagued as We are by thee.
Nor were We thus vexed by the Emperor Charles,
Or the Margrave William, or Theodoric of Verona,
Or the powerful Boppe, or Siegfried the invulnerable.
There are many mourners still for Aristotle and Avicenna,
Yet they leave Us in peace. When the mighty King David
And King Solomon the wise came to dying,
More thanks than cursing was Our share.
They who once lived are all of them gone;
Thou, and all who now are and are yet unborn,
Will follow behind. Despite all,
We, Death, here remain Lord!

31. *The Plowman*

Out of his own mouth a man is often condemned, especially he
who speaks now this way, now that way. You have said before that
you were something and yet nothing, that you are no spirit and yet
are the end of life and that all men on earth were in your keeping.
But now you say we must all pass away and you, Sir Death, remain
here Lord! Contradictory words cannot together be true. If we must
all leave this life, and if all earthly life must have an end, and if
you, as you say, are the end of life, then I ask: when there is no
more life, there will be no more dying and no more death. Where
will you go then, Lord Death? Not to Heaven, for none but good
spirits dwell there and you are, as you say, no spirit. If, then, there
is nothing more on Earth for you to do, and if Earth exists no
more, you must needs go straightaway to Hell, there to groan for all
eternity. And then, too, the living and the dead will be avenged
on you. No man can be guided by your contradictory words. Are
all things on Earth created and fashioned in a manner so evil, pitiful
and useless? Of that the Almighty God has never been accused. God
has ever loved virtue, hated evil, punished and forgiven sin down
to the present day. I think that He will always do so. Since I was a
youth, I have read and learned from books how God created all
things. You say that all being and life on Earth shall have an end.
But opposed to this, Plato and other philosophers say that for all
things the destruction of one is the birth of another, and that all
things are based on rebirth, and that events of Heaven and Earth
are conjoined in a whirl of everlasting change. With your double-

edged speech, upon which no one may build, you would affright me from my suit. Therefore, Lord Death, my Destroyer, I convoke us before God, my Redeemer. And may He deliver to you an evil Amen.

32. *Death*

Oft when a man hath begun to speak
He cannot stop till he be interrupted.
From such a die hast thou been stamped.
We have once said it, and will again say it,
And with it make an end to it:
The Earth and all that it contains is built on shifting sand.
And now, indeed, it is more changeable than ever,
For everything is changed about:
The back is made the front, the front is back,
The top is undermost and what is under is on top;
The masses have made perversion into law.
But We have brought them all, all generations,
To the constancy of flames.
To find a good, true and helpful friend
Is, on Earth, almost as possible as to grasp a beam of light.
All men are more disposed to evil than to any good in them.
And should one do the good, he does it out of fear of Us.
All the activity of men is vanity and noise.
Their body, their wife and children, their honor,
Their possessions and all their powers fly away,
Vanish in an instant and are scattered with the wind;
Neither shape nor shadow can remain.
Look about thee and behold what the children of men
Do hasten after here on Earth:
How they plumb mountain and valley,
Wood and wilderness, the depths of ocean and earth
For the sake of worldly goods;
How they dig deep mines and probe in the earth
To bleed her veins of the shining ores they prize
Above all else. How they hew down trees
And, like sparrows, weave together walls and houses.
Plant orchards and set graftings,
Plow their fields, stake their vineyards,
Build their mills, exact their taxes,
Hunt and fish, gather together great herds of animals,
And countless servants and maids,
Ride high upon their horses,

Stock their houses and their coffers full of precious stones,
Gold, silver, and voluptuous apparel,
Surrendering themselves by night and by day
To the lusts and raptures they are ever seeking.
What is all that?
It is all vanity upon vanity, and confusion of the soul,
As fleeting as a day already past.
With war and thievery they make their gains,
For the more they have the more they have robbed.
And what they have they leave as an inheritance
For new quarreling and dissension.
Alas, mortal man liveth always in fear, in misery,
In sorrow, in care, in dread, in terror,
In sickness and pain, in sadness and woe, in wailing and moaning,
And in adversity of sundry kind. The more of earthly goods,
The more compounded his adversity.
But the greatest burden is that he cannot know when, where, or how
We shall pounce on him and drive him hence
Along the way of mortal flesh.
It is a burden to be borne by masters and slaves,
Men and women, rich and poor, good and evil.
O painful certainty, how little thou art heeded by fools!
When it is too late, they would all of them be pious.
Therefore, O man, let go of thy complaint.
Enter what course of life thou wouldst,
Thou wilt find it frail and vain as any other.
But turn thyself from evil and do good,
Seek peace and pursue it ever,
Prize above all earthly things
A conscience that is clear.
And to prove Our counsel hath been true,
We shall stand with thee before God,
The Eternal, The Great, The Almighty.

33. *The Judgment of God*

Spring, Summer, Fall and Winter,
The four quickeners and helpers of the year,
Fell once into a great dispute,
Each boasting of his own good will
In wind, rain, thunder, snow
And weather of every grade and hue,
Each claiming that his work was best.
Spring said he vivified all fruit and brought abundance;

Summer that he brought all fruit its form and time of ripeness;
Fall said that for the other two he brought fruit home
Into cellars, barns and houses; while Winter said
He ate the fruit and drove away the venomous worm.
And each, in the eagerness of his claim,
And in the zeal of argument,
Forgot from whence his power came.
Now both of you do likewise:
The plaintiff mourns his loss as though it were his rightful due;
He gives no thought that it was loaned to him by Us.
And Death, as well, boasts of a warranted dominion
For which We alone indentured him.
The one bewails what is not his;
The other vaunts a power he does not himself possess.
Yet the quarrel is not without its sense,
And you have both fought well.
Sorrow drives the former to bring suit,
And, in the face of this, the latter is constrained to tell the truth.
Therefore:
To you, Plowman, honor;
To you, Death, victory.
Each man must give his life to Death, his body to earth,
His soul to Us.

34. *The Plowman's Prayer to God*

Ever watchful Keeper of the world, God above all gods,
Wonderful Lord above all lords, all-powerful Spirit above all spirits,
Wellspring of all good, Source of all holiness,
Crown and giver of crowns, Reward and giver of rewards,
O hear me!

O Light that needs no light, in whom all other light is darkness,
Light that breaks upon all shadow
Light that said "Let there be light!"
O Fire forever burning, O beginning and End,
Hear me!

Holy one above all holiness, Path without turning,
Best, Life of all life, Truth of all truth, Issuer of strength,
Perceiver of all evil, Helper of all in need of help,
Comforter and Rock of all celestial harmony,
Sculptor of the face of man, Law of the heavenly order, bright Sun,
Hear me!

Physician of all illness, sole Father of creation,
Almighty Companion from womb to grave, Hater of all corruption,
Judge and Unifier, Firm Knot which no man can unravel,
Hunter to whom no trail is hidden, Measurer, Arbiter, Conciliator,
O hear me!

Perfect Being in whose hand all perfection lies, Creator and Destroyer,
Host, Ministrant and Friend to all good men,
Mingler of the inconstant air, Kindler of fire, Lode-star,
Emperor in whose service none may fail, Cause of all causes,
Hear me!

Good above all goods, most worthy Lord Jesus,
Graciously receive the soul of my dearly beloved wife,
Grant her eternal rest, lave her with the dew of Your grace,
Keep her in the shadow of Your wings. Take her, O Lord, into
Your perfect peace.

I grieve for Margaret, my chosen wife. Grant her, Most Gracious
Lord, eternally to see into the mirror of Your divinity.

May all things that live under God help me to say with tranquil heart:
"Amen!"

Chapter 10

THE MOMENT OF GRIEF

JACOB NEEDLEMAN

Surely, few of us believe that life is a preparation for death. As historical events and scientific progress nullify our trust in traditional religious forms, this idea is one of the first to fall—that there will come a final moment when we will be tested and weighed in the balance of some higher universal purpose, and that the central concern of our day-to-day lives should be to ready ourselves. All our knowledge seems to lead us to the certainty that death is our destruction, meaningless, which only madmen glorify and whose factuality only cowards avoid. We know that we are cowards but at least we value those rare moments when life seems so rich that death loses its terror. For the rest, we refuse to brood morosely.

And so, when a philosopher like Plato tells us that we should spend our life learning to die, we cannot really listen to him, or even wish to. But in the time of grief we do turn to such thoughts and to many others which we avoid in the course of our lives. Are we simply looking for comfort in the form of some intricate denial of the death we have encountered? For, when we recover our customary balance, when we pass through this time, our attention is drawn far away from those thoughts.

Let us consider the possibility that in that moment of grief our consciousness comes into a new sort of relationship to the rest of us, and that it is precisely this relationship, and not the outer event, for which we are unprepared. And that a better meaning of the idea of preparing for death has nothing at all to do with the gradual relinquishing of vital experience. What we wish to explore is the thought that the preparation for death is a preparation to be alive.

Obviously, this line of thought will yield no consolation in the ordinary sense. It cannot lead to proofs of life beyond the grave or to prescriptions about heroic acceptance of our destruction. On the contrary, it begins and ends with the thought that we *do not know* what death is. The agony of the search for proofs and prescriptions is not rooted in our ignorance about death, but rather, in the fact that we are afraid to distrust our fears and imagination.

The point is this. It is a commonplace to say that man is afraid of the unknown. But is it really so? When I am afraid to enter a dark room, isn't it because my imagination makes me *forget* that I don't know what is in there? And if someone then reminds me about my imagination, doesn't the fear lift for an instant? In other words, if somehow I were able to stand in front of my imagination, to see it, then at least that portion of myself which saw it would not be afraid. But somehow I cannot wish to do this. In some way I value my imagination and the fears that are in it; I trust it; I believe that it gets me through life, or that it brings me my satisfactions.

If we think of death as being like that dark room, then many of the proofs and prescriptions in the literature of philosophy and psychology read like reactions to the imagination, rather than attempts to awaken us to it. In the main stream of modern thought, this usually takes the form of proving that the mind cannot exist without the body, or that there is no soul. Of course we can also find proofs that go the other way: that there is a life after death, an immortal soul, etc. Both sorts of effort are essentially the same, whatever the content of the particular proof. Each moves away from the fact of ignorance rather than toward it or into it.

The fact of ignorance is a fact about oneself, and to move away from it is to move away from oneself. This is to suggest that thought must be distinguished from self-awareness, since the thinking process is but one of the functions of that self or organism. Just as my fear lifts when I become conscious of my imagination, so it may be that if I can become conscious of my thought about death, I may begin to stand in a new relationship to that thought.

The ignorance about death is not an ignorance of some facts about the external world. Rather, it is possible to see this ignorance as the sensing of the inadequacy of thought, perhaps even the sensing of its surprisingly dependent place in the totality of our life.

It was also Plato who showed that our thought does not guide us, though we imagine it does; rather that thought always follows and serves some impulse, desire or fear in us, creatures of the cave. The same Socrates who in *Phaedo* offers his pupils several external proofs of immortality, also, in the *Apology*, reminds the whole Athenian community that no one but God knows what takes place after death.

Kierkegaard, a modern Christian pupil of Socrates, writes:

All honor to him who can handle learnedly the learned question of immortality! But the question of immortality is essentially not a learned question, rather it is a question of inwardness, which the subject by becoming subjective must put to himself. Objectively, the question cannot be answered, because objectively it cannot be put, since immortality precisely is the potentiation and highest development of the developed subjectivity. Only by really willing to become subjective can the question properly emerge, therefore how could it be answered objectively? . . . the consciousness of my immortality belongs to me alone, precisely at the moment when I am conscious of my immortality I am absolutely subjective . . . Immortality is the most passionate interest of subjectivity; precisely in the interest lies the proof . . . Quite simply, therefore, the existing subject asks, not about immortality in general, for such a phantom has no existence, but about his immortality, about what it means to become immortal, whether he is able to contribute anything to the accomplishment of this end, or whether he becomes immortal as a matter of course, or whether he is that and can become it. (*Concluding Unscientific Postscript*, pp. 155–156)

We thus come to the tentative conclusion that there is something valuable about this ignorance and that perhaps we should not be in too great a hurry to get rid of it. Whatever else they may be, are not the great sorrows of life also confusions? That is, don't they—and the death of loved ones more than any—bring us at least momentarily to the awareness that we do not understand? That we are ignorant? And are not our efforts to assuage our suffering often attempts to fly from that awareness back to our former "understanding"? When we suffer and we say "I don't understand" are we not searching for some way to fit what has happened into our old categories?

So the question arises: What would it mean to want a new understanding, rather than the retaining of our old understanding? Surely, the first thing it would mean would be the wish to remain cognizant of our ignorance and to see it as something which cannot be "corrected" by the selection (under the aegis of the old understanding) of external facts, proofs or exhortations.

However, it is surely life and not we ourselves that brings us to moments of this awareness of ignorance. If we are to speak of any preparation, it would have to be preparation for these moments.

We know we cannot change our emotions; we cannot, by thinking, change hate to love or erase our fears. In a minor sort of way, every emotional surprise in our life is thus such a moment as we are speaking of. Thus the material basis of any preparation lies right in front of us in the person of our everyday emotional life.

Our discussion having come to this, we can now connect it again with Socrates. In that same dialogue, *Phaedo,* which takes place on the day of Socrates' execution, he explains to his pupils that those who really apply themselves in the right way to the search for wisdom are directly and of their own accord preparing themselves for dying and for death. At this

> Simmias laughed and said, Upon my word, Socrates, you have made me laugh, though I was not at all in the mood for it. I am sure that if they heard what you said, most people would think—and our fellow countrymen would heartily agree—that it was a very good hit at the philosophers to say that they are half dead already, and that they, the normal people, are quite aware that death would serve the philosophers right.

Socrates answers:

> And they would be quite correct, Simmias—except in thinking that they are "quite aware." They are not at all aware in what sense true philosophers are half dead, or in what sense they deserve death, or what sort of death they deserve.   *Phaedo 64*

It is in precisely this context that Socrates explains this preparation as the turning of the attention toward the mind (or soul) and away from the pleasures and pains of everyday life. Most people are quick to see in this the thought that we should gradually relinquish the most vivid and valuable side of life. But, once again, does not this ready interpretation come also from the fact that we forget our ignorance about death? What could preparation mean if we are to continue, in our thought, to relate to our everyday emotions like undiscriminating beggars? If it is true that in our thought we are surprised by our emotions and confused by our powerful emotions, how else could we prepare ourselves than by searching for a new relationship to our thought? But we forget our ignorance, we forget that our emotions surprise us and lead us, we forget that they confuse us; we forget that we do not understand ourselves.

We think of the idea of preparing for death as preparing for something beyond the grave without our taking the initial steps of preparing for our fears and griefs. We reject the former idea as based on a presumption about life after death without realizing we live under the presumption that we stand in a right relationship to our fears and desires.

And so, when Socrates tells his pupils to despise everyday pleasures and pains, it is advice that follows from his (and the Oracle's) evaluation of ignorance. The Oracle said of him that he was the wisest in Athens because he alone was aware of his ignorance. We also recall the famous inscription "Know Thyself" which was Socrates' watchword as well. Together, these two formulae about Socrates' wisdom and self-knowledge can lead to the practical goal of becoming aware of our ignorance about ourselves. And thus, to despise our everyday emotions is to despise the illusion that we are not confused by our emotions, an illusion that often takes the form of believing it is the world out there which confuses us, or perpetrates injustice, or destroys us, or (on the other hand) rewards us and makes us happy.

A man would have to be a fool to think lightly of the anguish of the moment of grief. But precisely because such an emotion is overwhelming and sweeps everything else in us aside, precisely because of this the question of preparation becomes important.

If emotions are our source of life and yet not our responsibility it would seem that when we prepare for them we are preparing for being alive. It would follow that our search must be to struggle directly only with what is in our power to meet. Where, then, is our responsibility? What *is* in our power?

This question may perhaps reveal something about that weakening of trust in traditional religious forms which was mentioned at the beginning. For if the religions of our present culture take it as their task directly to legislate our emotions, the result may be for us only that we overlay the actual emotions which willy-nilly occur in us with imaginary feelings, i.e., thoughts about our emotions which are out of all congruity with the emotions themselves.

Nothing, of course, could be further from the awareness of ignorance, and nothing would more effectively block the growth of that awareness. For if I am told and if I believe that I ought to love my neighbor, how will I ever relate to my hatred of him? No wonder modern psychiatry seems realistic in reminding us of our actual emotions. But unfortunately, psychiatry, in passing judgment on our thought, just as effectively blocks our vision of confusion. Self-knowledge surely does not begin with the attempted refusal to judge my emotions, but with the search to see both my judgments and my emotions.

Yet what else but religion has the office of relating man with the question of death? In a sense, this is its main, perhaps its only task. It may be, however, just because we go to religion to escape our ignorance rather than to discover it, that it can become undermined by such things as psychiatry, science, and political events. Thus, when a great fear or anguish overwhelms us, we soon afterwards turn to religion either to have a counter-emotion evoked in us or to be commanded to feel something else, both of which serve the purpose of reinstating the illusion that we understand our emotions. And once it is reinstated, once we have "regained our balance," "passed through the difficult time," etc., we then avoid religion because it seeks to give us what we think we already have: a sense of moving in the right direction, or—to put it in the language of this discussion—a turning away from our emotions in the form of a "contented relationship" toward them.

Thus religion, psychiatry, and science all leave us unprepared for death. And the moment of grief, a moment in which we may be genuinely face to face with the enormous forces that act in us in the form of our emotions, fails ultimately to make the rest of our inner life a question. On the contrary, our reactions to that moment pull us out of ourselves in the search for philosophical systems, proofs, exhortations, consolations, substitutes— in short, the search for a return to our former quality of life, a life which those very moments reveal to us, momentarily, as far less than our human right, as far closer to the death we confusedly fear than to the real life that lies hidden within us.

A NOTE ABOUT METAPHYSICAL SPECULATION

When the fact of death compels us outward to more recognizably metaphysical questions about man's place in the universe, perhaps it need not be wholly at the expense of an awareness of ignorance. Let us, therefore, assume that there is a difference between fantasy and speculation, taking fantasy as the absolutizing of partial or relative knowledge, and taking speculation as the effort to maintain a sense of the relativity of our thinking and our concepts of the universe. Thus, it is not only grandiose metaphysical systems that are fantasies. Equally fantastic is the absolutizing of those common standards of intellectual satisfaction associated with logical consistency, ordinary language and pragmatic scientific theory.

How, then, are we to avoid fantastic thinking about death? And in what directions might metaphysical speculation about death take us?

One point is clear: for us, death is conceptually linked to a great many other things such as time, identity, consciousness, life, matter, change, birth. It would, therefore, be a great mistake to think about death without trying to see how these other ideas present themselves in our minds.

We may take as example what seems a truism: Death is the end of life. Yet this simple proposition contains many questions which, if totally avoided, leave us with nothing more than an empty verbal equation. *What* is that of which death is the end?

How do we understand life? Biologically? Personally (my life)? If biologically, do we think of life as a complex trick of matter, an intricate organization of what is essentially dead? Does it seem more *natural* that things should die rather than that they should live? What concept of reality underlies this thought?

Or are we willing to settle for an unbridgeable dualism of the living and the nonliving in our universe? If so, what becomes of our *uni*verse? And in such a universe, how could anything die, that is, change from living to nonliving? What is lost or what is ended in such an event? How, in fact, do we understand an *end*? Disappearance? What is that—vanishing into nothingness—or disappearance from our view?

Furthermore, if we think of life as purposive activity, how do we recognize purpose? Is *our* activity the only sort of purpose that could exist? What is our standard of time against which we measure the accomplishment or effort towards purpose? Is there life that exists on totally different scales of time—incommensurably smaller or greater—than our own? If so, how would we ever perceive it?

For that matter, how can we perceive our own time scale? From what perspective, from what *place* could we ever perceive our scale of time? Or are we condemned forever to stay within it, never directly perceiving how or if our beginnings are related to our endings? Is there in *us* the possibility of another order of time within which we can see the processes and changes which constitute the time of our everyday lives, both as individuals and as mankind? If not, is there no other order or time other than our own? Or are we so cut off from the time of galaxies, planets and molecules that it is foolish to think about them in this way? What sort of a universe would that be? And are we necessarily so cut off?

Or should we avoid these questions as unanswerable or meaningless? Unanswerable, meaningless to whom? What sort of answers do we insist on? Why? What sort of meaning would we like to find? Why do we stop looking when we fail to find it? What sort of purposes is our thought supposed to serve? Are these purposes consonant with what exists in the universe? What kind of certainty are we looking for? Why do we get weary of questions, and more questions? Why do we want to stop? What kind of resting-place is the sense of certainty we prize? Is it that of fantasy?

Perhaps we take death as the end of *my* life. What kind of end can *I* have? What is it which ends? Can I believe in my own death? Can I imagine it? If not, why? Is it because I have no understanding of what I am? Can I even imagine my own life, not to mention my own death? Do I assume, only because of the rules of grammar and dictionary definition, that death is the end of experience? The end of consciousness? What are these? Is consciousness some weird, metaphysically unique phantom in a blind unconscious universe? Is there a consciousness that is different from thought? If so, how could I begin to *think* about it? Do I even have it? or does it, can it, have me? Is it *I*?

And what do *I* ever experience? Is our past already dead? Is what dies, when I die, only the final member of a bundle of perceptions? Or is there a self that persists "through time"? If we would like to believe the latter, how do we experience it? Do we remember our life? What is there to do the remembering —one of the bundle? Or something above and beyond the bundle? And, again, if we believe the latter, who or what is believing? Another member of the bundle? That is, is this, too, fantastic thinking, a taking of the part for the whole?

There may be an interesting relationship between the notion that my self will be either destroyed or preserved in death and the degradation into fantasy of the impulse toward metaphysical speculation. The fantasist asks: What is the place in the universe of this being, man, who is destroyed by death? Or, alternatively: What is the place in the universe of this being, man, who is immortal? Fantasy would seem to be inevitable as long as we rely on part of our thought while questioning the other part. But in speculating about our place in the universe, is it not a fact that we have no real idea of what purpose our thought is to serve?

That our lives are dominated by fantastic thought may be because there is so little relationship between the *impulse* to speculate about our place in the universe and the *content* of our "speculative thought." If the emotion of the moment of grief represents one such impulse, surely another is what the ancients called *thaumazein*—what we speak of as "wonder."

Most of us remember the rare moments when we have experienced this emotion: perhaps on a night away from the city, looking up towards countless worlds; perhaps as children directly observing some living thing; it would be futile to try to put this emotion into words. But what is it we forget when this moment passes and we are trying to think about the questions which we then associate with that moment: What is the meaning of my smallness? How can I know my part in this magnitude which I sense? Isn't this what we forget: That at that moment when we are presented with the emotion of wonder, that emotion and that state of mind *are themselves an element in the answer to our questions.* We know this at the moment—though perhaps not in so many words—and we forget it later.

Might it not be that such an emotion and state of mind is itself a kind of knowledge that truly takes us out of ourselves toward the universe? Might it not be that, just as in the moment of grief, this emotion is a brief individual connection with what, to thought, seems so far above us or outside us? What do we trust when this emotion is no longer present? What do we then take to be knowledge? Is our fantastic thinking a mere expenditure of the knowledge or force with which we were temporarily connected? When we think of metaphysical systems which speak of man as a microcosm, embodying in himself in some way and to some degree all of the reality of the universe, do we value or even remember that our questions about the universe came to us originally in the form of an answering direction, and that this partial answer itself came in the form of a certain quality or force of questioning? Isn't it so, however, that our thinking flies away from that moment, forgets it by classifying it and distrusting it?

Thus, in this light, metaphysical speculation can be the study and the search for questions, or, rather, for questioning, the study of what we desire and the possible attempt to be alert for help and direction when it appears. Do we want thoughts about death and immortality, or do we want immortality? Do we want answers or do we want to be?

Chapter 11

SCIENTIFIC APPROACHES TO THE STUDY OF SURVIVAL

GARDNER MURPHY

S cientists still remain reluctant to turn the searching light of scientific investigation on eternity, immortality, and related subjects which are at the very core of the soul's "invincible surmise."

However, among the world's thousands of scientists, a few are making an effort to lead trained investigation into imaginative study of these areas, employing the same research skills and ingenuity that have brought about far–reaching discoveries made in recent years.

What better path to travel? What more rewarding target? And what more fitting basis on which to commence work than the honest admission by the agnostic scientist that he does not know and cannot prove that there is no "hereafter."

Gardner Murphy, an outstanding scientist now engaged in just such efforts to see beyond the curtain, contributes the following thoughts not as assurance that there is a hereafter but as assurance that we certainly do not know there is *not* one; and makes the plea that we undertake determined and appropriate studies to unlock the secrets which lie in the beyond . . . if such there be.

A.H.K.

"To see life steadily and see it whole" includes looking honestly at death. Most of us not only fear death, we are afraid to talk about it, or to ask what there is beyond the biological termination of our individual existence. When it is seriously maintained, as it is by some branches of modern scientific investigation, that personality, or some aspects of it, may survive death or may belong to a time-space reality not limited to biological existence, utter incredulity usually spreads over the face of the listener; and tart remarks about ghosts, haunted houses, mediums, and the cycle of the bizarre and the occult stifle the serious progress of

139

the conversation. But in spite of this incredulity, there is complex and challenging evidence that relates to the issue of continuity beyond death.

Although there is very little chance that we will survive death in our familiar form or that any *aspect* of us is changeless, there is still a chance that we shall discover some extraordinary things about personality, if we look at the evidence. It is not the philosophical or religious approach that is considered here; it is the empirical evidence considered in relation to the important issue of the place of human personality in a cosmic context.

Certain evidence exists that is usually referred to by the broad term of *spontaneous cases*. Spontaneous experience usually consists of a vision of a dying person that conveys specific information about his identity and personality.

A well-corroborated example of a fully externalized apparition coinciding with the sudden death of a distant person is given by Mrs. Sidgwick in the English *Proceedings of the Society for Psychical Research*.[1]

The original report is long and detailed, but may be summarized here: The percipient was Lieutenant J. J. Larkin, of the Royal Air Force, and the apparition was that of one of Larkin's fellow officers, Lieutenant David M'Connel, killed in an airplane crash on December 7, 1918. Lieutenant Larkin reported that he spent the afternoon of December 7 in his room at the barracks. He sat in front of the fire reading and writing, and was wide awake all the time. At about 3:30 PM, he heard someone walking up the passage.

> The door opened with the usual noise and clatter which David always made; I heard his "Hello boy!" and I turned half round in my chair and saw him standing in the doorway, half out of the room, holding the door knob in his hand. He was dressed in his naval cap, and there was nothing unusual in his appearance . . . In reply to his "Hello boy!" I remarked, "Hello! back already?" He replied, "Yes. Got there all right, had a good trip." . . . I was looking at him the whole time he was speaking. He said, "Well, cheero!" He closed the door noisily and went out.

Shortly after this, a friend dropped in to see Lieutenant Larkin, and Larkin told him that he had just seen and talked with

Lieutenant M'Connel. Later on that day it was learned that M'Connel had been instantly killed in a flying accident which occurred at about 3:25 PM. Mistaken identity seems to be ruled out, since the light was very good in the room where the apparition appeared. Moreover, there was no other man in the barracks at the time who in any way resembled Lieutenant M'Connel. It was also found that M'Connel was wearing his naval cap when he was killed—apparently an unusual circumstance. Agent and percipient had been "very good friends though not intimate friends in the true sense of the word."

Several hundred cases of this type have been investigated and published. The issue of "coincidence" is hard to state properly. Although actuarial data on the likelihood of death show that cases coinciding with death are far more numerous than could be expected, this is not a very real issue to the scientifically minded. What is more interesting and important is the specificity of the information given, for example, the wearing of the naval cap in the above example.

One may ask whether these cases really have any bearing on the question of survival after death. They may just be cases of "telepathy between the living." However, there are many cases in which the apparition appears some time *after* death, but without knowledge of this fact on the part of the perceiver, and there are a few cases in which the apparition is seen by more than one person. G. N. M. Tyrrell[2] has amassed considerable evidence to show that the data suggests the subconscious collaboration of two personalities—as if there were an intention to communicate or to be open to such communication. Hornell Hart[3] and his collaborators have shown that the psychological characteristics of hallucinations of the living are strikingly similar to those of apparitions which appear after death.

But spontaneous cases give less adequate evidence of purpose than that which can be secured by a more systematic approach. In most societies there are devices for allowing the hands or the organs of speech to communicate impressions which are believed to come from the deceased. Such means can also include automatic writing, the Ouija board or complex processes of inducing a trance in which dream or reverie may convey what is regarded as evidence of postmortem communication. It is not surprising, of course, that the ready state of the receiver and his eagerness for communication should be followed by speech, gesture, and action interpreted as giving proof of survival. The issue is whether any of the information thus communicated could have, been available beforehand to the person in a trance or indeed to anyone present. One could say that apparent communications are merely a form of "play acting" in which knowledge of the habits of the deceased is dramatically represented, but this still would not touch upon the real question that interests psychical research; namely, whether there are *bona fide* communications which give detailed and characteristic evidence of continuing personality.

There is much good material at hand. One record[3] involves two deceased communicators who planned to provide evidence of their own continued individuality and scholarly interaction by giving a complex classical reference which had not been asked by the investigators. After a great deal of elaborate library work, it was discovered that the evidence concerned a series of intertwined themes in which these two distinguished classical scholars had been interested. It is difficult, in such a case, to say that this was a telepathic communication from one of the persons present. It cannot safely be said that the personality of the deceased invades the body of the living. The person in a trance is still himself, and psychological analysis of the process of communication strongly suggests that there is a kind of weaving back and forth between communicator and receiver, just as there is in human conversations.

Evidence of this sort will, of course, not be regarded by most persons as "proof." Even if there is a great desire to believe, and even if there is a great deal of material at hand, our society is strongly against acceptance of such interpretations. The material, moreover, is scattered and does not lend itself to easy interpretation. There is some real evidence of survival after death, but in what form or how the pieces are put together is certainly not clearly indicated by such evidence as we have.

There is, of course, a tendency to build a cult out of this material, and it is not surprising that beliefs in personal survival take a form which follows the religious tradition of the believer. This is dramatically evident when one looks at survival evidence that has been gathered in India, Ceylon, Burma, the Middle East, Alaska, and Brazil in the recent work of Dr. Ian Stevenson[4] of the Department of Neurology and Psychiatry at the University of Virginia. The material, though varied, reveals common attitudes and patterns of belief related to reincarnation. Typically, a small child announces to his parents that he does not really belong to them, that he belongs in a village many miles from where he lives, usually a village which he has never visited. He names persons, houses, streets, events in the other house, and demands to be taken there and to resume his own normal life. One can do a great deal of detective work but still find it quite difficult to explain how these little children pick up and so adroitly use detailed information regarding other towns, especially in these regions, in which there is very little village-to-village communication. There is less material like this in Western culture, in which the Christian tradition of individual survival beyond death, rather than the belief in reincarnation, characterizes the early experience of all who face death. There are, of course, many philosophical devices for reconciling a belief in continued disembodied existence with the more typical reincarnationist lore of the sort that comes down from Pythagoras. There are, in fact, several other ways of looking at the survival of physical death, all of which present serious intellectual problems.

If it is true, then, that there are many states of mind and body which suggest that some aspects of human nature are less narrowly dependent upon biochemical and physiological realities than simpler reflex functions are, it may be natural to ask whether functions relating to creativity, long-range planning, and capacity for conceptualization of a high order, may not represent forms of contact of man with elements in the cosmic structure that he does not understand well, but may slowly be learning to reach. There is no room here for dogmatic philosophy. It is natural and legitimate that the first studies of personality should be made with a literal concern for simple bodily function as a cause, or at least a support, of psychological function. It is equally natural that the close study by psychiatry and psychology of the more complicated realities should arouse doubts depending upon the temperament and the individuality of the thinker.

There is apparently a close relation between these evidences of personal survival and the evidences for unusual modes of psychical functioning, altered ego states, out-of-the-body states, cosmic consciousness, and a number of new ways of defining the limits of human personality. The possibility exists that the transcending of ordinarily held time-space limits, as we function here and now, may have something to do with time-space dimensionality in relation to continuity of some aspect of personality beyond physical death. The character of the issues is open, and points to the need for more sharply defined hypotheses, especially those relating to quite fundamental biological and physical science dimensions and the way in which personality is conceived in terms of these dimensions.

Whatever the reasons may be, it is of the utmost importance in the study of this issue of bereavement and parapsychology to grasp that there is no "scientifically correct" position to take, no predetermined conclusion. Some persons derive great personal comfort from their conviction that there is evidence for the reality of continued existence beyond death; for others there is no comfort at all. Despite these individual differences, this is a well-defined scientific problem and reason for believing that considerably less sense of despair is intellectually justifiable after thorough study of the available evidence for survival. It will at the same time be pointed out that the conditions under which we, after our own physical death, might meet and carry on with our loved ones after death might be utterly different from anything that we can imagine. It certainly is not sound mental health practice though it may be a philosophical comfort, to believe that after death we shall go on through a long span of years essentially just as we were.

We are reminded by the evidence presented by thousands of sensitive men and women in all times and places of the infinite variety of attitudes and modes of appreciation which we may take towards the universe. Nothing is "proven" by these histories. They serve as science, art, and religion may sometimes serve to redefine a way of looking at our own individuality and that of the persons whom we respect and love. The attempts at a new scientific definition of the relation of personality to the physical organism, and the attempt to define the mode of self-enhancement or self-exaltation that comes with experiences of profound exaltation, may yet reveal some sort of continuum.

Let us return to our initial theme as a conclusion. If concept of time proves to be different from what it is now, human existence in the form of recognizable individuality may be accessible after death to scientific investigation and communication. Is it not worth while then to investigate such matters?

REFERENCES

1. *Proc Soc Psychical Res (London)*, 33:151–160, 1923.
2. TYRRELL, G. N. M.: *Apparitions.* New York, Pantheon, 1953.
3. MURPHY, GARDNER (with collaboration of L. A. Dale): *The Challenge of Psychical Research: A Primer of Parapsychology.* New York, Harper, 1961, pp. 250–270.
4. STEVENSON, I.: Twenty cases suggestive of reincarnation. (*Proc Amer Soc Psychic Res,* vol. XXVI, 1966.

Chapter 12

REFERENCES TO LIFE AND DEATH, TRIBUTE AND MEMORY

SIDNEY NATHANSON AND WALTER DEBOLD

IN THE OLD TESTAMENT

Sidney Nathanson

There is but one step between me and death.   SAMUEL I, 20:3

Lord make me to know mine end, and the measure of my days, what it is; let me know how short-lived I am.   PSALMS 39:5

We bring our years to an end as a tale that is told.   PSALMS 90:9

The days of our years are three score years or even by reason of strength four score years, yet is their pride but travail and vanity for it is speedily gone and we fly away.   PSALMS 90:10

Man is born unto trouble, as the sparks fly upward.   JOB 5:7

Our days upon the earth are like a shadow.   JOB 8:9

To everything there is a season, and a time to every purpose under the heaven: a time to be born, and a time to die.
ECCLESIASTES 3:1ff

I shall go to him, but he shall not return to me. SAMUEL II, 12:23
I go the way of all the earth: be thou strong therefore and show thyself a man.   KINGS I, 2:2

Set thine house in order; for thou shalt die, and not live.
KINGS II, 20:1

146

If a man live many years, let him rejoice in them all; and remember the days of darkness; for they shall be many.

ECCLESIASTES 11:8

He will swallow up death forever, and the Lord God will wipe away tears from off all faces. ISAIAH 25:8

Comfort ye, comfort ye, my people, saith your God. ISAIAH 40:1

Thy sun shall no more go down, neither shall thy moon withdraw itself: for the Lord shall be thine everlasting light, and the days of thy mourning shall be ended. ISAIAH 60:20

For thou wilt not abandon my soul to the netherworld; neither wilt thou suffer thy godly one to see the pit. PSALMS 16:10

Into thine hand I commit my spirit; thou hast redeemed me, O Lord, thou God of truth. PSALMS 31:5

Mark the man of integrity and behold the upright: for there is a future for the man of peace. PSALMS 37:37

He will cover thee with his pinions and under His wings shalt thou take refuge; His truth is a shield and a buckler. PSALMS 91:4

He will give His angels charge over thee, to keep thee in all thy ways. PSALMS 91:11

A good man leaveth an inheritance to his children's children.

PROVERBS 13:22

Righteousness delivereth from death. PROVERBS 10:2

The Lord shall keep thee from all evil: he shall keep thy soul. The Lord shall guard thy going out and thy coming in from this time forth and forever. PSALMS 121:7,8

Surely there is a future and thy hope wilt not be cut off.

PROVERBS 23:18

Her children rise up and call her blessed, her husband also, and he praiseth her. PROVERBS 31:28

The spirit of man is the lamp of the Lord, searching all the inward parts. PROVERBS 20:27

Till I die I will not put away mine integrity from me.   JOB 27:5

One generation passeth away, and another generation cometh: and the earth abideth forever.   ECCLESIASTES 1:4

Remember also thy creator in the days of thy youth, or ever the evil days come and the years draw nigh, when thou shalt say, I have no pleasure in them; or ever the sun and the light, and the moon, and the stars be darkened and the clouds return after the rain: and the dust return to the Earth as it was: and the spirit to God who gave it. This is the end of the matter; all hath been heard: fear God and His commandments, for this is the whole duty of man.   ECCLESIASTES 12:1,2,7,13

REFERENCES TO DEATH AND BEREAVEMENT IN THE OLD AND NEW TESTAMENTS

Walter Debold

He will destroy death forever.   ISAIAH 25:8

Where is your plague, Death?   HOSEA 13:14

Do not neglect to honour his grave.   ECCLESIASTICUS 38:16

Let grief end with the funeral.   ECCLESIASTICUS 38:19

Do not abandon your heart to grief.   ECCLESIASTICUS 38:20

Jesus said: I am the resurrection. If anyone believes in me, even though he dies he will live, and whoever lives and believes in me will never die.   JOHN 11:26

But we believe that having died with Christ we shall return to life with him: Christ, as we know, having been raised from the dead will never die again. Death has no power over him any more. When he died, he died, once for all, to sin, so his life now is life with God; and in that way, you too must consider yourselves to be dead to sin but alive for God in Christ Jesus.   ROMANS 6:8-11

If we have died with him, then we shall live with him.
If we hold firm, then we shall reign with him.
If we disown him, then he will disown us.
We may be unfaithful, but he is always faithful,
for he cannot disown his own self.   2 TIMOTHY 2:12-13

But Christ has in fact been raised from the dead, the first fruits of all who have fallen asleep.   1 CORINTHIANS 15:20

Happy are those who die in the Lord! Happy indeed, the Spirit says; now they can rest for ever after their work, since their good deeds go with them.   REVELATION 14:13

God would not be so unjust as to forget all you have done.
HEBREWS 6:10

I have told you all this so that you may find peace in me.
JOHN 16:33

The love of Christ overwhelms us.   2 CORINTHIANS 5:14

When we were baptized in Christ Jesus we were baptized in his death.   ROMANS 6:3

If in union with Christ we have imitated his death, we shall also imitate him in his resurrection.   ROMANS 6:5

But when Christ is revealed—and he is your life—you too will be revealed in all your glory with him.   COLOSSIANS 3:4

Christ suffered for you and left an example for you to follow the way he took.   1 PETER 2:21

If by the Spirit you put an end to the misdeeds of the body you will live.   ROMANS 8:13

We carry with us in our body the death of Jesus, so that the life of Jesus, too, may always be seen in our bodies.
2 CORINTHIANS 4:10

All I want is to know Christ and the power of his resurrection and to share his sufferings by reproducing the pattern of his death.   PHILIPPIANS 3:10

The life and death of each of us has its influence on others; if we live, we live for the Lord; and if we die, we die for the Lord, so that alive or dead we belong to the Lord.   ROMANS 14:7-8

Life to me, of course, is Christ, but then death would bring me something more.   PHILIPPIANS 1:21

And then, if my blood has to be shed as part of your own sacrifice and offering—which is your faith—I shall still be happy and rejoice with all of you, and you must be just as happy and rejoice with me.   PHILIPPIANS 2:17-18

We want you to be quite certain, brothers, about those who have died, to make sure that you do not grieve about them, like the other people who have no hope.   1 THESSALONIANS 4:11

Joseph of Arimathaea . . . boldly went to Pilate and asked for the body of Jesus.   MARK 15:43

Just as all men die in Adam, so all men will be brought to life in Christ.   1 CORINTHIANS 15:22

There will be no more death and no more mourning or sadness.   REVELATION 21:4

Death is swallowed up in victory. Death where is your victory? Death where is your sting?   1 CORINTHIANS 16:55

As one man's fall brought condemnation on everyone, so the good act of one man brings everyone life and makes them justified.   ROMANS 5:18

For the wage paid by sin is death; the present given by God is eternal life in Christ Jesus our Lord.   ROMANS 6:23

PART III

BEREAVEMENT

Chapter 13

PSYCHIATRIC IMPLICATIONS IN BEREAVEMENT

JAMES P. CATTELL

𝒯he loss of a loved person suddenly and violently alters one's view of the world and, more importantly, provides drastic alterations in one's view of himself. "Who am I without this concrete and operational extension of my identity? How can I function without this person, whose sterling qualities I had come to take for granted? How can I ever be whole without him?"

Hamlet, grieving over his father and feeling that he had lost his mother and his kingdom to his usurping uncle, seriously considers suicide in the soliloquy that ends:

> And thus the native hue of resolution
> Is sicklied o'er with the pale cast of thought.
> And enterprises of great pith and moment
> With this regard their currents turn awry
> And lose the name of action.

This discourse provides a full view of the paralysis that afflicts the bereaved. The loss of the loved one is irrefutable. The point in question is the loss of an important part of one's identity and of one's ability to function as an individual.

The reaction of the bereaved person is inextricably linked with his earlier experiences in life; he is moved by all the subtleties of his relationship with the loved one, the circumstances of the loss, and the general characteristics and specific responsibilities of the current situation. The loss of a loved one is only one of a wide variety of losses that the average person may experience. Inasmuch as the reactions to loss are similar to those following the death of a loved one, it is pertinent to indicate a few.

153

Losses may occur in the physical realm; i.e., they may consist of any change that significantly alters the appearance and functioning of one's body and one's body-image concept; and in the socio-professional realm, i.e., there may be a significant change in one's social, academic, professional, economic, or freedom status. Amputation, paraplegia, colostomy, loss of sight and hearing and, to some extent, heart attacks, are illustrative of the first category. Loss of social status, academic failure, apparent or real professional incompetence, loss of income or savings, and incarceration in prison or concentration camp, illustrate some of the possibilities in the second category.

FACTORS INFLUENCING REACTION TO LOSS

The reaction to loss is influenced by a variety of historical factors, both early and more recent, as well as by many aspects of the contemporary scene. Generally speaking, the closer and freer the relationship between child and parents in the early years, and the more opportunity for healthy emergence as an individual and for gradually evolving independence, the greater the adult person's eventual ability to sustain significant loss. Conversely, factors such as a broken home, whether through death, divorce, or protracted absence of one of the parents for medical, legal, military or other reasons, can distort the child's opportunity for healthful, close relationships. These can impair his developing realistic concepts about the world and about himself and his potential for independent functioning. Several authorities have enunciated the striking similarities between the reactions of infants to the protracted absence of the mother and the reactions of adult depressives. An early loss, though temporary, sensitizes or programs the individual to a loss in adult life, and he often responds by mourning for both.

Studies of amputees by Lawrence C. Kolb, and of paraplegics by this author, have demonstrated that both groups accepted their disabilities more philosophically and entered into rehabilitation more eagerly if they had had a history of the stable kind of background described. If their growth and development had been characterized by pride in performance and self-mastery, they brought these attitudes to the task of adapting to the world despite their disabilities.

Factors of this kind are obviously influential in determining the quality and intensity of the relationship between a person and the lost loved one.

The relationship *with* the lost person would, of course, have varied with one's relationship *to* him or her. The concepts, attitudes, and patterns of behavior that each partner brings to a marriage are modeled on observations and experiences from infancy until the time of marriage and modified by the climate of the marriage itself. The person who has felt free to develop resources in various areas of behavior, to maintain warm and lasting friendships, and who has achieved relative independence, would have much to bring to a marriage. He would be prepared to fulfill his responsibilities while enjoying its rights and privileges, provided he had a mate with whom all this would be possible.

The person who has lived a restricted and constricted life; who has been timorous about venturing anything new; whose relationships had been characterized by marked ambivalence and were subject to interruptions or dissolution, and who has remained dependent on some parental figure, would have much less to contribute to a marriage. His expectations of his spouse would include a combination of everything that his parents had provided for him and all that he had failed to provide for himself in terms of development of his resources, satisfaction in living and basic identity. He finds himself in the position of being unable to live without his wife, yet unable to live with her.

The reactions of a person to the loss of a relative other than a spouse would vary according to how important the deceased had been to his self-concept and his day-to-day living. The loss of an infant is less devastating to a young and healthy mother who has other children than it would be to a heretofore barren woman of thirty-nine whose marriage is in jeopardy. The relative health of the person, in terms of emotional equilibrium, would of course influence the reaction in both instances.

Circumstances of the Loss

To the extent that the relationship with the lost object had been truly devoted and giving, the circumstances of the loss are of little significance in the grieving person's reaction. To the extent that there had been ambivalence, overdependency and fear of life, the circumstances seem to influence the reaction. Then there may be guilt and self-recrimination about some error of omission or commission. These emotions are usually focused on circumstances that could not have affected the outcome (e.g., having given medicine a few minutes late) or that called for clairvoyance (e.g., not having urged an earlier plane flight).

Erich Lindemann, a leading investigator of acute grief reactions, including survivors of the 1942 Cocoanut Grove fire in Boston, has noted that there may be little or no grief reaction for weeks or months if the bereaved is confronted with important tasks and a need to maintain the morale of others. A teenaged girl had no perceptible grief reaction to the death of a widowed mother, because several younger siblings depended on her for care.

A woman in her midfifties was suddenly widowed by her husband's unexpected heart attack. He and the children had long been the hub of her universe, but the younger child had recently married. The mother was on excellent terms with both children and their spouses but respected their privacy, knowing that she was vulnerable to attempting to make a career of their lives. Earlier, she had been active in various organizations in the suburbs, but, having moved to the city, had devoted herself to her family. Thus, she was suddenly presented with a life that had no apparent meaning.

In broader terms, the loss of a spouse entails a major change in role for a person of either sex, but particularly for the bereaved woman. Socially, she and her husband had been regarded as a unit, although appreciated individually up to a point. Without his presence, the unit is dissolved and friends are perplexed as to what to do. More often than not, they will deluge the widow with social invitations—usually long before she is prepared to venture into the world again. If she does, she may find that friends are too cordial, oversolicitous but obviously cautious about saying the wrong thing. She has enough of her own anxiety without being subjected to that of others. After the too early flurry of invitations, to which she has not responded very graciously, she may find herself tacitly abandoned because, as less than a unit, she no longer fits into the social scene.

If she is a relatively young and attractive person, her women friends may suspect that her presence in their social circles might jeopardize their marriage. When she is ready to find new social contacts, she may discover that the opportunities have disappeared and that she is limited to spinsters and widows.

Particularly if she has a career, daily contact with men would continue as before, but again her role in their eyes may gradually change. However much they may have respected her as a married woman, she may come to be seen as hungry for love and sex on any basis and fair game for them. These factors provide a further disruption in her already convulsed world and further undermine her tenuous self-esteem and identity.

Analogous factors have an essential bearing on the future of a twelve-year-old boy, an only child whose parents were killed in a plane accident. His future could be bright or catastrophic, according to the home situation available to him.

REACTIONS TO LOSS

Bowlby, who has written extensively on grief and mourning, has delineated three phases of mourning. He has described a behavioral sequence, following the loss of a loved object, that is observable in humans of all ages and in a number of species of animals. In man, there is also a sequence of subjective experiences that begins with anger and anxiety, followed by pain and despair and that may end in hope. The course of both sequences may vary remarkably, and rage, protest and yearning may alternate with feelings of emptiness and despair. The physiological (nonpathological) sequence begins with craving, angry efforts to recover the lost object, and appeals for help. This is followed by a period of apathy and disorganization of behavior that allows the individual to relate to new objects and, eventually, once again to find some satisfaction in living.

Concomitant with the rational awareness that the loss is final and irremediable is a denial of this, as well as conscious and unconscious efforts to recover the loved one. This occurs in dreams and fantasies, and has been regarded as analogous to a child's response to the temporary absence of the mother. The angry and aggressive behavior that is seen in young children and animals during such an absence is useful in coping with anxiety until the return of the mother. In addition, it may speed the time of reunion and provide some assurance that such separation will not be repeated. However, this hostility in the truly bereaved cannot serve any of these purposes. It may be turned against the self and experienced as depression, guilt, and self-deprecation. It may be experienced as conscious or nearly conscious reproaching and blaming the lost object for having deserted one.

An important aspect of the disorganization of behavior is characterized by the experience of depersonalization. This refers to feelings of unreality, change, and strangeness. It may be experienced in relation to the self, the body or the world. The sensation is very painful and is usually accompanied by a failure to perceive feeling and emotion.

Some cogent remarks that may contribute to an understanding of the phase of disorganization have been made by Edith Jacobson. She has stated,

> we may tend to underrate the extent to which the consistency and homogeneity and hence the stability of our self-image depends on the compatability, harmonious interplay and collaboration of those innumerable *identifications* with all the familiar, personal and impersonal, concrete and abstract objects of our past and present life and environment . . . We know that abrupt changes from the familiar to new, strange and unfamiliar scenes and environment can bring about mild, fleeting experiences of depersonalization.

She was referring specifically to the abrupt and devastating changes to which concentration camp internees had been subjected. Their losses included just about every aspect of life as they knew it. With the loss of the loved one, often the central identification of the bereaved, everything else that was familiar becomes unfamiliar, and feelings of unreality are frequently experienced.

In commenting on the reaction to the absence of a nucleus for organized behavior, Lindemann noted

> There is restlessness, inability to sit still, moving about in an aimless fashion, continually searching for something to do . . . Activities do not proceed in the automatic, self-sustaining fashion which characterizes normal reactions . . . There is . . . a painful lack of capacity to initiate and maintain organized patterns of behavior.

For the bereaved, the days can be harrowing and filled with all of the disquieting reactions noted; however, there are mitigating circumstances that can provide some relief: the necessary duties and tasks entailed in living, contact with tradespeople, domestics, neighbors and others, visits to and from friends and relatives, and telephone conversations, as well as the opportunity to pursue various diversions. Most important, it is daylight and, particularly in reference to a spouse, a time of expected separation.

Evening comes. It progresses into night. The time of the daily reunion is left empty. Even if one joins friends or family for the evening, there is the inevitable time of parting, of going to one's home and bedroom, alone. Then come the utter loneliness, the despair, the tears, the memories, the fantasies, the self-recriminations, the anger at fate and at the lost one—in effect, the bald confrontation of one's unconscionable situation. None of the social diversions of the day is accessible. Efforts to avail oneself of evening's limited possibilities—reading, listening to music or watching ancient movies on television—have little success. Any pathway that once brought ease and peace is now a plague and ghostridden.

Man's reaction to the dark and nighttime is as old as man. It is a time when he confronts his ultimate aloneness. Hamlet, in one of his midnight vigils with his father's ghost, characterized his return as: "Making night hideous." In one of the lyrics from Maxwell Anderson's and Kurt Weill's "Lost in the Stars" are the lines

> All day long, you won't catch me weeping
>> But God help me when it comes time for sleeping
> When it comes time for sleeping here alone.

Many young children fear the dark, even under optimal family circumstances and before they are able to conceptualize aloneness. In early years, darkness means a separation from mother, but there is the gradually recognized conviction that there will be reunion when daylight returns. The bereaved has this expectation of reunion and may feel that a sleepless vigil will somehow magically facilitate it. Nevertheless, one knows that the morning sun will bring another day in which he finds himself as bereft as yesterday, and faced with an eternally bleak prospect.

Another deterrent to sleep is the anticipated possibility of dreaming. What kind of dreams will there be? Will there be happy reconciliations and pleasant reliving of the past? Again, the dreams may dramatize some of the bereaved's hostility and be anything but pleasant. Whatever the content, there is the inevitable awakening and the emptiness that accompanies it.

Hamlet's dilemma in the soliloquy about *being* is experienced nightly by the bereaved about *sleeping,* and the soliloquy fits most appropriately into the context. This contributes to a quantity and quality of desperation that leads one to demand surcease.

The anniversary of the death of the loved one is noted personally by the bereaved, and more publicly according to the ritualistic practices of his particular religion. Memorial flowers near the pulpit mark the practice in Protestant churches; the celebration of a mass or some equivalent is the pattern followed by Catholics; and those of the Hebrew faith enunciate the first anniversary with the unveiling of a grave-marker, and subsequent ones by a visit to the grave, a practice often followed by those of other beliefs.

There have been instances of the bereaved's replicating the symptoms of the fatal illness of the lost one at various times. The occurrence of such symptoms may be especially striking during the period that marks the anniversary of the onset of the final acute illness and the death. Such a constellation may serve as a primitive substitute for true mourning, however unsuccessfully. In other circumstances, the bereaved may deny the loss until he has an overwhelming reaction or a reactivation of past grief on the anniversary.

In the ordinary course of events, many lives are highlighted or undermined by a series of other anniversaries: the birthday of the individual or of the loved one; the wedding anniversary; the ritual celebrations surrounding the winter solstice (Thanksgiving Day, Chanakuh, Christmas, New Year's Eve and Day, Twelfth Night), and the vernal equinox (Easter, Passover) as well as other semifestive family days such as those that occur between Friday evening and Sunday evening. Mourning is often renewed or underlined during these times when the absence of the lost one is more keenly perceived.

REORGANIZATION AND RESTITUTION

I have discussed some of the factors that influence the individual's voyage through the process of angry and supplicative efforts to recover the lost object, his subsequent withdrawal, apathy and relative disorganization, and some of the determinants of his ability to realign his self-concept and his world-concept with the new state of affairs.

The grief work is necessary for a time, but enervating. Implicitly, it abandons the pleasure economy of the bereaved and incurs a mounting deficit in that life-sustaining area. Thus, one might say that nature is on the side of daring to seek new objects, interests and sources of self and world identification and appreciation.

The relative success of the positive venture is multiply determined but there are two major components: inner strength, based on endowment and experience, and the opportunities available. The latter is particularly important to the child or adolescent, whose opportunity to experience the vicissitudes of reality and to develop ego strength have been limited. The adult, in whatever decade, is theoretically a free agent and this is true in actuality to the extent that he is willing to venture anew.

The courageous ones, however bound and dependent they had been, can discover unrecognized resources, self-reliance, and some of the delight of developing these—often contributing to the benefit of those less fortunate because of age or station in life.

To return to William Shakespeare's soliloquy for Hamlet, the final recourse to loss is to "find the name of action" or to die. Hamlet, having waited too long, did both.

Chapter 14

LINDEMANN'S PIONEER STUDIES OF REACTIONS TO GRIEF

ALAN ROSELL

Dr. Erich Lindemann carried on an intensive study of grief based on the experiences of many people who lost relatives or close friends in the unfortunate Cocoanut Grove fire in Boston.*

There are four main points which this study tries to clarify:

1. "Acute grief is a definite syndrome with psychological and somatic symptomatology.
2. This syndrome may appear immediately after a crisis; it may be delayed; it may be exaggerated or apparently absent.
3. In place of the typical syndrome, there may appear distorted pictures, each of which represents one special aspect of the grief syndrome.
4. By appropriate techniques these distorted pictures can be successfully transformed into a normal grief reaction, with resolution."

The investigation consisted of a series of psychiatric interviews with 101 patients. The records of these interviews were analyzed in terms of symptoms reported, and the observed changes of the mental status throughout the series of interviews.

SYMPTOMATOLOGY OF NORMAL GRIEF

There is a uniform picture seen in persons suffering from acute grief, the most striking characteristics being, (1) a marked

---

* LINDEMANN, ERICH M.D. Symptomatology and management of acute grief. *Amer J Psychiat*, 101:141–148, 1944.

tendency to sighing respiration, especially when the patient was made to discuss his grief, and (2) a complaint about lack of strength and a feeling of physical exhaustion, accompanied by such digestive symptoms as inability to eat, repugnance toward food, or abdominal discomfort.

The bereaved may demonstrate a sense of unreality and detachment from others, and there may be an intense preoccupation with the image of the deceased. Feelings of guilt about what they should have done and what they neglected to do for the lost person are common among the bereaved. Often there may be a loss of warmth and friendship for others and a tendency to respond with irritability and anger. These feelings and actions are often disturbing and interpreted by others as a threat of approaching insanity.

The bereaved person often shows restlessness, inability to sit still, aimless movements, and a search for something to do but at the same time displays a lack of initiative. He follows a daily routine but finds it an effort and sees little significance in it.

The duration of grief seems to depend upon the ability of a person to readjust to the environment from which the deceased is missing, and upon the formation of new relationships. Some try to avoid the intense distress and the emotional expression of grief. Others are able, as soon as the grief is accepted and the memory of the deceased can be dealt with, to find relief of their inner tensions and hostilities.

MORBID GRIEF REACTIONS

Morbid grief reactions represent distortions of normal grief patterns.

The most common example of this is *delay* or *postponement* of mourning. The person may show little or no reaction to the loss for weeks, months, or even years, if the bereavement occurs at a time when the patient is confronted with important tasks or concerned with maintaining the morale of others. Patients in acute bereavement over a recent death may actually be preoccupied with grief over a person who died years ago.

In other cases the bereaved may show alterations in conduct of several types as follows:

1. "Overactivity without a sense of loss.
2. Acquisition of symptoms belonging to the last illness of the deceased (hysteria or hypochondriasis).
3. A recognized disease of psychosomatic origin; including ulcerative colitis, rheumatoid arthritis, and asthma.
4. Alteration in relationship to friends and relatives with progressive social isolation.
5. Furious hostilities against specific persons, e.g., doctor or surgeon may be bitterly accused of neglect of duties and the bereaved may assume foul play has led to the death.
6. Repression of these feelings of hostility and complete absence of emotional display.
7. Lasting loss of patterns of social interaction in cases where there is a lack of decision and initiative.
8. Engaging in activities which are detrimental to his own social and economic existence. Such persons give away belongings, are easily lured into disastrous economic dealings, lose their friends and professional standing and by a series of stupid acts find themselves without family, friends, social status or money.
9. Deterioration into a state of agitated depression with tension, agitation, insomnia, feelings of worthlessness, bitter self-accusation and obvious need for self-punishment. Such people may be dangerously suicidal."

MANAGEMENT

Proper psychiatric management of grief reactions may prevent prolonged and serious alterations in the person's social adjustment as well as the onset of potential medical disease.

The psychiatrist can be an aid in helping break the bond to the deceased and finding new patterns of rewarding interaction. Although religious precepts are helpful in providing comfort, they do not provide adequate assistance in overcoming the person's grief. The psychiatrist can help the bereaved to accept the pain, review his relationship with the deceased, understand his fears, express his sorrows, verbalize his feelings of guilt and find an acceptable formulation for his future attitude toward the memory of the deceased.

Chapter 15

JACKSON'S NINE AREAS OF CONCERN

AUSTIN MEHRHOF

In his book, *Understanding Grief*, Edgar N. Jackson points out nine areas of emotional concern which may present themselves to the bereaved person. He emphasizes the ways a normal person may comprehend and cope with one or more of these concerns. They are as follows:

1. These feelings and emotions are natural and will not continue indefinitely.
2. You may want to review verbally your relationships with the deceased.
3. You may want to verbalize the nature of your own feelings and how they have changed.
4. You may encounter new feelings which may lead you to believe that you are losing your mental balance. The fact that you recognize this should be reason enough for you to dismiss this concern.
5. In order to gain a clearer picture of your future course, you may want to discuss with someone what you are doing and what you can do to deal with your changed feelings.
6. You may encounter feelings of hostility towards the deceased and find that discussing these will be valuable in discovering the cause.
7. Discussion may also prove valuable in helping you to establish a concept of how you will think and feel about the deceased in the future.
8. You may feel a need to verbalize feelings of guilt . . . although it must be kept in mind that such verbalization might serve only to reinforce these feelings; hence such an approach should be kept in proper perspective.
9. You may find that talking about new possibilities in your way of living may make the transition from possibility to reality much easier to attain.

It is evident then that each of these nine areas which may be a cause of concern to the bereaved may be alleviated to some extent by talking about them to someone who is a trusted and sympathetic listener and, if need be, a trained counselor—medical, religious, psychiatric or social service.

Chapter 16

EVIDENCES OF NORMAL GRIEF

PAULA J. CLAYTON

O ur project was an attempt to define normal reactions to death by a study of the consecutive symptoms of bereavement in people who were selected by means other than one which necessarily involved a consultation with physicians, either internists or psychiatrists.

Forty relatives of Caucasian patients who died at Barnes Hospital in St. Louis, Missouri, were interviewed from two to twenty-six days after the death, and twenty-seven were reinterviewed from one to four months later. The age range of these relatives was from twenty to eighty-nine. Among the twenty-four women and sixteen men there were twenty-one Protestants, thirteen Catholics, three Jews, one Ethical Culturist and two with no religious affiliation. The subjects had incomes ranging from $2500 to over $10,000. The relationship of the subject to the deceased was that of the wife, fourteen cases; the husband, five; the mother, six; the father, three; the grandparent, two; the daughter, two; and the son, eight. The length of the illness of the deceased varied from less than three months to ten years.

Each relative who was interviewed was asked to list his symptoms and feelings. Only three symptoms, sadness, difficulty in sleeping, and crying, occurred in more than one half of the relatives. Five of them denied feeling sad. One, a wife, felt relieved of many burdens by her husband's death. He had been invalided by a series of strokes. Long periods of hospitalization had been financially and physically difficult for the family. She had been informed that nothing further could be done for him at the hospital, and was preparing to move him to a nursing home. She felt guilty. His sudden death probably did come as a relief to

168

her. A thirty-year-old man, himself a victim of Hodgkin's Disease, showed little concern over the sudden death of his seventy-nine-year-old mother. Another woman's husband had suffered from two chronic illnesses, diabetes and rheumatoid arthritis. She felt sorry and helpless about his disability and illness, but it had never occurred to her that these illnesses would be fatal. When he died suddenly of a myocardial infarct, she denied feeling sad. The other two were sons respectively of a deceased father and a deceased mother, and both took the deaths calmly.

Loss of appetite and weight, loss of interest in television, friends, and current events and difficulty in concentration were other symptoms that occurred frequently, but also in less than one half the relatives. Irritability and attacks of anxiety, accompanied by shortness of breath, palpitations, weakness, trembling, apprehension and fearfulness, also occurred in these relatives. More severe psychiatric symptoms, such as self-condemnation, guilt, suicidal thoughts, and depersonalization, derealization, hallucinations, and delusions were rare. This set had few physical complaints either. Those who had never used a sleeping medicine or a nerve pill before the bereavement usually did not use them now. Women, in particular, who had used these medicines before, tended to use them again in the bereavement period. This also applied to drinking. Nondrinkers did not begin to drink in the bereavement period; most social drinkers did not increase their drinking. However, heavy drinkers (defined arbitrarily as those who took three or more drinks a day) and frank alcoholics increased their drinking either during the terminal illness or the bereavement. No striking differences were noted when bereavement symptoms were analyzed in relation to sex, age, length of the deceased's illness, or relationship to the deceased. The parents of deceased children seemed to respond most severely, but the group was too small for statistical analysis.

At the follow-up, twenty-two of the twenty-seven (81%) reported feeling better since the first interview, four (15%) were not improved according to our symptom inventory, although they claimed that they felt better, and one (4%) was worse. Improvement dated from six to ten weeks after the death. The symptoms that improved most strikingly were the three occurring in most of the relatives: depressed mood, sleep disturbance, and crying.

Some statements at follow-up were

"I look at other widows in church and see that they made it" (a widow in her seventies).

"I was okay the first month after his death; I rearranged the house, but I can't eat the foods my husband enjoyed" (a 75-year-old widow who was worse at follow-up).

"I felt affected by my mother's death, more than I expected, but all of the symptoms have cleared in the last two weeks" (a 37-year-old-married son).

"Within the last month I've felt better. I've forgotten the unpleasant things about her death and now remember only the good things." He talked about sex and remarriage (a 62-year-old-widower whose wife committed suicide).

"I visit my father's grave often and talk to him. I cry there. Otherwise I'm fine. I've gone back to church" (a 39-year-old married son).

"I've felt better in the last two weeks. I'm more sociable. I still feel alone in the evenings" (a 50-year-old widow).

"This is always a hard time of year for me. I had a still birth in this month." She inquired about giving to the leukemia fund (a 40-year-old mother who had lost a 5½ year old girl).

"I'm feeling better since our last talk, but I still feel depressed. I learned to drive and took a job, but I had to quit. I was too nervous" (a 27-year-old widow).

"Between the death of my wife and the trouble with my son I feel at wit's end. Sometimes I feel like I can't take it. I can't handle the three children, a housekeeper, and a job" (a 43-year-old lawyer).

"I'm trying to remember but the memories are fading too fast" (a 56-year-old widow who had learned to drive and reactivated her interest in social activities since the first visit).

"I can accept my grandson's death. At my husband's death three years ago I wasn't depressed. I could visit the grave and all. I've noticed though that a lot of women lose weight during this period" (a 60-year-old grandmother).

"I think I've accepted it. I wish though when it rains on her grave that I had had the body cremated. I keep her clothes. I wonder if I want to make myself depressed" (a 27-year-old mother of a little girl who died).

There was no significant increase in patients experiencing three or more physical symptoms. Chronic symptoms accounted for the major portion of the symptoms reported. One exception, an attorney, had a family history of mental illness. At the first interview, he was worried about the hereditary aspect of arteriosclerosis and myocardial infarct (the cause of his mother's death). At follow-up four months later, he denied any of the specific somatic symptoms asked about and had not visited a physician. For the first time he reported palpitations after overeating, and was concerned about a soft-tissue injury to his chest wall that had occurred the previous week. He thought people could develop the same symptoms as their deceased relatives and was still wondering about myocardial disease. He anticipated having more frequent physical check-ups in the future. Only one other subject, a married woman with an anxiety neurosis, reported a symptom that seemed similar to that of the deceased. On learning of the sudden death of her father from a cerebral vascular accident, she developed severe neck and head pains for a brief period. At the follow-up, although she still complained of headaches, she felt they were like those she had usually had. She remembered being "hysterical" at the time of her father's death, but did not remember the specific headache she had described at the time.

Only two relatives displayed hostility. One widow showed hostility toward the doctors because she suspected them of experimenting on her husband. At follow-up, this hostility had shifted to her in-laws. She felt "they stayed away from her for some reason." One family, after the death of a six-year-old daughter, was extremely critical of the hospital, although they felt the doctor had done all he could.

Twenty-five per cent of the subjects in this series reported a serious medical illness, such as cancer, Hodgkin's Disease, high blood pressure, and heart disease. At follow-up, twelve (44%) subjects had visited their physicians. Six (22%) felt their symptoms were related to grief; four had consulted a physician because of depression, nervousness, weight loss, etc., and two because of previous stomach and leg pains that flared up "because of nerves." On the insistence of the author, one patient sought psychiatric help. Through telephone conversations with the subjects, interviews with relatives and conversations with their private internists, we learned that the other thirty-nine (98%) did not consult psychiatrists following the initial interview. The patient who did, as a direct result of this research, had had psychiatric help previously.

The following is the history of a woman who had previously suffered from depression and who was depressed at the first interview, but was well at follow-up.

This woman, aged thirty-four, gave a history of a nervous breakdown previously, with symptoms of depression, crying without reason, weight gain, loss of interest in her husband, children, house and church, and suicidal thoughts, even to the point of taking a gun in her hand. She had seen a psychiatrist and had achieved recovery at home. In her own words she "hibernated for three months."

Her husband died when she was thirty-five, leaving her with three young children and many debts. He had had rheumatic heart disease, was hospitalized many times, had had cardiac surgery seven years prior to his death, and was never free of symptoms. During his terminal illness he was irritable and difficult to live with. Most of his wife's depressive symptoms started then. When first seen, five days after his death, she answered "yes" to almost the entire symptom inventory. She denied early morning awakening, but she had all the other vegetative symptoms of depression in addition to the psychological ones. She admitted to auditory and visual hallucinations; she believed she actually saw her husband walk down the hall and heard his voice. At the funeral she had told a relative, "Take him to breakfast and give him salt-free foods!" During the two-hour interview, she was talkative, dramatic, and demanding. She found concentration difficult and her conversation was so disconnected that, when interrupted, she would lose the trend of her thought. She appeared depressed and cried often. She was self-deprecatory: "People are tired of hearing my complaints."

She said that she talked to her children as if her husband were alive, saying, "Your father won't like that." Her physician had prescribed chlorpromazine. The interviewer recommended that she come to the clinic for further help. Seven days later, she was seen by a screening psychiatrist, treated with imipramine and meprobamate, and was asked to return in one week. At the first interview, depressive symptoms were still present, but her hallucinations and suicidal ideas had disappeared.

She returned to the clinic several times during the next two months. Feeling compelled to train herself for a job, she had returned to beauty school. She admitted some difficulty in concentrating. She took out a life insurance policy and planned to make a will. Several days before her husband's birthday she had felt depressed and tearful. She also kept her husband's complete wardrobe as if he would return, but denied that this was the reason.

A follow-up interview took place approximately three months after his death. She had been off medication since her last visit to the clinic three weeks before. She said she felt well. She still had initial insomnia and slept poorly, but all other somatic symptoms had cleared up, and she was gaining weight. She said that until very recently she had felt depressed and tearful in the evening, but this was improving. Her only other complaints were of occasional migraine headaches and backaches.

When asked how her recent bereavement compared to her previous nervous breakdown, she said, "They are not the same at all. With the present situation, I had a fear of being unable to carry on. I didn't think I could carry on my responsibilities. Before, I didn't care if I carried them on or even if I lived. Hell couldn't have been any worse than that." She concluded by saying, "I can't mourn forever."

Chapter 17

PSYCHIATRY: ITS ROLE IN
THE RESOLUTION OF GRIEF

NORMAN PAUL

In the middle of a Geometry I class, Karen Harper was summoned to the principal's office. Her Uncle George was there.

"I've come to take you home, Karen," Uncle George spoke gravely. "There's trouble at home. Your mother will tell you all about it."

"Don't stop to gather up your books, Karen," the principal said. "I'll have them sent over to your house. Just get your coat."

Karen's first thought was that her brother Johnny was really sick. He'd stayed home from the third grade that morning because of a slight temperature. She put on her coat quickly and drove home with Uncle George.

Her mother and Aunt Alice were sitting on the sofa in the living room, Aunt Alice patting Mother's shoulder. When Karen came in, Aunt Alice and Uncle George withdrew into the dining room.

Mother said, "Come sit down, Karen."

"Is Johnny worse?" Karen wanted to know.

"It's Daddy, darling," the mother said. "Daddy suddenly became ill at the office and, well, I've something terrible to tell you—he's dead. We're not sure yet, but it seems to have been a heart attack."

Karen felt her knees shake and her stomach turn around as though she would be sick. She couldn't say anything except "Oooooo."

"It's a dreadful, dreadful blow," her mother said, and her lips seemed to quiver. But she pulled herself together and hugged

174

Karen. "We'll be brave, though, won't we? Daddy would want us to be brave."

The next few days had no pattern. Karen didn't eat much of what Aunt Alice cooked. When she felt hungry, she would take something from the refrigerator, and once she made Johnny some soup and a peanut butter sandwich. Uncle George was on the telephone most of the time, talking with the doctor, with the minister, with the newspapers, and with the funeral director to whose chapel her father had been taken. The doctor came to see them, and she heard him say to her mother, "Absolutely no warning whatever. He had his regular check-up just two months ago and there was nothing wrong."

The minister came and said a prayer and made arrangements for the funeral. Aunt Alice answered the doorbell whenever it rang and sometimes let in a very close friend or neighbor. "Oh, Gloria, what can I *say?*" they would ask her mother. Mostly everybody was quiet and kind. Mrs. Gordon, across the street, asked Karen, "Would it make you feel better to come over and have dinner with Jane tonight? She misses you at school and feels very sorry about your trouble." But Karen didn't want to go.

Some cousins arrived from New Jersey with her mother's mother. Daddy's parents were too old and too sick to make the long trip from Florida. The church organist came to ask about Daddy's favorite music for the funeral service.

Once Karen said to Aunt Alice, "Did anyone try to resuscitate Daddy? I hope they just didn't assume he was dead when there was still a chance. He looked perfectly all right to me at break-fast." Aunt Alice said that everything humanly possible had been done. It didn't seem real to Karen, though. She half expected to see her father walk through the door each evening. Once she set the table and laid a place for him, but Johnny said, "He won't come. He won't even come for my birthday party."

It was Karen's first funeral. Whenever a family friend had died, she had not been taken to the funeral because she was too young. Aunt Alice and Uncle George left their children with a baby sitter because they were only seven and nine. Two girls from the tenth-grade homeroom and two from her Sunday School class came and said very sadly, "Hello, Karen, we're sorry." But the other two hundred people at the church were adults. The flowers were beautiful, the music was beautiful, and the minister said wonderful things about her father. Afterward, at the cemetery, when the coffin was being lowered into the ground, she wanted desperately to cry. She noticed, though, how hard her mother was trying to keep erect and quiet under her black veil; Karen felt she should do the same, if only for Johnny's sake. When it was over, everybody said goodbye except a few relatives and very close friends; they came back to the house where Aunt Alice served lunch. By late afternoon, she and Johnny and their mother were alone.

She missed only five days of school. During that time, a letter had come from the tenth-grade secretary that said, "We all sympathize with you in your great loss and look forward to having you back again." When she returned to her homeroom the first day, the teacher said quietly, "Welcome back, Karen. It's good to have you here again."

The principal talked with her during lunch period and said, "This has been a great shock for you, Karen. But your life is all before you, and I know a girl of your courage and intelligence will be able to go on and do her best." The guidance counselor said that, if there were ever any problems, Karen should feel free to visit her at any time.

In order to take care of Johnny, she no longer stayed after school for art club on Wednesdays and Thursdays. Her mother had decided to get a part-time job as an accountant. "It's what I was trained to do," she told Karen, "and now it will come in handy. I want things to go on just as though Daddy were still here. Between Daddy's insurance and my job, you and Johnny will have the kind of life he would have wanted for you."

It was hard to believe that her father was dead. Twice she dreamed about him. In one dream, he was painting her bedroom again and asked, "Shall we have the walls blue this time? Alice blue, baby blue, powder blue, sky blue?" In the other dream, she was asking him to sing in the student-parent choral recital and he said, "Sure. My voice isn't first rate, but it will be fun." And then in the dream he sang "I am the Captain of the Pinafore." Sometimes Karen's mind would wander in Latin class. While someone read from *The Gallic Wars*, she would muse, "Suppose all this is a dream, a long dream, and I'll wake up, and Daddy will be back." In church one Sunday the light shining through the stained glass windows made her think for a moment that it was Daddy passing the collection plate. She almost cried when it turned out to be someone else. "Why did you have to go away," she thought, "just when I need you more than ever?"

In her thoughts, she often blamed her father for dying and leaving them with so much sadness and no chance for happiness ever again. Johnny's birthday party was terrible. There were eight boys in paper hats around a birthday cake, but who could really feel glad? "Couldn't he have waited until after the birthday?" Karen wondered. Christmas was terrible too—a tree, some presents, a turkey dinner; but Uncle George sat at the head of the table and didn't carve the turkey very well. "I would have to be this unlucky," Karen thought. "Couldn't he have waited to die until after Christmas?"

By the beginning of the new term in February, Karen was absolutely fed up with school. She had always studied hard because her father and mother wanted her to do well and to go to college, but, with Daddy out of the picture, what was the use? Her mother was so wrapped up in the new job and in trying to figure out the income tax and the check stubs (things that Daddy used to do) that she didn't have much time to listen to Karen's news from school. Karen dropped her fifth course, Latin, and got so bored with biology that she cut two labs in a row. Instead, she played solitaire in the girls' locker room. In March, she felt that geometry was useless and hardly did any homework. "I'm unprepared," she said when the teacher asked her to demonstrate a theorem at the blackboard. She quarreled with the director of the chorus over the program for sophomore assembly. "Honestly," she said, "I'm just sick and tired of the whole thing. It's just too much to sing another stupid old Gilbert and Sullivan number." Sometimes she stayed home from school with a headache, but mostly she went and just didn't pay much attention. She wrote silly notes to Jane Gordon during English classes.

Once the teacher intercepted a note and talked to Karen after class. "Don't you want to do well in this course?" she asked, and Karen said, "Not particularly." It was the rudest thing she had ever said to a teacher. She changed her seat in the lunchroom, because she was tired of the kids she used to eat with.

Once the guidance counselor sent for Karen and asked how things were at home, how they were all getting along. "Just fine," Karen said. "I guess we're back to normal." The counselor wondered whether Karen was worried or tired and mentioned that her grades were slipping. "Well," Karen said, "I just haven't been interested in school this term. All my subjects are pretty boring."

Her mother seemed worried about the interim report card, the worst Karen had ever received. "I can't understand it, Karen," she said. "I know Daddy's passing away has been a great sorrow for us all, but we can't let it make us stop trying. I was just a few years older than you when my father died. Naturally I felt sad, but I knew I just had to keep going and that time would heal everything."

"Oh, I don't care," Karen said. "School isn't everything."

By May, it seemed that she would fail two of her four subjects, and Mrs. Harper was called to school. While they sat with the guidance counselor, Karen hardly listened, but she tuned in occasionally to hear her mother say, ". . . just as usual, we've kept the house, same routine . . . . no illness, she's fine . . . no outside strains that I know of . . . just about normal . . . to the movies with some girl friends occasionally, no serious social distractions that I know of . . . . "

"Yakkety-yak," Karen thought to herself, "why can't she ever let me alone?"

Because Karen failed biology and geometry, Mrs. Harper insisted that she attend summer school. Karen went but hated every minute of it. To relieve the monotony, she made some new friends there. They all began to go around together in school, and out of school too, to the movies and to dances and to the swimming pool. Her mother disliked her new companions and complained that they were noisy and rude, that the boys smoked and the girls wore too much make-up. She especially disliked a boy called Jim, but he was the most fun of all, always thinking up new places for the whole crowd to go. Karen and her mother had some terrible arguments about what time she should get home from movies and dances. Karen suspected that her mother was trying to confine her to home and school without any diversions, and this made her angry. She resolved that, when regular school began again in the fall, she would do as little work as possible and not let herself be browbeaten by her mother into a round of study and homework.

During the first weeks of the fall term, she hardly did any work at all, and she felt this would teach her mother not to interfere in her life so much. One day, instead of going to American History, she left school and went down town to the movies with Jim and the other kids. Her cutting class was discovered, and, once more, Mrs. Harper was called to school, this time to the principal's office.

✲   ✲   ✲   ✲   ✲   ✲

Here let us interrupt the story of Karen Harper. It is a piece of fiction, but it incorporates elements from real situations that my patients have talked about. Karen, aged fifteen, formerly a good student and a sociable, cooperative person, has become a "case" in the guidance counselor's files. Her academic work has declined greatly, and she appears not to care. Her relations with other students, with teachers, and with her mother have become abrasive. Although she is not yet a serious disciplinary problem, her inattention, anger, and willingness to cut classes clearly suggest more trouble in the future. The school, seeing these symptoms, has sought to confer with Mrs. Harper in the hope that home and school together can find the root of the problem and take steps to solve it.

Obviously the reader will have guessed that Karen's troubles are in some way related to her father's death. What he may not understand, though, is how the loss of a loved person can lead towards such a remote effect as poor school performance several months later. What has really happened to Karen? What will become of her in the future? Are there effective ways of helping Karen now?

The death of her father was a serious loss for Karen. She had enjoyed a warm, close relationship with him that was interrupted suddenly and without preparation. Furthermore, in losing her father, she really suffered a double loss, since her mother felt obliged to take a job outside the home at the expense of time shared with Karen and Johnny. On the credit side, Karen would seem to have many elements in favor of her being able to withstand this loss and to continue an effective life at home and school. Her family has remained a close unit, occupying the same house. With Mrs. Harper's part-time job, they have sufficient income to maintain a standard of living very nearly equal to what it was before. They have relatives, friends, and neighbors who are interested in them. They are assisted by such supporting structures as their church and a school that attempts to cope with personal as well as academic problems. Karen's life retains most of the routines that were there before Mr. Harper's death. All of these benefits, though, have not been able to sustain her through this crisis in her life. Although ostensibly adjusted to her new situation and accustomed over the months to being without her father, Karen is unable to perform well at school or to get along comfortably with her friends or her mother.

Although the loss of loved persons has always been recognized as one of life's inevitable and intense experiences, it is only in recent years that systematic studies of such losses and their effects have been undertaken. There have been researches into the nature and function of mourning, those overt behaviors and hidden reactions which a bereaved person experiences. The overt and visible aspects of mourning consist of formal and ceremonial practices that the society or subculture may prescribe for such occasions, as well as individual, spontaneous expressions of grief. "Grief" refers to the feelings of the bereaved, which he may express overtly in various ways or which he may experience silently and invisibly. The findings of those who have studied mourning can help to illuminate Karen Harper's situation.

Data collected by Parkes[1] and Lindemann,[2] for example, reveal a close relationship between grief that is unresolved and various degrees of personal disability. Parkes concludes, ". . . grief may prove to be as important to psychopathology as inflammation is to pathology." Deutsch, in summarizing some of her work, maintains that, "The process of mourning as reaction to the real loss of a loved person must be carried to completion."[3]

It is appropriate, then, that we examine Karen's mourning for her father to assess its completeness.

First, however, it is necessary to understand what "complete mourning" means. An analytic description by Bowlby[4] has pictured mourning, in both its overt and hidden reactions, as covering a series of three overlapping stages. The first stage, set in motion by the news of death, is characterized by a kind of numbness and disbelief as the bereaved person attempts to deny the reality of what has occurred. A second stage involves the disorganization of the bereaved one's personality as the death is reluctantly accepted as fact. Outwardly, he may weep, move about restlessly, decline to eat or sleep, grow indifferent to his personal appearance and to the impression he makes on others. Inwardly, he will feel that the bottom has dropped out of his world and that nothing worthwhile remains. His feelings will include profound sadness, loneliness, helplessness, and anger both towards the deceased who has removed himself and towards those who remain alive whereas the loved person is dead. Eventually, this state of disorganization should give way to a third stage in which the personality of the bereaved undergoes reorganization. He sees his loss in a new perspective, as something that has occurred in the past, whereas he still has future time in which to live. He feels a sense of weary relief in having worked through the bitter emotions of grief, and is ready to approach his new situation more calmly.

These three stages, then, can be considered as constituting the complete process of mourning. Bowlby maintains, however, that an individual can become fixated at any point in the process: he can continue to reject the fact of death; he can remain disorganized, torn by intense emotions; or he can reach a stalemate in an early stage of reorganization that is insufficient for his effective response to the demands of living. I would go a step further and say that a bereaved person can achieve a third stage that is merely an imitation, a pseudoreorganization which masks the fact that the first two stages have not been thoroughly traversed.

Karen Harper's disability seems to reflect this state of pseudo-reorganization. The "back-to-normal" assumptions that she and her mother have made about her life seem to be unconscious pretenses screening the incomplete mourning of the first two stages.

Karen did, of course, experience some of those reactions that characterize the first stage of grief. She initially felt unable to accept the reality of her father's death, wondering whether anyone had fully checked to make certain the heart attack was fatal, expecting his return home, dreaming of him in lifelike situations. Once she thought she saw him in church—a fantasy resting on her failure to accept her loss. She also experienced some second-stage reactions, though these were brief and attenuated. For a while, she did not care about eating or seeing friends. She felt sad before and during the funeral and, at times, afterward. She felt anger and resentment towards the father who had abandoned her and caused a break in her hitherto secure environment. These feelings were sporadic and always, to all appearances, brought under control. Karen's personality did not undergo anything so cataclysmic as the disorganization of grief. Karen has, in effect, attempted to take a short cut through grief "back to normal." In her own view, she is reorganized. What she has attained instead is the pseudoreorganization that masks incomplete grief and carries with it the disability that is erupting in her poor school performance and her detached apathy at school and at home.

Karen's is not a unique situation, but is, in fact, almost a prototype for many disabilities encountered by the psychotherapist. Her incomplete mourning follows the pattern of many in contemporary society. First of all, Karen had little experience of death prior to her own father's death. She had not been taken to any other funeral, in accordance with an attitude that shields the young from unpleasant reminders of their own mortality. She had never been in mourning herself nor been a witness to the mourning of others. In this naive state, she was confronted with her father's funeral, a proceeding conducted, in the modern manner, from the impersonal establishment of a funeral director, thence to the church, thence to the cemetery. At the moment of his death, Mr. Harper was extracted from his home permanently.

The funeral observances provided an occasion for focusing grief upon the loved person, and Karen was able to feel sad in company with those nearest her. Yet, at every moment, she felt constrained against letting this sadness show too conspicuously because self-control seemed to be required. During the days and weeks following the funeral, she received many expressions of sympathy. These, though, were couched in vague and abstract terms, as though grief were too delicate for verbal intrusions. Karen's mother, whatever her private reactions, behaved around Karen as though their reduced family ought to pick up the pieces and move forward as before. She attempted to minimize and overcome for her children whatever differences the death of their father might bring. Indeed, she cited for Karen her own loss of her father at a comparable age and her own quick and apparently effective recovery from this loss. Karen, then, in the morass of her own grief, felt similarly obliged to keep the family going, to return to school, to pick up her familiar routine. Her grief was expressed only in sporadic reveries and daydreams.

It is ironic that the culture which has provided Karen with a better standard of living, health, and education than most of the world's children has simultaneously deprived her of another vital need—the opportunity to complete her grief within a socially acceptable context. In some, more primitive societies, every death is an occasion involving the entire community, including the smallest children. All participate in rituals and ceremonies that mark the passage from life to death. And mythic explanations about the difference between the living and the dead are intrinsic parts of the culture. Some societies would have permitted Karen the free expression of her grief; she might have been allowed to wail, to throw herself on the ground, to weep over the corpse, to make a pilgrimage, to fast, to disfigure herself or her clothing as outward manifestations of inner feeling. These vents for expression have their uses in helping the mourner to complete the mourning process. Our more urbanized and secular society, with its smug reliance on rationalism, has eradicated such useful customs and has put nothing in their place.

What, then, will happen to Karen as she progresses through her life, unknowingly carrying the burden of her unresolved grief? There are, of course, too many variables to allow for an intelligent prediction. We can assume with some confidence, though, that her imagined reorganization will always involve some measure of disability. Perhaps Karen will follow her mother's pattern. She may decide to resume her life as before, move through school to work and to marriage in what appears to be a reasonably satisfactory adjustment. But trouble will remain beneath the pseudoreorganization, trouble that can, at any time in the future, emerge to spark new difficulties. Mrs. Harper's grief for her own father was unresolved, a precedent she has set for Karen; Karen may pass on the precedent to her children. The festering of these fragmented experiences over the generations is bound eventually to erupt into some visible disability.

Alternately, Karen may not take her mother's course but continue to be detached from school and family, more and more frequently identified as a "problem." If her behavior provokes discipline and penalties, she may harden into a state of alienation, and display behavior that is openly hostile. Karen has been denied a full sense of the difference between life and death, and this lacuna in her understanding could have terrible results. When such a difference is glossed over, a young person can adopt a callous attitude towards human life, including his own. Some of the casual flirting with suicide among this generation of young people may reflect their unpracticed insensitivity to what death really means.

A third and most desirable alternative is that Karen will be helped now or in the near future. If she continues to be a problem, she may be referred for psychiatric treatment by her school's counseling services or brought to a psychiatrist by her mother. The treatment she receives will depend on the methods her doctor uses. I should like to describe briefly and in a somewhat oversimplified form the procedure I would follow with Karen, based on my experience with similar cases.

My approach is to undertake an out-patient course of therapy that involves not only the individual but the entire family. Karen would be referred as the labeled patient and I would see her alone from time to time. The therapeutic sessions, however, would more often be group meetings—Karen with her mother, Karen with her mother and Johnny. I should want to involve Aunt Alice and Uncle George and Mrs. Harper's mother.

If it might prove useful, I should like to call in friends or neighbors who have been in close touch with the Harper family. The choice and sequence of groupings would be dictated by attempts to provide opportunities for the expression of feelings that have been suppressed in the family's own pattern of interpersonal relations.

Karen would originally be referred because of her troubles at school. A review of her history, though, would very soon suggest that Karen's difficulties were rooted not in school but in her father's death and that, although it was Karen who was named the patient, the whole family's pattern of reactions was potentially disabling.

My underlying hypothesis in working with families is that there is often a direct relationship between abrasive relationships within a family and unresolved grief over the death of a loved person. A parent may have suffered the loss of one of his parents or a sibling many years ago, long before his current family came into existence. If his grief was not completely resolved, his feelings about the deceased may remain unchanged all through the years, lingering with him to influence his adaptation to his new family. A family's inability to cope with an original loss may produce a family style that is variably unresponsive to a wide range of changes. Such families often contain a psychotherapy patient. It seems as though the family needs a scapegoat or "problem" on whom to focus its attention so as to maintain its unity against the threats of change and of the passage of time.

I would, then, begin to see the nuclear family—Mrs. Harper, Karen, and Johnny—joined from time to time by relatives and close friends. Since their problems are associated with unresolved grief, I should introduce a corrective grief experience, which, even though belated, may help to dislodge the family's pattern of interrelationships and move family members towards a better sense of themselves and of each other.

According to a therapeutic procedure I have used frequently, I would make direct inquiries about Mr. Harper's death, aiming my questions toward Karen. A review of the details of her experience would eventually expose some of Karen's distress and agitation. It would not be surprising, at this point, for Mrs. Harper or some other relative to try to prevent further evidence of Karen's distress with such responses as, "You can pull yourself together now" or, "That's all over and done with now," or "don't listen to the doctor, Karen, because he doesn't understand this particular situation." Family members, including the mourner himself, unwittingly conspire to deprive the mourner of his right to grieve. I would explain to them that people typically have difficulty in sharing the pain of grief with each other; then I would pursue the inquiry about Mr. Harper's death. By this time, Karen would probably be weeping, evidence I could point to in emphasizing for the family the heavy influence of Mr. Harper's death.

I would also inquire about losses in the more remote past and, at this stage, would expect details about the death of Mrs. Harper's father to emerge. A review of this experience would probably induce long-delayed expressions of grief in Mrs. Harper, and possibly in her mother, if she were able to be included in these sessions. My role as therapist would require detailed review of the loss experiences as they were lived, and the encouragement of expressions of inner feelings by all the belated mourners. Other family members would then be invited to reveal the feelings generated in them by observing the reactions of grief.

It is at this point that others may finally respond empathically to the mourner in his belated grief. Providing a setting that nurtures empathy is, indeed, one of the invaluable benefits of family therapy. Empathy is an interpersonal phenomenon that occurs when the empathizer, or subject, recognizes that he shares kindred feelings with another person, the object. Olden defines empathy as ". . . the capacity of the subject instinctively and intuitively to feel as the object does . . . the subject temporarily gives up his own ego for that of the object."[5] There is a kind of empathy that involves intellectual needs and another kind that involves only verbalized feelings and attitudes. In family therapy, however, the goal is affective empathy which seeks to meet emotional needs and which involves all feelings, not merely those that can be verbalized.

Affective empathy presupposes the existence of honest, direct communication without value judgments and includes the empathizer's accepting, for a brief period, the other's total emotional individuality. In other words, the empathizer accepts the existence within himself of not only the simple emotions of the other but also of the other's whole state of being—the history of his desires, feelings, and thoughts as well as other forces and experiences that are expressed in his behavior and have produced his current response to his situation and to those around him. The empathizer is not only aware of the other's various experiences, but finds himself sharing the reliving of those experiences. The object senses the empathizer's response and realizes that, for a brief point in time, they have fused. If he then takes the initiative and communicates more of his experiences, he provides a basic stimulus for what can become an affective empathic process.

It is imperative to make a clear distinction between empathy and sympathy. Although these terms are often used interchangeably, they describe different and mutually exclusive kinds of interpersonal experience. The two words share a common measure of meaning in that both express a preoccupation with the assumed affinity between a subject's own feelings and those of the object or other person. In sympathy, however, the subject is principally absorbed in his own feelings as projected into the object's special, separate experience. In sympathy, the subject is likely to use his own feelings as standards against which to measure the object's feelings and behavior. Sympathy, then, bypasses real understanding of the other person; he becomes the subject's mirror image and is thus denied his own sense of being. When Mrs. Harper tried to comfort Karen by pointing to her own loss of a father, she was sympathizing, seeing Karen's problem and feelings only in terms of her own experience. "I lost a father and I got over it," she might have been thinking. "If I've been able to withstand the loss, so can Karen. Perhaps my method of working hard and trying to forget will help her. Karen should not stop exerting her best efforts at school."

If her response had been empathic instead of sympathetic, Mrs. Harper would have accepted Karen as a separate individual, entitled to her own feelings, ideas, and emotional history, for whom another's loss would have no necessary value as precedent. She would have had no presuppositions about what Karen *should* feel, but would solicit the expression of whatever feelings Karen might have, for brief periods experiencing those feelings as though they were her own. The empathizer oscillates between such complete involvement and a detached recognition of the shared feelings. To the other person, these periods of objective detachment do not seem to be periods of indifference as they would in sympathy; instead, they are evidence that the subject respects himself and the object as separate people. The empathic relationship is generous; the empathizer does not use the object as a means for gratifying his own sense of importance, but is himself principally concerned with encouraging the other person to sustain and express his feelings and fantasies. Thus, the empathizer makes clear the other's right to his own individuality without apology, thereby avoiding the induction of guilt in the object, a common ingredient of sympathetic interactions. Being told that her mother, despite a heavy loss, carried on bravely would be likely to make Karen feel guilty if she were less "adequate" in similar circumstances.

Karen received much sympathy but no empathic responses at the time of her father's death. Within the family therapy sessions, this omission will be repaired by the therapist himself and, if the sessions work well, by other family members. From the start, the therapist presents himself as an empathic model, entering into the feelings of resistance to a review of the loss and, ultimately, the poignant review of the loss itself. In accepting the reality of the belated mourner's resistance and grief, the therapist encourages him and other family members to experience empathy. The therapist's role also includes empathizing with other family members in their resistance to sharing the grief experience and in their efforts to block a cathartic review by offering expressions of sympathy. He does this by imagining himself to be alternately the belated mourner and the other family members, thus feeling within himself everyone's disinclination to review a painful experience. His empathic stance will facilitate the belated mourner's expression. The process of countering family resistance may have to be repeated session after session, but eventually family members tend to freely offer empathic responses.

Reciprocating expressions of empathy lead to a lessening of family tensions, a sense of relief, and expressions of good will and love for one another. Karen, free to expose all her feelings about her father and his death, and Mrs. Harper, able at last to expose her long dormant distress over losing her own father and the newer anguish of her husband's sudden death, will be drawn closer in their empathic sharing of sorrow. For the first time, Karen and Johnny will observe their mother expressing intense feelings. This is a forceful lesson in empathy, one in which children and parents can acquire a sense of emotional continuity between generations.

The therapist should assure every family member that these exposed feelings are natural. Because of social taboos, there is one emotion that they may have particular trouble in accepting—hostility towards the deceased. A bereaved person, as Karen illustrated, often feels angry towards a loved person who has died, who has taken away his presence, who has shattered the environment, and who has abandoned the survivor to shift for himself. But, in our culture, it seems ungenerous to think or speak ill of the dead; thus such hostility is often deflected from the deceased towards some living member of the family. Karen's resentment of her mother probably reflects this displacement of hostility. Once the anger and its real object are brought out into the open, the family can understand the situation more clearly.

The Harper family may, however, find itself entering a state of confusion, and with good cause. They initially sought psychotherapeutic treatment for a daughter who had become a school problem, but this presenting complaint has long since been overshadowed by another, more pertinent consideration—the family's burden of unresolved grief and the resulting disabilities in their interpersonal relationships. To recognize that Karen is not the source of the difficulties but that the family must share the responsibility for them will be painful, particularly for Mrs. Harper. The confusion within the family which this recognition triggers is somewhat like the second stage of mourning, the stage of disorganization.

The therapist must be alert to a variety of psychological and psychosomatic reactions that usually emerge at this stage—anxiety states, depression, mood swings, and gastrointestinal disorders that simulate organic disturbances. I should not be in the least surprised if, at this juncture, Mrs. Harper started frantically to turn to others for counsel—physicians, her clergyman, the family lawyer, friends. These "busy work" pursuits are often undertaken to block the recognition of regrets that the family has wasted much time in useless discord. The therapist's empathy towards a resistance to sharing such regret usually leads to genuine declarations of remorse.

Although they will not realize it, the Harper family will be slowly preparing for the loss of the therapist through their corrective grief experience. Their belated completion of mourning for the original loss will enable them to cope more adequately with new losses, including the loss of the therapist on whose catalytic presence they may have grown somewhat dependent.

I would use another technique to encourage successful termination, the main goal of treatment, whether for individuals, couples, or families. The availability of easily operated audiotape and video-tape equipment now makes possible a useful self-confrontation procedure. I would, in the course of the treatment program, try to accustom the Harper family to having their therapy sessions recorded in my office. Later, they could play back the tapes at home. Mrs. Harper and Karen (and Johnny too) would be able to observe how they interact with each other in mutual and spiraling provocations. By assessing a disturbance and her own part in it, each could learn to avoid being provoked on future occasions.

Again, the therapist must empathize with the resistance of family members towards hearing how they actually sound, and seeing themselves involved in family arguments. An individual often has the greatest difficulty in empathizing with the self revealed on tape, a feeling comparable to the disgust or embarrassment some people feel when reading letters they wrote long ago. Once this resistance is overcome, however, and Karen and her mother achieve increasing self-control, they will feel free to explore the relevance of the past to the present under circumstances in which the effect can be most enduring, i.e., at home and with the therapist absent.

If the therapeutic work succeeds (and the successes of such work have been most encouraging), each of the Harpers should acquire an increased empathic understanding of himself and the others. Each, too, should have a more realistic understanding of the attitudes of other persons. Mrs. Harper will realize that Karen is not really angry with her and not really permanently disenchanted with school. Karen will realize that her mother's new pattern of work and home does not mean that she is alternately ignoring her children and trying to confine them too closely. Johnny will share fully the family's feelings, no longer artificially sheltered from the strains of his environment because of his age. All will recognize that their new life is and must be very different without Mr. Harper and that no pretenses can minimize that difference. The treatment will have aimed towards developing firmer individual identities through the establishment of each member's sense of self, while simultaneously reinforcing the viability of the family.

The reader will have observed how important empathy is in the treatment process. Empathy is important to every person because it allows him to feel that he is not alone in his passage through life. Children frequently admit the existence of empathy; sometimes they speak of their feeling that one or another parent is "with them inside." A large part of our cultural heritage, however, as presented both at home and at school, acts to inhibit rather than to nurture the empathic potential. Adults frequently resist empathy. Harold Pinter, the playwright, expresses his insight into this resistance in saying: "To enter into someone else's life is too frightening. To disclose to others the poverty within us is too fearsome a possibility."[6] He emphasizes a double aversion—to empathizing with someone else and to becoming the object of empathy. The aversion is especially strong against empathizing with such uncomfortable feelings as guilt, terror, and helplessness, feelings typical of bereavement. Before a person can empathize with someone who has these feelings, he must have been able to accept their existence within himself. But one may be unable to do this because of a natural tendency to avoid pain and distress. We have all heard reactions from theatre audiences to certain empathic experiences on the stage or screen, expressions like "schmaltzy," "corny," or "childish." These suggest that the dramatic portrayal of feeling has been recognized by the viewer as one of his own feelings, but that he wished to cancel this recognition with verbal reactions that minimize and negate the feeling.

There have been few studies of empathy, or even allusions to it, in scientific literature, perhaps because it is difficult for scientists to cope with an essentially nonintellectual experience and because, being human, they share in the general aversion to empathy. Sullivan reflects upon this aversion:

> I have had a good deal of trouble at times with people of a certain type of educational history; since they cannot refer empathy to vision, hearing, or some other special sense receptor, and since they do not know whether it is transmitted by the ether waves or air waves or what not; they find it hard to accept the idea of empathy . . . So although empathy may sound mysterious, remember that there is much that sounds mysterious in the universe, only you have got used to it; and perhaps you will get used to empathy.[7]

The artist, poet, or playwright is perhaps better suited than the scientist to discourse upon experiences of empathy and their relationship to frustration, loss, love, and tenderness. A work of art or a theatrical presentation can resolve for us, the audience, temporarily and imperfectly, the conflict between our deep hunger for empathy and the façades we erect against being touched by real people. In *A Long Day's Journey Into Night*, for example, we can empathize with the characters without risk because we know that our engagement will be confined within the limits of the play. We know, too, that our empathy as spectators will involve little pain, for we are not asked to expose our own distress. And we know that the actors will not be hurt by their revelations of emotion because they are merely assuming their roles. Empathy is so vital a nutrient that human beings deliberately seek it in fiction. Would it not be desirable that they be encouraged to satisfy their hunger for empathy in real life?

The Harpers will be helped to empathize with themselves and each other through family therapy. It would, of course, be better if they could manage to do this spontaneously within the family and did not require corrective experiences in treatment.

* * * * * *

Let us look again at Karen as she was on the day of her father's death and her experiences thereafter to see how empathy might have influenced her progress through her troubles. From the moment when she was summoned from class to the principal's office, Karen was exposed to an atmosphere of disaster without clear explanation of what the disaster was. The reticence of the principal and Uncle George is understandable, but this was only the prelude to many later verbal avoidances. Friends talked about Karen's "trouble" and "loss" and the "terrible blow" she has suffered. If, instead of these euphemistic abstractions, those around her had spoken of Karen's father, of what he had been like, of how sad it was that he should die suddenly, of how much she must miss him, they would have offered her opportunities to talk about her grief directly and expansively, verbally reviewing her relationship with her father and ventilating in words and actions her feelings about losing him.

Other avenues of expression were also blocked for her. Karen's mother wanted her to be "brave," and she herself served as a model of bravery in the face of adversity. This setting of a standard of restrained, undemonstrative sadness, even at the funeral, made it necessary for Karen to indulge in expressions of grief only when she was alone, and sometimes only in fantasies. Obviously, Mrs. Harper had intense feelings of loss that she was attempting not to expose; as a corollary, she required that Karen not expose her feelings. A sharing of their innermost sorrow and desolation would have permitted an empathic understanding and the resolution of their grief. Parents are the most enduring models for their children's behavior and attitudes; it would have been appropriate for Karen to learn from her mother the value and reality of such empathic understanding.

The pretense that life could proceed as before tended to diminish the importance of Mr. Harper's death, again robbing Karen of the chance to sense the impact of this sorrowful event. Mrs. Harper, Karen's school friends, her teacher, and the principal, all expressed the view that Karen should continue as though nothing had happened to her. Karen knew instinctively that her life had changed terribly, but there were no opportunities for her to express this sense of difference. The nuclear family is, in our society, that social unit which should most readily be able to nurture empathy. An open recognition within the Harper family that no efforts to equalize income, no determination to succeed at school, no exercises in cheerfulness to compensate for the absence of a husband and father would have helped Karen to accept the fact that one phase of her life was over and that the new one would not be the same. She could, then, have reviewed her relationship with her father in the perspective of past experience as a chapter regrettably but certainly closed.

The case of Karen Harper illustrates an hypothesis in which I have great confidence: that, just as unresolved grief is at the root of psychopathological blight, so empathy may be the principal element of the healing process. Family therapy has been able to encourage empathy and thus to treat the disabilities arising from unresolved grief. But prevention is better than cure in psychological as well as physical disorders. This leads us to a vital question: What social patterns can we devise that will provide modern man with a climate for empathy to resolve his grief? Man did not stop nomadic hunting before he domesticated food animals and instituted agriculture to insure that he would not lack food. Through some noxious oversight, however, he has discarded the cathartic mourning rituals of his ancestors before acquiring a substitute to insure that he will not lack the means for assuaging his grief. We must address ourselves to filling this gap in the pattern of social behavior. In the meantime, though, within our families and among our friends we can informally work towards freeing our capacities for empathy from the crippling restraints that so often enclose them.

REFERENCES

1. PARKES, M.C.: *Brit J Med Psychol,* 38:1, 1965.
2. LINDEMANN, E.: *Amer J Psychiat,* 101:141, 1944.
3. DEUTSCH, H.: *Psychoanal Quart* 6:12, 1937.
4. BOWLBY, P.: *Int J Psychoanal* 42:317, 1961.
5. OLDEN, C.: *Psychoanal Stud Child,* 8:111, 1953.
6. PINTER, H.: *Evergreen Review,* Winter, 1964, p. 81
7. SULLIVAN, H.S.: *The Interpersonal Theory of Psychiatry.* New York, Norton, 1953, pp. 41–42.

Chapter 18

ANTICIPATORY GRIEF

JAMES A. KNIGHT; FREDERIC HERTER

There appears to be a timetable of grief, oriented to both the date of the onset of a fatal illness as well as the date of death of the loved one. This timetable of grief, somehow built within us, is one for which we should indeed be thankful, for it sequentially relates the period of bereavement to a finite period of time.

No amount of foreknowledge or grieving will do more than mitigate the event of death when it comes. But the presence of grief in anticipation of the loss alters its subtle progression; the inevitable change has foreshadowed one's feelings; one is powerless, and a measure of resignation has crept in. A sorrowful reality is about to ensue; and actual death comes as an affirmation of our preknowledge. Sharp grief has already been experienced; but the sharpest edge of grief comes at this time. However, because of his anticipatory grief, the bereaved more readily finds his way back to peace, according to the dictates of his own situation and the ensuing circumstances. Those about him should somehow be brought to the same realization, so that they will understand all the bereaved's reactions to the ultimate event and will become better able to assist, rather than hinder him in working through his grief.

Thus, without recognition of the influence of anticipatory grief, no consideration of the complexities constituting the emotional and physical state of bereavement would be complete. Once the bereaved and those about him become aware that grief in anticipation of the

EDITOR'S NOTE: It is noted that, because of professional interest engendered by this volume, a separate book for the medical and paramedical professions took shape, a book which looks upon loss and grief from a far broader perspective than that of the experiences which follow death alone, but rather emphasizes the anticipatory grief on the part of the patient and those about him concerning loss of body part and/or functions, and so forth, problems which oftentimes are a part of the progressive illness which terminates in death. This book is entitled *Loss and Grief: Psychological Management in Medical Practice*, to be published by the Columbia University Press. Many of the writers in *Death and Bereavement* have also contributed to *Loss and Grief*.

death of a loved one does, in fact, occur, a giant stride toward recovery will have been made.

A. H. K.

Anticipatory grief is a most important reaction which is all too
frequently overlooked. Understanding and recognition of this
phenomenon enable those who comfort and work with the families of the dying to make their ministrations much more effective.
Four instances will be considered, the most pertinent and important, in the context of bereavement, being the fourth.

The grief reaction is only one of the forms of separation reaction. All separations are not a result of death. Genuine grief
reactions can also be seen in individuals who have not experienced a bereavement but who have experienced separation.
The families of service men in time of war often suffer a genuine
grief reaction on the departure of a member of the family into
the armed forces. Such separations occur under a threat of death
but are not due to death. A common picture growing out of this
type of situation is a syndrome which has been designated *anticipatory grief*.[1]

I

For example, in time of war, a woman may be so concerned
with the adjustment that will have to be made by reason of the
potential death of her father, brother, or husband that she goes
through all the phases of grief, including a review of all the
forms of death which might befall him and anticipation of the
modes of readjustment which might be necessitated by the death.
While such a reaction may form a safeguard against the impact
of a sudden death notice, it can turn out to be a severe handicap
at the occasion of reunion. Detailed studies have been reported
on the effect of wartime separations.[2]

The phenomenon of anticipatory grief can be seen as it related
to one serviceman upon his return home from the war. On arriv-
ing home, he discovered that his wife did not love him any more
and wanted a divorce. In such situations, it was often found that
the wife had mourned the potential loss of her husband so

effectively that she had actually emancipated herself from her ties to him. The readjustment then had to be directed toward a new interaction and a new integration of the husband back into the family.

Separation from significant persons in one's life may be brought about by war, chronic illness, distant employment, or any number of circumstances. An appreciation of the complications which may arise out of anticipating grief should enable us to deal more effectively with certain critical problems in interpersonal relationships.

II

I am acquainted with a physiologist, on a university faculty, who for the past ten years has had Hodgkin's Disease. When his illness was first diagnosed, it was thought he would live for only a few months, but he recovered sufficiently to return to his teaching and research. Periodically, though, he has had a severe exacerbation of his illness which has required hospitalization for weeks or months. During each of these periods of hospitalization, he has not been expected to recover. Yet, he has recovered and returned to his family and to work. During his remissions, each of which usually lasts for several months, he performs most of his duties at a high level of effectiveness and continues to do creative work in research.

Each time he is discharged from the hospital and returns home, a genuine crisis in interpersonal relationships develops. Hostility seems to flow in every direction. His wife and four children seem to have great difficulty integrating him again into the life of the family. Thus diverse complications arise which almost break the structure of the group.

In discussion of this problem with the brilliant and perceptive wife who, like her husband, is a university professor, it became obvious what was happening. Each time the husband and father went to the hospital, the wife and children expected him to die because of the gravity of his condition. They began to mourn his loss. In order to prepare themselves for the seemingly inevitable death of their loved one, they began to mourn for him in advance. When he did not die, but returned home after weeks or months, the family members had already to a great extent broken their ties to him. Then they were faced with the problem of reintegrating into their lives the person they had already given up.

The wife was helped to see what was happening. She was amazed that she and the children did not realize what they were doing. Now that she understood the situation, she was able to prevent the storm which had previously followed each of her husband's discharges from the hospital.

III

The family's reaction to the prospective death of a child can also be compared to separation anxiety. The process of mourning usually begins before the child dies. The family must be allowed this period of mourning, which involves self-examination, self-condemnation, and also guilt. They need their pastor's and physician's permission to indulge in the various aspects of mourning. Both pastor and physician can permit the child's parents to voice their guilt and reassure them by the gentle and understanding manner in which they answer their questions, such as: Should I have called the doctor sooner? Did the child inherit the disease from one of us? Did his recent injury contribute to this illness? Do you think my spanking him may have brought this on? Intellectually, parents know that these questions are unreasonable or unrelated, but they ask them because they are so deeply involved emotionally. Ventilation of their fears and anxieties and reassurances from those around them serve to ease their discomfort.

The process of anticipatory mourning, the gradual detachment from the child of the family's emotional investment, is observed in most cases in which the course of illness is longer than three or four months. The kindest effect of this anticipatory mourning is a muting of the grief reaction, so that the terminal phase and death of the child can often be received with an attitude of philosophic resignation.

J. A. K.

IV

There is a final area of anticipatory grief that is of overriding importance to the theme of this book, and which many bereaved and even some workers in the field fail to understand and appreciate realistically. This concerns the extent to which grief is experienced in advance of the actual death of a loved one and is especially true if he has been sick for a long time and is now terminally ill. Here, bereavement is imminent; the inevitability of coming death has been faced over an extended period. At the same time that the approaching loss is profoundly affecting the bereaved-to-be, the situation is further complicated and compounded by evidences of grief in the patient himself related to his illness and fear of death.

A. H. K.

* * *

Grief following long-anticipated death presents special problems of its own. There is no initial shock phase. Preparations have already been made in detail. Friends and relatives have long since been informed of the impending end. Expressions of sympathy, acts of support have already been conferred. Grief has found its fullest expression long before death and has been gradually replaced by a resigned acceptance of the facts. The life alone has already begun and the attendant adjustments in thinking made.

Death, under these circumstances, comes anticlimactically, without drama. A transient resurgence of grief may ensue, but it is dulled by long months of anticipation. More often, the end is marked by a sense of relief; of release from a protracted phase of anguish and suffering into a new life of relative normalcy. It is not unnatural that this suppressed relief should be accompanied by feelings of confusion and guilt. To the outside world, a posture of grieving must be assumed out of proportion to the actual sense of loss. In our culture, any overt expression of relief is inappropriate. Hence, honest emotions are sublimated to a degree, and a charade is played out.

Whatever conflicts may arise can be lessened significantly by a simple awareness of the nature of anticipatory grief, and once again the physician can play an important role by anticipating this reaction and preparing the family for it.

F. H.

REFERENCES

1. LINDEMANN, E.: Symptomatology and management of acute grief. *Amer J Psychiat, 101*:141, 1944.
2. ROSENBAUM, M.: Emotional aspects of wartime separations. *Family, 24*:337–341, 1944.

Chapter 19

GRIEF IS

JOSEPH BESS

Tragic, heroic, stately, consummate, august, ennobling, dignified, impressive, lofty, courageous, majestic; passionate, compassionate, empathic, sympathetic, commiserative, stoic, resigned, reticent, silent, clandestine, covert, taciturn, implicit, impenetrable, occult; pathological, guilt-ridden, obsessive, agonizing, overwhelming, chimerical, fanatical, delusive; egoistic, self-centered, narcissistic; projective, personal, idolizing; universal, impersonal, eternal; ambivalent, ambiguous, paradoxical, rhapsodic, enigmatic; amoral, irreligious, obdurate; religious, mystical, transcendent, prayerful, soulful; philosophical, rational, logical, enlightened; poetic, rhetorical, musical, artistic, aesthetic, orphean, elegaic, exquisite, eloquent, plaintive, symphonic; mystical, fantasticized; sublimated, disguised, transmuted, inaudible, suppressed, inarticulate; ironical, burdensome, onerous, maudlin, brooding, lamentable, languishing, cumbersome; dispirited, melancholic, morose, saturnine, cheerless, disconsolate; inconsolable, irreconcilable, intractable, refractory, recalcitrant, despairing, dolorous, uncontrolled, irrepressible; struggling, rebellious, mutinous, dissentious, contentious, belligerent, aggressive; purposeful, willful, volitional, resolute, sedulous, determined, ceremonious, empirical, bacchic, ritualistic; pessimistic, negative, gloomy, cynical; beleaguering, defiant, intrepid, chivalrous, valiant, indomitable; solicitous, rapacious, suppliant, beseeching, importunate, apologetic; chastened, lacerated, castigated, abused, wounded; abstruse, incomprehensible, ineffable, recondite; transient, ephemeral, desultory, vacillating; perfidious, treacherous, vengeful, diabolical, caustic; banal, conformist, trite, commonplace, prosaic, platitudinous, materialistic; expedient, useful, serviceable, advantageous; vitalizing, energizing, reviving, inspirational; unbelieving, incredulous, skeptical; cowardly, cringing, obsequious, groveling; fearful, apprehensive, anxious, terrified, panicky, tremulous, timid; invincible, impregnable, insuperable, audacious, brazen, ingenuous; symbolic, interpretive, allegoric, analogous, metaphoric, figurative; passive, acquiescent, docile, pliant, submissive; blasphemous, abusive, infamous, scandalous, virulent, opprobrious, accusatory, damnatory; appreciative, complacent, thankful, gratified, consoled, heartened; communicative, patent, confidential, confessed, avowed, acknowledged, assertory; angelic, celestial, divine, ethereal, holy; grave, composed, serene, sublime, placid, austere, tranquil.

Chapter 20

MOURNING

H. ROBERT BLANK

The normal initial response to the loss of a loved one is a manifest grief reaction, a depression, characterized by dejection, tearfulness, restlessness or retardation, insomnia, and the expression of feelings of hopelessness, helplessness, emptiness and guilt. The guilt feelings are based on the bereaved's fantasied or actual derelictions. All these signs are not always apparent, and they vary in intensity, not only because of individual differences in temperament and personality, but also because of cultural sanctions regarding the expression of emotion in general, and mourning rituals in particular.

In general, experience teaches us that the expression of grief through tears and talking is healthier than its suppression. To share painful feelings with a friend or respected counselor facilitates the mastery of these feelings. And the bereaved who are ashamed of such feelings and their expression (typically, men) need reassurance that to have such feelings and talk about them is healthy and desirable, not an indication of weakness.

The bereaved also needs reassurance about hostile feelings toward the deceased for abandoning him. Such reactions are universal but are usually repressed. When they do emerge, the bereaved is extremely disturbed by them and ashamed to talk about them. It is easier to talk about one's own guilt than to talk about current anger or rage toward the deceased.

Usually the overt signs of grief are no longer evident to the ordinary observer after a week or two; the bereaved has resumed his work, and his life is under reasonable control. We all know, however, that the internal, private, painful work of mourning has just begun. What is the normal duration for this prolonged and painful process—that is, for the bereaved fully to accept his loss and to direct all of his energies toward the problems and satisfactions of living? If one is to avoid blundering in giving advice to the bereaved, or avoid making unrealistic demands on him, it would be safe to assume one year to be the minimum duration of mourning, and one to two years the average duration. Variations depend, of course, on the maturity and temperament of the bereaved, and the quality and the duration of the relationship with the deceased.

REACTIONS TO SUDDEN LOSS

Grief is preceded and complicated by a shock reaction when the loss occurs without any warning, e.g., as a result of accidental death. The shock reaction has two components: one is a denial, "It can't be true." The other is a form of depersonalization, a state of emotional anesthesia, in which the bereaved feels numb or unreal or that the world is unreal. This condition is frequently described as "weird," "I feel like a zombie," "It is like living in a dream." In extreme cases, these symptoms are severe enough to immobilize the bereaved's movements and speech so that he appears to be mute and immobile. Frequently, the observer notes that the bereaved is dazed, walking slowly and talking with great difficulty.

The state of shock is really a protective mechanism against overwhelmingly painful feelings of grief. The denial and emotional anesthesia permit these painful feelings to emerge bit by bit. Hence, it might take a day or two before the emotional anesthesia is gone and the bereaved feels the full impact of his grief.

At the opposite pole are the frequent cases in which death has occurred after a prolonged, painful, wasting illness, when the patient, in the final months, weeks, or days is in a drugged, stuporous state most of the time and often unable to communicate coherently. In such cases death is commonly accepted by the family with relief because they know that their loved one's hopeless suffering has come to an end. As one who has experienced both sudden bereavement and, more frequently, losses due to prolonged illness, I can say that the more unexpected the death, the more acute and disturbing the grief; the more prolonged the illness, the more one can accomplish the most painful part of mourning in anticipation of the loss.

Even though the stage of shock is often alarming and medical attention is necessary, it should not be interpreted as pathological. It is a normal reaction of an emergency, self-protective nature, a defense against overwhelming sudden loss.

ABNORMAL AND PATHOLOGICAL MOURNING REACTIONS

Grief reactions of unusual, often incapacitating severity or duration, and a variety of strange, even bizarre behavior patterns, are often seen in bereavement states.

Certain factors in a person's history predispose him or her to abnormal reactions to the loss of spouse, parent, sibling or lover:

1. Alcoholism: this, more than any other factor, is correlated with suicide following death of the spouse.
2. Death of a parent or sibling in the bereaved's childhood or early adolescence.
3. Homosexuality.
4. Psychiatric hospitalization.
5. Past history of depressive reactions to relatively minor misfortunes or frustrations; for example, to an automobile accident in which no one was seriously hurt, or to failure to obtain a promotion.
6. Prolonged conflict with the deceased.
7. Marked dependency upon the deceased.

Awareness of these factors can help in anticipating abnormally severe or pathological mourning reactions, so that prompt medical or psychiatric help may be provided. It is essential that such knowledge be part of the basic training of every physician, nurse, clergyman, counselor, and other professional persons. Such knowledge will make it possible to provide early effective treatment for otherwise incapacitating depressions and other mental illnesses.

Chapter 21

BEREAVEMENT

W. DEWI REES

The reaction of people to personal bereavement is both varied and stereotyped. It is varied in the sense that no two people react to a similar situation in an identical way. It is stereotyped in the sense that all human reactions fall within a particular range of pattern which is capable of being discerned and assessed. The range of reaction to personal bereavement varies from a nil response at one extreme to such intense grief or depression at the other that the bereaved person contemplates or actually attempts suicide. These reactions form the extreme limits of response and are experienced by a small minority of people. The reactions of most bereaved people fall within a central range of response, which contains a number of common factors and which varies in duration from a few days to a few months.

Much remains to be learnt about this normal range of response. Its pattern and intensity probably varies with the age and sex of the bereaved and with his kinship to the deceased. Social factors are also important as is apparent when we consider the increased anxiety associated with financial worries for a widow left in penury compared with a widow receiving an adequate pension. The response of bereaved people also varies with the age and previous state of health of the deceased. The sudden and accidental death of an adolescent son is always a grievous and shattering blow to the parents. It usually causes much more intense and prolonged grief than the death of the very old relative, whose physical and mental deterioration has been noted and watched for years with sorrow and whose final demise is accepted as a kindness to the dying and a relief to the relatives.

This pattern of normal response is often associated with a variety of factors, such as temporary loss of appetite, loss of weight, altered sleep pattern and a tendency to think about and miss the deceased. Crying is more usual in women than men, but occurs in both sexes. Loneliness is for many a particularly difficult and important problem. Sometimes it is made worse by the bereaved tending to avoid social contacts or by the failure of family friends to maintain a previously close relationship. The frequent visits of friends, relatives, doctors and clergy to the dying person often contrasts sharply with their subsequent failure to visit the bereaved.

A surprisingly large number of bereaved people "see" their dead relatives, after these have been cremated or buried. Some describe this phenomenon as something they see in their mind's eye, thus rationalising it. Others state quite definitely, that they really consider that the deceased is with them. This visual experience is not uncommon amongst people who are otherwise coping adequately with their bereavement and pursuing normal lives. Because of this I include it among the range of normal reactions to bereavement. It is an experience about which bereaved people do not talk unless directly questioned and one from which they often derive great comfort. It is a reaction which is not spontaneously disclosed to either priest, doctor, friend or relative and one which I was completely unaware occurred amongst my patients during my first ten years of medical practice. Sometimes it continues for very many years; it seems more common amongst those people who were living with or remained actively associated with the deceased, than with those whose ties had remained less close. The climate of opinion in modern Western civilization is obviously such that many people feel that they are unable to disclose to others one of the most interesting and important experiences in their life. This is particularly sad, as they often feel happier for having discussed it and learnt that it is not so very uncommon.

To an increasing extent people now die in hospitals and not in their own homes. The reason for this is usually sociological and not basically medical. The concept that "they can look after him better in hospital" is often true only to the extent that it simplifies the situation for the doctors and nurses, and relieves the relatives of an important responsibility. Often in fact, the dying person is better cared for at home than in hospital. At home he is looked after by the relatives with the help of the doctor and nurse. In hospital he is looked after by the doctors and nurses, while the relatives are excluded from any effective care or contact with him. They are welcomed as visitors and observers but not as active participants. The direct care by people of their dying relatives is a considerable help in preparing them for the subsequent bereavement. The realization that one is doing everything possible in the terminal care is a great help in subsequently accepting the fact of a relative's death. This care requires considerable patience. Often it entails sleepless nights, anxiety and moments of anguish, but the continuity of contact and the realization that one is caring for one's own, make the effort worthwhile. I find also that the status of a person dying in hospital is different from that at home. In hospital the patient is often a peripheral personality and subservient; at home he is usually the central figure and often the dominant figure in the house. Many people whose relatives have died in hospital have subsequently told me that they would have preferred them to die at home. No relative of a person who died at home has told me that they would have preferred the death to have occurred in hospital.

This is an age of skepticism and of changing cultural and ethical forms. Doctrines taught for centuries by the various world religions are now considered irrelevant and meaningless by countless people. Those who have the solace of religion in bereavement are fortunate. Other effective help is also now available in the form of modern psychotropic drugs, particularly for those who find that life has become empty and meaningless and who remain anxious and depressed.

Chapter 22

GUILT

GLENN MOSLEY

One of the most effective ways to *cope with grief* is to understand that the feelings of guilt, resentment, of not having done enough, desertion, deprivation, anger, fear and countless others, are shared by almost all who grieve. Since death is not a subject for casual conversation, two people in a family may be grieving for the same person and experiencing almost identical emotional reactions, but because they do not feel free to bare these emotions completely, they may assume that their own reactions are abnormal.

For example, there may be feelings of guilt because the bereaved believes he could have done more to prevent the loved one's death: "I could have insisted on calling the doctor sooner; I should not have allowed him to refuse surgery five years ago; he should have been in the hospital sooner; he should have had more rest and longer vacations."

The bereaved may even feel *resentment* "because he left me, just when I need him most." The bereaved rarely feels he can openly admit such an emotion, so he bears it in silence. The death of a parent, husband, wife, or a child with whom one has had an intimate relationship brings a pervasive feeling of loss. What is less well recognized is that this feeling of loss may be taken as a personal slight, the feeling that the departed has run away, deliberately deserted his family. On a deep emotional level, such feelings of desertion, deprivation, and resentment are to be expected. If we are aware that these negative-appearing emotions are not abnormal, we can cope with them more positively.

In addition to thoughts about his own death, it is not uncommon for a person to have thoughts about the death of a loved one from time to time. He fantasies his reaction to such a loss as well as fantasying the loved one's reaction to the situation, were it reversed. This should not be confused with the death wish, but it often is.

Chapter 23

ATTITUDES
TOWARD DEATH IN OUR CULTURE

EDGAR N. JACKSON

Every culture must find ways for dealing with the existential facts of life. Primitive cultures depended largely on rites, rituals, and ceremonies to give personal meaning to life at the same time that they met psychological needs of the individual and preserved social viability for the group. In more modern times, religion has functioned as the acceptable channel through which meaning for life could be sought. Religious institutions became the custodians of the useful forms of ritualized behavior at the same time that they served philosophical and theological purposes in guiding the quest for meaning.

When periods of rapid change occur, there is the possibility, and sometimes the hazardous probability, that the meaningful ways of doing things that satisfied deep and often unconscious psychological needs may be lost. We are faced with just such a set of circumstances in our day, for our basic values have been changing rapidly, and the changes have been so close to us that objectivity concerning them has been difficult. We have had little opportunity to assess meanings, and what they portend for us. Let us give ourselves to such a search for objectivity now as we look at the meaning of the attitudes we reflect culturally as we try to cope with death in our day.

Death is an existential fact. Man is a mortal creature. Yet in our culture, for the first time in history, we are trying to deny this fact. A sociological survey in California showed that the majority of persons felt death was a form of illness to be overcome with medical research rather than the sure mark of man's mortality. A group of physicians in New York admitted that they tended to think of death as accidental and their language even demonstrated this in terms of "cerebral accidents," "circulatory accidents" and "coronary accidents." Increasingly, death is considered to be an unwarranted intruder into the affairs of man rather than the signal of his nature as a mortal being.

This attitude tends to bring about modifications in our thinking that may be subtle but are nonetheless relentless. We establish a value system that glorifies youth, beauty, health, and vigor. To see how far this has gone, just observe or read advertisements. Even Geritol® does not mention old age, but speaks of restoring youthful vigor to iron-poor, vitamin-deficient blood, the implication being that one shot brings back the surging hot blood of youth, or "your money back." This is clearly an appeal not to rational judgment but to a generally accepted value system operative in our society.

The practical effect of this denial of the reality of man's nature as a mortal being is at least three-fold. In the first place, it tends to make religion irrelevant, for if religion seeks to give meaning to life and to death, we are addressing ourselves to a generation that has no interest in what we are trying to say, for it has already found its answers in its denial. It has carried nihilism to the ultimate.

In the second place, any answers arising from denial of our mortality are the expression of a rapidly contracting view of life. Many people are less and less interested in the past with its traditions and its answers, and at the same time they deny the reality of the future—for somewhere in that future lurk the ideas of aging, suffering, and death. The present becomes increasingly the focal point. A philosophy of life as traditionally understood becomes less and less important, and the "now" expands to encompass more and more of life. Even the power of faith as an audacious venture of the spirit of man becomes largely irrelevant, for there is no yesterday, no tomorrow, only the glory of today. Life becomes not primarily a quest for meaning but rather a satisfaction of appetites. This attitude, in short, resembles a rapid retreat to animalism. There are no longer any moral problems to be met, for one does not really need to look ahead to consequences. Warnings about nuclear war, unsafe cars, overpopulation, air pollution, inflation, and lung cancer fall largely upon deaf ears, for many persons have adjusted themselves psychologically to a way of life free of painful tomorrows as well as any concern about the consequences of today's actions.

The third effect of denying our mortal nature expresses itself in the form of new social and cultural patterns which fortify our constricted philosophy of life. We must get rid of the aged, and those who are on the verge of doing something as inconsiderate and troublesome as dying. We give them their social security and send them over the mountains or to the hinterlands into a new type of segregation, the rest home or "senior citizen" reservation. Then, if they must die, they will at least do it unobtrusively. The architect creates homes for the small family unit with small living space as protection against intrusion, and with large enough garages to keep people so rapidly in motion that they do not have a chance to slow down and look at life or death. As if this is not enough, one family in four that buys a home has it already equipped with wheels, ready to go. Thus instability, loss of roots, and escape from traditional human values becomes the prevalent mood of life, sadly reduced by its effort to escape an honest confrontation with its own mortality. But no one specifically can be blamed for what has happened. These changes have come about more by happenstance than design. They are due to the increasing specialization of our society, the growth of existential anxiety, and the breakdown of communication between human beings.

That ours is an age of specialization is already a time-worn cliché! But what it means is less often explained. In the matter of death and dying, it becomes quite clear. Today, nearly all death and dying occur in the presence of those who are technically skilled but emotionally uninvolved, the doctors, nurses, state police, and medical corpsmen. Those who are emotionally involved are largely excluded, so that the focus of their emotions is oftentimes diffused and unrelated to the reality. When this happens, it is more difficult to express genuine and commensurate feelings. Instead, they are diverted, repressed or denied. But when we are dealing with powerful emotions, we know they cannot be easily denied. Rather, they take detours and show up in other forms, such as psychogenic illness, personality changes, and maladaptive behavior.

This remoteness from reality, at the time of death, this removal of the focus of emotion creates inner confusion and anxiety. Anxiety is a difficult state to cope with, for it shows itself in many ways, often camouflaged. Persons involved often have the feeling they can control distress-creating events by more denial.

Thus, instead of experiencing real death and real grief, we indulge in escape from reality, which only increases our anxiety. Anxiety tends to show itself through characteristics related to age and experience. Children show it in behavior. Youth shows it in rebellion. People in the full vigor of life may become dependent on alcohol; the aged seek their escape through physical symptoms. The reactions may show up in a variety of ways. As head of a psychiatric clinic serving children and their parents, this writer found that behavior motivated by basic anxiety could result in organic illness, in aggressive destructiveness, or characterized by a quiet withdrawal into a loss of ability to function in home, school, or play.

With adolescents, anxiety may appear in the self-destructive games they play, like "chicken," in which they race their cars toward each other to see who will pull out first. Although they would probably say that they are proving they have no fear of death, it might be more accurate if they said, "Look, folks, we are so overwhelmed with anxiety about death that we are willing to make a plaything out of life in order to try to allay it."

By 1970, one half of the population of this country will be twenty-five years of age or younger. Thus we know how significant this group will be in shaping the values we will live by for generations to come. Most deaths occur in the over sixty-five age group. The teenagers and young adults will be arranging for the events surrounding the deaths of their parents and other adults. They will be the parents of the group one to four years of age and, in their own major age group, they will undoubtedly experience a large number of accidental and military deaths. How they react will be significant. Yet the unhappy fact is that the largest number of suicides today is said to occur among college age youth, and the next largest among high school students. This seems to indicate that our compounded anxiety not only tends to destroy meaning for life but makes life intolerable. It appears that, unless something constructive is done, the problem will become worse rather than better, and could lead to neurotic states, maladaptive behavior, and a progressive loss of the capacity to feel sympathy or express love.

But, fortunately, those who have been exploring the nature of the problem psychologically, sociologically, anthropologically, and medically have not been content with diagnosis alone. They have given us some helpful prescriptions as to what can be done to relieve the problem. Let us look now at some of these suggestions for wisely managing acute deprivation experiences, and learning to grow through grief.

First, it is unsound to try to intellectualize an emotion. Emotions have their own validity. Grief is an emotion and must be understood as such. One of the reasons that the intellectual community has recommended unwise reforms as far as a realistic approach to death is concerned is that it has the inclination both by training and experience to approach problems from the rational point of view. Often this is a form of escape. Emotions tend to be nonrational, and the complex emotions that come with acute loss must be accepted for what they are. When we intellectualize, we tend to change the focus of attention and set the basis for consideration where we want it rather than where the persons we serve need it. We tend to feel uncomfortable with a person who is suffering, and in so doing, we deny his right to such feelings, at least in our presence.

I have on my desk a letter from a pastor in a nearby state who exercised his privilege of disagreeing with me on the subject of emotions and death. He vigorously supported limited and private ceremonials. Then his daughter was killed in an automobile accident. For her funeral, he insisted on an elaborate set of ceremonials, and wrote to say that he could not have gone through the tragedy without the time and opportunity to adjust to the reality of what had happened. In effect, he seems to be agreeing that he had been trying to intellectualize and realized at great personal cost that the emotions had to be met where they existed. The difficulty here, of course, is that it is impossible to feel strongly in advance of the event that precipitates deep emotion.

Also, it is important to realize that everything which is done at the time of death is done for those who still live and feel. As John Donne pointed out long ago, the funeral is for everyone, for it is a simultaneous process by which the reality of death and the mortal nature of man are honestly faced, and whereby the viability of the continuing community is affirmed. Although there is death, it never overcomes life. The significance of the rituals of death is for those who desperately struggle to find some meaning in the process by which death overcomes life, whose faith affirms that life is always master of death. The acts that are carried out, the ceremonials that are performed, are meant to provide the climate for acting out and working through the deep feelings that exist in the living. These may be as varied as identification, rejection, hostility, love, anger, loneliness, guilt, doubt, and fear. Whatever they are, they are authentic for the persons who feel them, and they have to be expressed or they fester and infect the whole being.

Dr. Erich Lindemann has emphasized the importance of facing reality in coping with grief. Escapes are always temporary, and illusions are the stuff of which disturbance is bred. In an age when many of the approaches to mind and emotion are prone to deny reality, it is doubly important to use the resources available for facing what has happened with openness and honesty. The human organism has certain built-in mechanisms for escaping the painful. We can faint when we have acute physical pain, or we can employ denial in the face of painful emotional situations.

Dr. Lindemann says that one of the most important resources is the moment of truth that comes when death is faced openly and the total being is obliged to contend with the devices of denial. When a person says, "I just want to remember him as he was," he is denying the one important fact that must be faced before control of grief can be properly begun. The dead person is not as he was.

One of the psychological facts we have to cope with is the

heavy investment of emotional capital in the objects we come to love, and the need to withdraw that emotional capital when there is no longer a possibility for a significant human relationship. Part of our fear of death is that it is unconsciously communicated, or contaminating, so we try to avoid it in self-protection. But in avoiding the physical fact of death, we prolong the process of identification and make it difficult or impossible to withdraw from the relationship. When that happens, the human personality may be injured for a long time to come. The sooner reality is faced, the more quickly the person, as a general rule, is able to express the appropriate feelings and engage in the natural and healthy process of emotional withdrawal.

In our times, it is fashionable to refrain from showing strong feelings, as if only weak people demonstrate their emotions. We know this is not true, for it is generally the strong who are capable of the deepest and most profound emotions. Grief is a feeling, growing out of the extension of one person into the life of another. Such an expression of identification could be considered the reverse side of love. There is no simple, easy or painless way of coming to terms with these deep feelings. The pain is real, but it is released more quickly if it is met openly and faced for what it is. It is prolonged endlessly if ignored or denied. We must learn to respect our deep feelings and the deep feelings of others, and help to create the channels through which these valid feelings can be wisely expressed.

Chapter 24

BEREAVEMENT AND THE AMERICAN FAMILY

PAUL J. REISS

𝒯he manner in which Americans organize their family relation-ships has an important bearing on the meaning of bereavement. In the United States, great emphasis is placed upon the immediate family, consisting of father, mother, and children. Whereas in other countries and in earlier centuries in this country groups of relatives beyond the immediate family were of considerable importance, American urban family life has tended to focus rather exclusively on the immediate family. Relationships with relatives and in-laws are maintained, of course, but usually only involve visiting on holidays or an occasional "get together." For most people, relatives are not involved in their occupations or business or in matters of education or religion. The immediate family is the important economic, residential and social unit; relatives are of secondary importance.

Our society firmly believes in the independence of the immediate family in relationship to relatives and in-laws. For children to leave the parental household when they marry and establish their own independent family is accepted as the right and proper thing to do. As the married children leave the homes of their parents, contact with the parents, brothers and sisters is naturally lessened, as their main attention is now devoted to their own growing families.

The death of parents usually occurs when children have already established their own families and have been living apart from the parents for a number of years. While the death of a parent in such circumstances may well represent a loss, it certainly does not in most cases greatly alter the pattern of life, which has already been established independent of the parents.

With increased life expectancy, the death of a brother or sister is also most likely to fit the same situation, in which there has been a separation over a period of years while each has been giving primary attention to his own family.

When children get married and establish their own families they have a new interest with which to replace the family within which they grew up. The same is not the case, however, with the parents of the married children, who find that to some extent they have had to lose their own family of children to marriage and separation.

Increased life expectancy, coupled with the younger age of parents when their children have left home, has created a whole period of family life when the couple are by themselves. The fact that women have a life expectancy which is now about seven years longer than that of men, added to the fact that women generally marry men two years or so older, means that the first death to occur is very likely to be that of the husband. Approximately two thirds of all married women become widows and remain widows for an average of about sixteen years. The experience of the loss of a spouse is, therefore, much more frequently an experience for women than for men.

Improvements in mortality, then, have greatly reduced the likelihood that a person will experience the death of his parents, brothers or sisters while he is young; after he has married, he is also less likely to experience the death of his own children, even after they have married. In addition, the independence of each immediate family has meant that the death of a person's parents, brothers, or sisters occurs years after he, as well as his brothers and sisters, have established and given primary attention to their separate families.

Although these factors have reduced the effects of bereavement in other family relationships, they have actually heightened the problem in the case of the death of a husband or wife. The most serious loss of a personal relationship for most people is the loss suffered through the death of a spouse. Through the emphasis placed upon the immediate family, American family patterns have increased the importance of the marital relationship. Unlike many other societies, the marital relationship in the United States takes precedence over all other relationships with family members, relatives, in-laws, or friends.

Social and behavioral scientists have long recognized the importance of close personal relationships for the development and stability of the individual person. In the type of complex society which has developed in the United States and other industrialized, urbanized societies, about the only personal relationship which an individual is able to maintain over an extended period of time is the one with his spouse. As a consequence, we place great importance upon marriage, expecting it to do a great deal for the individuals involved, compensating by itself for the lack of meaningful relationships elsewhere in the society. It is significant that American couples today report that companionship is the most important aspect of marriage for them. In no other society is one's spouse expected to be so exclusively one's companion, friend, confidant, and emotional support.

This pattern which stresses marriage as companionship is further reinforced in the later years, when the children have departed from the home, when retirement from occupations cuts people off from their business, professional, or work relationships, and when the frequent moving of people around the country often leaves the couple in a community of strangers. In this situation, the married pair for a number of years must depend upon each other to an even greater extent for the meaning of life and the personal satisfactions which can only be derived from a close personal relationship with another person.

Therefore, although trends in mortality and family life patterns have mitigated the problems associated with the death of other family members, the problems of bereavement in the case of husband or wife have been rendered more severe.

PART IV

PRACTICALITIES OF RECOVERING FROM BEREAVEMENT

It is not our intention to present an in-depth discussion of the funeral. Space permits only a brief summary of certain legal and other aspects of orientation, as outlined below. The reader is referred to a chapter in *But Not to Lose* (Kutscher, A. H., New York, Frederick Fell, 1969) for additional information regarding the religious, sociological and psychological implications of the funeral in bereavement as well as to the vast literature already available on this most significant subject.

Chapter 25

FUNERALS, CUSTOMS, RITUALS

PAUL E. STEWARD

When death occurs, practical and legal aspects must be considered. There are laws and regulations governing final disposition which must be observed, and certain documents must be completed stating the cause of death and other vital statistics. Only qualified persons are permitted to handle such details.

Society has legislated what may and may not be done with the body of the deceased. Laws determine who may and who may not make final disposition of the body. They determine some of the procedures which must be used. Some cities and counties, all states and countries have their own laws, rules, and regulations which must be met and adhered to. The health departments protect society from possible contagion, by governing how a body is cared for.

They also devise legal documents which must be filled in with vital statistics and medical information and filed with the local registrar. These certificates are used in many ways. Some of the more important uses are to show trends as to causes of death so that enlightment may be brought to bear to eliminate or reduce the great killer, and for other vital statistics.

The legislature enacts laws based on police powers to license and regulate persons who deal with the disposition of the dead. They establish educational, moral, age and citizenship requirements which must be met before the person may be licensed. They also set rules and regulations by which they must operate.

The funeral itself is a religious and social experience. From time immemorial, man has been buried with dignity and ceremony. Archeologists have found records of former civilizations indicating such practices as burial facing a certain way to de-

225

note belief in a life after death. We are all familiar with the Egyptian burials, mummifications, and monuments, burial of the Pharaohs with their retinue of servants to wait on them in their afterlife. We read in the Old Testament how Moses took the bones of Joseph out of Egypt. We also read how Joseph of Aramathaea wrapped the body of Jesus in linen and laid it in a stone sepulchre. We return the bodies of soldiers who were killed overseas for proper ceremonies and burial. We dig at great risk to recover bodies of the victims of a mine cave-in for burial.

It seems to me that there are unexplained forces working within each one of us which compel us to react to death in his own way. No one can predict how he will feel or what he will do. Each will do what he has to do at the time. Because of this no two funerals are exactly alike. A funeral is a personal experience and no one can experience it for someone else. The best one can do is try to channel this experience within certain guidelines and assist with a common support. Religion has helped to give meaning to our actions and limit the time wherein these actions can take place with the approval of society in general.

The funeral director is usually a knowledgeable, experienced individual who sympathetically and empathetically organizes the funeral according to the wishes of the immediate survivors, recognizing the legal, social and religious responses necessary.

Chapter 26

SERIOUS MUSIC SELECTIONS

$\mathcal{C}$he following selections suggest music that is available for use at a memorial service or during the early stages of bereavement. It is not meant to be complete, and emphasizes only music by well-known composers of our Western tradition since the sixteenth century.

Since grief is a wholly personal experience, the music selected for a memorial service may be in some way associated with the deceased. Perhaps a word of caution is, therefore, to be wisely interposed at this point: if the music played at the funeral is something which had an intimate meaning for the bereaved and the deceased, the psychological association may later be deleterious for the bereaved. He may never hear it again with pleasure, remembering that it accompanied the loved one on the last journey. His delight in this music for its own sake is spoiled; he cannot enjoy the feeling formerly shared when it was played; he loses the restorative influence of a happy memory, depriving himself, in the months and years to come, of the loving remembrance that can be evoked by listening to a familiar melody that has deep associations for him.

Perhaps, then, other music befitting the sad occasion of services for the departed should be selected. The list which is offered here contains not only distinctive funeral music but great religious music from innumerable sources, as well as symphonic or choral excerpts of a solemn and noble character, suitable, although not intrinsically meant for this use, on the occasion of death. Every taste can be satisfied with some choice from such a compilation of profoundly moving music.

Amram, David	*Dirge and Variations—viola and piano
Anerto, Giovanni	*Missa Pro Defuncti—chorus
Bach, J. S.	*Christ Lay in Death's Dark Prison (Cantata No. 18)—chorus
	*Come, Soothing Death—chorus
	*Death, I Do Not Fear Thee—chorus
	*Come, Sweet Hour of Death— (Cantata No. 161)—chorus
	*God's Time is the Best (Cantata No. 106)—chorus
	*Trauer Ode (Funeral Ode)—chorus
	*Mass in B Minor—chorus
	*The Passion According to St. John— chorus
	*The Passion According to St. Matthew —chorus
	*Any of the organ Preludes and Fugues
	*Selections from "German Organ Mass"
Barber, Samuel	*Adagio for Strings
Barnby, Joseph	*Crossing the Bar—chorus
Beethoven, Ludwig van	*Cantata on the Death of Emperor Joseph II—chorus and orchestra
	Elegy—chorus
	*Funeral March from Symphony No. 3 (Eroica)—orchestra
	*Missa Solemnis—chorus and orchestra
	*Selections from "Mount of Olives"— chorus and orchestra
Berlioz, Hector	*Symphonie Funèbre et Triomphale— orchestra
	*Requiem—chorus
	*Death scene from Romeo et Juliette— orchestra
Billings, William	*Selections from his Hymns and Anthems—chorus
Bloch, Ernest	*Baal Shem—violin and piano
	*Selections from Sacred Service— chorus and orchestra

Blow, John	*Ode on the Death of Mr. Henry Purcell—chorus
Brahms, Johannes	*Chorale Preludes—organ
	*A German Requiem—chorus and orchestra
	*O Death—from "Four Serious Songs"—voice and piano
	A German Requiem—organ score
	*Tragic Overture—orchestra
Britten, Benjamin	*Sinfonia da Requiem—orchestra
	*Lachrymae—viola and piano
	*War Requiem—chorus and orchestra
Bruch, Max	*Kol Nidrei—cello and orchestra
Bruckner, Anton	*Mass No. 2—chorus and orchestra
	*Mass No. 3—chorus and orchestra
	*Psalm 150—chorus and orchestra
	Requiem—chorus
Buck, Dudley	Crossing the Bar—voice and piano
Byrd, William	*Mass in Three Parts—chorus
Campra, Andre	*Requiem—chorus and orchestra
Cherubini, Luigi	*Requiem in C minor—chorus and orchestra
	*Requiem in D minor—chorus and orchestra
Chopin, Frédéric	*Marche Funèbre from Second Piano Sonata
Dowland, John	*Lachrymae—chorus and orchestra
Dubois, Theodore	*Adoremus Te, Christe (from "The Seven Last Words")—chorus
Durufle, Maurice	*Requiem—chorus and orchestra
Dvořák, Antonin	*Requiem—chorus and orchestra
Eberlin, Ernst	Grief Is in My Heart—chorus
Fauré, J. B.	Crucifixus—voice and piano
Fauré, Gabriel	*Elegie—cello and orchestra
	*Requiem—chorus and orchestra
	Requiem—organ score
Franck, César	Panis Angelicus—chorus
	Cantabile—organ
	Chorales—organ

Gallus, Jacobus	Lo, Now Is the Death of the Just Man —chorus
Gaul, A. R.	They That Sow in Tears (from "The Holy City"—chorus
Guilmant, Alexandre	Marche Funèbre—organ
Guion, David	Prayer—voice and piano
	Prayer—chorus
Gounod, Charles	The King of Love My Shepherd Is— voice and piano
	Messe Solennells—chorus and orchestra
	Requiem I
	Requiem II
	Requiem III
Grieg, Edvard	Ase's Death (from "Peer Gynt")— orchestra
	Ase's Death (from *Peer Gynt*)—piano solo
	God's Peace Is Eternal—chorus
	Two Elegiac Melodies—orchestra
Handel, G. F.	Trust in the Lord (after the Largo from "Xerxes")—chorus
	Selections from The "Messiah"—chorus
Haydn, Franz Joseph	*Symphony No. 44 (Trauer)—orchestra
	*Seven Last Words of Christ—chorus and orchestra
	Darkness Obscured the Earth—chorus
Hindemith, Paul	*When Lilacs Last in the Dooryard Bloom'd—chorus
	*Trauermusik—viola and strings
Holst, Gustav	*Dirge for Two Veterans—chorus
Kabalevsky, Dmitri	*Requiem—chorus and orchestra
La Forge, F.	Before the Crucifix—voice and piano
	Before the Crucifix—chorus
diLasso, Orlando	*Requiem—chorus and orchestra
LaRue, Pierre de	*Requiem—chorus and orchestra

Liszt, Franz	Funeral Music for Mosonyi's Death—piano solo
	To the Memory of Petofi—piano solo
	The Funeral Gondola I—Piano solo
	The Funeral Gondola II—piano solo
	Richard Wagner, Venice—piano solo
Mahler, Gustav	*The Farewell from "Das Lied von der Erde" (Songs of the Earth)—voice and orchestra
	*Kindertotenlieder—voice and orchestra
Malipiero, Gian Francesco	Sinfonia del Silenzio e della Morte—orchestra
	Missa Pro Mortuis—chorus
Malotte, A. H.	The Lord's Prayer—chorus
	The Lord's Prayer—voice and piano
	The Lord's Prayer—organ
	23rd Psalm—voice and piano
	23rd Psalm—chorus
Mendelssohn, Felix	*Funeral March—orchestra
	If With All Your Hearts—chorus
Monteverdi, Claudio	*Lament from "Arianna"—chorus
Morely, Thomas	Thou Knowest, Lord—chorus
Mozart, W. A.	*Ave, verum corpus—chorus and orchestra
	*Masonic Funeral Music—orchestra
	*Requiem—chorus and orchestra
Mueller, Carl F.	Create in Me a Clean Heart—chorus
Mussorgsky, Modest	*Songs and Dances of Death—song cycle
Noble, T. T.	Souls of the Righteous—chorus
Palestrina, Giovanni	*Messa Papae Marcelli—chorus
	O Gentle Death—chorus
	The Strife is O'er—chorus
Poulenc, Francis	*Elegie for Horn and Piano
Purcell, Henry	Now, O Lord, I Lay Me Down—chorus

	*Music for the Funeral of Queen Mary —chorus and orchestra
	*When I am Laid in Earth from "Dido and Aeneas"—aria
Rachmaninoff, Sergei	*Isle of the Dead—orchestra
	Vocalise—voice and piano
Ravel, Maurice	*Pavane Pour Une Infanta Defunte— orchestra
Rheinberger, Joseph	Vision—organ
Roberts, J. V.	Peace I Leave With You—chorus
Rodney, Paul	Calvary—voice and piano
	Calvary—chorus
Saint-Saëns, Camille	Requiem
Salter, S.	Gethsemane—voice and piano
Schubert, Franz	*Death and the Maiden—voice and piano
	*Death and the Maiden—slow move- ment of string quartet
	The Lord is My Shepherd—chorus
Schuman, William	*Carols of Death—chorus
Schütz, Heinrich	*A German Requiem—chorus and or- chestra
Shelley, H. R.	The King of Love My Shepherd Is— voice and piano
	The King of Love My Shepherd Is— chorus
Sibelius, Jean	*Swan of Tuonela—orchestra
	*Valse Triste—orchestra
Stravinsky, Igor	*Elegie—for unaccompanied violin or viola
	*In Memoriam, Dylan Thomas—chorus and orchestra
Sullivan, Arthur	God Shall Wipe Away All Tears— chorus
Tallis, Thomas	*Lamentations of Jeremiah—chorus
Vaughan Williams, R.	*Dona Nobis Pacem—chorus and or- chestra

Verdi, Guiseppe	*Requiem—chorus and orchestra
Wagner, Richard	*Gotterdammerung: Funeral Music—orchestra
	*Trauermusik for wind instruments
Zechiel	Entrust to Him Thy Footsteps—organ

Any hymns from Protestant and Catholic hymnals.

Recordings are available for those selections marked with an asterisk.

Chapter 27

ACCEPTANCE

GLENN MOSLEY

There are times when the bereaved, while making funeral arrangements, decides that he will be strong, and have the casket remain closed. There are some religions which encourage having the casket closed and there are some people who can truly accept the fact of death within a few hours, and who do not need to see the remains of the loved one again. More often than not, however, the closed casket represents an effort to evade the reality of death. As in the case of unnecessary sedation, all that is effected is that the bereaved has only put off until a more difficult time the acceptance of the reality of the death. It is more difficult because friends and relatives depart almost immediately after the funeral, and the bereaved is left without their support.

When one is greatly disturbed by the death of a loved one, it is important for him to be able to express his feelings freely. Much conspires to prevent such expression. Particularly when one is ashamed of feelings which to him indicate weakness or unworthy thoughts, it is well for him to attempt to share these with an understanding, accepting friend, relative or professional counselor. There is no real merit in concealing such feelings. The clergyman, especially one who has added skills in personal counseling to his religious training, may well be the one to whom the person with a deeper problem may turn.

The author once knew a lady whose doubly devastating grief came through an accident which took the lives of her husband and her only child, an adult son. Because of the family's involvement in religious work, hundreds of people visited the funeral chapel and attended the religious service for the two beloved

234

men. The bereft wife and mother somewhat misguidedly undertook to show all who came just how strong her religious convictions had made her. She was quite a comfort to the many mourners who came. Besides, she never cried in public; she seemed to exude a faith that precluded grief.

However, three weeks after the funeral, she lost all control of the urinary tract. Nature, God, Universal Wisdom, whichever name we choose, was no longer allowing her to ignore the grief she felt. Months of talking with an understanding therapist helped her to clarify her feelings concerning the deaths of her two loved ones and also to accept the fact of her own eventual death. Once her anguish and distress were channeled into healthful forms of expression, her life literally restored itself, regrouped its energies, and perfect physiological functioning was restored.

Chapter 28

THE CONDOLENCE CALL

REGINA FLESCH

OUR CHANGING CUSTOMS

> At no time are we so indifferent to the social world and all its code
> as when we stand baffled and alone at the brink of unfathomable
> darkness into which our loved one has gone. The last resource to
> which we would look for comfort at such a time is the seeming
> artificiality of etiquette. Yet it is in the hours of deepest sorrow
> that etiquette performs its most real service. All set rules of social
> procedure have for their object the smoothing of personal contacts,
> and in nothing is smoothness so necessary as in observing the solemn
> rites accorded to our dead.[6]

These words of Emily Post show a profound understanding
of custom worthy of an anthropologist. Every system of society has developed social procedures regarding the ceremonies
of birth, marriage and death which bind the individual to the
group, emphasizing that he is, indeed, a social being. In more
rigidly structured societies, as in some primitive cultures, appropriate behavior for the bereaved and for other members of
the group is prescribed by ritual. There is an article by Edmund
Volkart and Stanley Michael[10] about the Ifaluk people, who
obey the custom of showing visible pain upon the death of a
family member. Their display of distress coincides with the
funeral, and, also by custom, disappears as soon as the funeral
is over. Various interpretations are offered by students of social
life for this highly ritualized response to death. Whatever interpretation one accepts, the paths of both the bereaved and participants in the funeral seem to be made easier through these dictates
for appropriate behavior.

Formerly, in our Western civilization, there were, among

certain groups some approximations of highly ritualized behavior connected with mourning; some of these customs still are maintained in various forms. The traditional Irish wake and funeral required strict adherence to an established pattern, down to the actual words and wailing which followed the corpse to the grave.[2] Participants in this kind of funeral came back to the house for food and drink after the funeral. In this Irish society, a bereaved family must have felt a close tie to the group which provided so dignified an expression to their grief. The public display of grief by the bereaved, accepted as it was by the group, would diminish the need for withdrawal and concealment of emotion by the bereaved.

Orthodox Jews also follow rigidly prescribed behavior for the bereaved after the funeral. According to orthodox Jewish custom, the bereaved family sits together for seven full days and nights (shiva), an open practice which makes virtually impossible the hiding of private grief. To these orthodox mourners, custom dictates not only what the bereaved should say and do, but also what greeting their callers should use when they come to express their sympathies to the bereaved. An English student of mourning, the anthropologist Geoffrey Gorer, believes that these strict rituals are profoundly useful to bereaved families and sympathizers and that their disappearance from contemporary British and American society is a serious loss.[4]

The breakdown of custom concerning funerals and mourning is attested at almost any funeral today, where somber garments, for instance, frequently are replaced by clothing acceptable at any other social function. Books of etiquette have very little specific advice about appropriate behavior for either the bereaved or friends at this crucial time. There appears to be a general agreement that a condolence call is obligatory after a death in the family of a friend, but close reading of the text leaves a strong impression that the call should be made and terminated as quickly as possible.[9] Precisely what the caller should say or do on these occasions remains unspecified, as the bereaved family frequently appears to delegate to a friend the task of meeting callers. Close and sympathetic contact between the bereaved and their social group, as exemplified in the Irish wake and the orthodox Jewish shiva, is not fostered, to say the least, by our current customs.

This throws the mourner back upon his own resources, to find his own way, at a time when his resources are most depleted by his grief. What is needed, of course, is a period of time for a "formal withdrawal from society, a period of seclusion, and a formal re-entry into society."[4]

The absence of ritual obliges us to develop understanding, so that the complex feelings of bereavement and mourning may not create obstacles to comfort and consolation in the bereaved and sympathizers. Gorer writes,

> Nowhere is the absence of an accepted social ritual more noticeable than in the first contacts between a mourner and his neighbors, acquaintances or work mates after a bereavement. Should they speak of the loss, or no? Will the mourner welcome expressions of sympathy or prefer they pretend that nothing has really happened? Will mention of the dead provoke an outburst of weeping in the mourner, which might prove contagious?" [p. 57.]

Elsewhere in his book, Gorer criticizes our society for "failing to provide . . . members with the support which most societies make available."

Hence, our discussion that follows will concern itself with feelings about condolence calls, both in the bereaved and in the callers.

FEELINGS OF THE MOURNER
ABOUT THE CALL

Let us be clear at the outset that our discussion will deal only with condolence calls to the bereaved, made by those who are not members of the family. Obviously we cannot discuss all complex responses in the bereaved, following a death in the family, nor is it our purpose to consider how the bereaved deal with these responses, and gradually resume social life. Grief, like any other pain, has very private aspects, which we cannot examine here. Our concern here is only with calls of condolence, and with some feelings that the bereaved family members often have about these calls and about those who call.

1. Our society not only provides few guides to proper behavior during mourning, but compounds this error by subtly frowning on displays of grief,[4] giving approval to those who successfully hide their grief. In the author's interviews with recently bereaved families, the single instance encountered of open copious weeping without apology on the part of the bereaved was that of a family newly come to this country, emigrants from the southern Mediterranean area. Not yet sufficiently acculturated to feel ashamed of any display of emotion, they frankly showed how they felt. To a person who mourns, suppression of feeling represents one more burden when he already has many to bear. Suffering from a latent fear of losing control, he may yet be constrained to accept condolence calls, however hesitantly, rather than to defy custom by withdrawal from outside contacts. Even individuals who, for whatever reason, do not grieve deeply for a lost relative, fear the display of inappropriate, socially unacceptable behavior, and thus tend to avoid such opportunities. In our society, our conventions imply that to show grief is undignified and undesirable and thus the mourner's natural tendency to concentrate on his sorrow and withdraw from human contacts must be controlled if he is to maintain his status in the environment of grief.

2. In a society in which it is not quite acceptable to show grief, how can there be intelligent practices regarding the duration of mourning? It is the essential nature of the sorrow of bereavement that the sufferer can hardly conceive of a time when the present acute pain may be eased. To hear a would-be comforter declare, "You'll feel better in a week or two" is a painful experience to the mourner, who often wants to cling to his suffering, for at least that is part of what he has lost. Bereaved families perceive and resent the subtle pressure extended by our culture in the direction of rapid termination of mourning.

As examples of this pressure, the author is reminded of our accepted tendency to wear our mourning clothing for ever shorter periods of time. Some experiences related by families in mourning strain one's belief. One twelve-year-old boy, whose teacher had observed him staring blindly out the window only four weeks after his father died an accidental death, was reprimanded in the classroom for failure to concentrate. "Four weeks is enough time to get over it," was the teacher's comment, which the fatherless child repeated to his mother. Her reaction is easy to imagine. In another example, a woman calling on a mother, visibly grieved over the death of a lovely, teenaged daughter, reproached the mother for her continued grief. "If you do not stop, won't the other children think you don't care about *them?*" she asked. Clearly, it had not occurred to this caller that the other children, seeing their mother grieve, might think instead that they had a devoted mother who felt a profound and continuing attachment to her children.

In the writer's experience, wide individual variations in the duration and intensity of mourning may be related to many elements, such as the age of the deceased, the closeness of the relationship, the degree of interdependence in the relationship, and even the nature of the death. It is understandable that families in mourning should resent dicta from individual "sympathizers" about the length of mourning, since in this area there are no definite lines of behavior acknowledged by everyone. The prescribed custom of wearing mourning clothes, and the right of withdrawal from social activities for a year were, at least, a protection against unwelcome advice.*

3. John Donne's much quoted "No man is an island" and "Every man's death diminishes me" are perhaps the most familiar statements of the diminution of self-esteem which the bereaved person feels. When the death is that of a family member, how much more of a loss of self is involved! Even when aged parents die in the fullness of time, their children often feel the loss is irreparable, although they have long ceased to be dependent. The death of a spouse is felt commonly as a loss in self-worth

* Some of the literature on funerals reveals what seems an unfortunate tendency to regard the funeral as therapy and to equate it with a therapeutic experience. One can accept that the funeral is a necessary social custom, with both desirable and undesirable aspects. However, to call a social rite "therapy" appears to the author to be a distortion of the concept of therapy, which means treatment of an ailment. A funeral service may be appropriate, beautiful, and comforting to the mourners, and still have no bearing on the duration and intensity of mourning or the healing of sorrow. The phase "therapy of the funeral" lends support to the notion that when things are done properly, grief should be dispelled rapidly. Such a misconception tends to foster withdrawal on the part of the mourner.

and even of social status. Bereaved marital partners are extremely sensitive about their social acceptability and desirability
after the spouse is gone. Similarly, the loss of a child may mean
to the parent that he has less to give and receive from life, and
that he is worth less as a person. These feelings may be recognized by the mourners as irrational; nevertheless they may persist. The loss of self-esteem, awareness of injury, and feeling of a
loss of social status all contribute to the mourner's extreme sensitivity with regard to human contacts. As one bereaved mother
put it, "You must learn to protect yourself from those who tear
you down."

In the author's opinion, only through open recognition that
such feelings are universal and natural can the stricken mourner
accept his own hypersensitivity as a temporary phase which he
must live through.

The nature of the unconscious is such that, not far beneath
this hypersensitivity, lurks the unspoken, treacherous feeling that
something one did or did not do, could have prevented the loss.
Thus, one hears from one mourner after another, the pitiful
questions, Why did this happen to me? What did I do that was
wrong?—questions raised without any expectation of answers.
The idea of being singled out for grief or punishment is, of
course, a misreading of reality, which is induced by the mourner's
strange, unfamiliar frame of mind. This frame of mind may sometimes unconsciously distort the mourner's perception of the actions or intentions of others.

The author recalls one family which had lost a dearly beloved
adolescent daughter through accidental death. The heartbroken
father related that one of the things that was hardest to bear
was the indifference he encountered in the community. "No one
came after she died." Inquiry revealed that the girl's classmates
and teachers had attended her funeral and continued to visit
the family. Neighbors, friends, relatives, and clergymen also
stopped in to offer help and sympathy. The father's feelings of
neglect represented an unconscious distortion, in accordance
with his own sense of loss of worth and hope. Mourners cannot
change their feelings, but they can be helped to acquire a broader
intellectual orientation and the awareness that these feelings are
universal, deceptive, and transitory.

4. A most important element in any grief, and perhaps the least discussed, is the rage that accompanies bereavement. In the author's interview experience, it is indeed rare to encounter grief not accompanied by rage. The rage may be directed almost anywhere, against the agent causing death, against medical science for ineptitude, even against the Almighty for allowing the death. In contemporary psychology, this is seen as natural, the outcome of frustration. The loved one, the source of former satisfaction, no longer is present, as the object and minister in one's emotional life. The emotion centered on the lost person no longer has a target and must be frustrated; the anger of the frustrated mourner is as natural as gravity.[1]

Popular writing does not depict the bereaved as angry or prone to anger, and religious writings, to which many mourners turn, tend to emphasize the acceptance of death without question, with reliance on religious faith. Yet throughout the centuries, profoundly devout and religious persons have questioned "God's ways to man," even reproaching the Almighty as did St. Theresa of Avila, for "treating so badly the few friends He had." Jewish legend tells of a rabbi who lost all his many sons. A sympathizer remarked, "Whom the Lord loveth, He chastiseth." "I do not want His chastisement and I do not want His love," replied the grieving father. Perhaps it should be emphasized for the bereaved that profound religious faith may coexist with altercation with the Lord.

Mourners who know their own anger and tendency to become irritable with others, even with those who mean well, are in a better position to control their behavior. When custom fails, self-control and self-understanding become essential. "Know Thyself," always a good precept, is a beneficial commandment when feelings are aroused that generally are taboo to the average person.

FEELINGS OF THE SYMPATHIZERS
ABOUT THE CALL

The sympathizer, no less than the bereaved family, has complex feelings which create obstacles between himself and those with whom he has come to condole. These obstacles to communication also are in part the products of cultural omission and confusion. Here we shall review only problematic feelings of the caller relating to the call itself. Any attempt to explore possible personal responses to a death would be hypothetical and here, extraneous.

1. Just as the bereaved family has a wish to withdraw, so has the caller. Like the bereaved family, the caller has been partially indoctrinated against the display of feeling, with a consequent reluctance to become involved in an emotional crisis. To the would-be caller, it often seems best to believe that grieving individuals actually prefer to be left alone, rather than to share or to talk about their sorrow. This belief in a preference for solitude is facilitated by the caller's understandable wish to avoid the sight of another's pain. Only the callous can be unaffected by another's suffering, and the callous usually do not set out to make condolence calls.

The caller who arrives at the door really ready to express his sympathy, not simply to leave a card (in accordance with the recommended procedures of some volumes on etiquette), first must conquer his hesitation, due to the mourner's anticipated unwillingness to see visitors. He must overcome the latent conviction that the individual prefers to be alone, that the expression of sorrowful feelings somehow is undesirable, and that he himself is in for a difficult interview, in which he rarely feels comfortable, not knowing what to say or do. The author has found that the best way to overcome these inner obstacles to calling upon a grieving family is to recognize that the family wishing to be left alone usually makes that wish clear. Furthermore, it is important for the caller to remember that pain suffered in solitude is heavier to bear than is pain shared. The privilege of entry into a house of sorrow can be earned only by the willingness to share the feelings in that house, without embarrassment, discomfort, or annoyance. If the wish to console and bring comfort is genuine, whatever the caller says will be received well. The sympathizer's presence symbolizes the support of the living community, as much as the reality of the loss, and thus has a true therapeutic function.

2. Misconceptions about the duration of mourning and appropriate behavior during mourning are likely to exist on the part of the caller no less than of the mourner. Procedures outlined in current books on etiquette encourage the brief call, as soon as possible after news of a death, without repetition of the visit. However, the time when supportive calls are most needed is after the funeral, and after obligatory condolence calls have been paid. Here, social custom provides no guidelines for the bereaved family or for their friends. Individuals who have talked with the author about their personal reluctance to continue contact with bereaved families attribute this reluctance to ignorance as to what to say and do, surprising in socially sophisticated adults who are at ease in almost any conceivable situation. Yet these knowledgeable people ask for precise instructions on behavior, just as would an adolescent, going out for the first time into a new social situation. The caller instinctively recognizes the extreme sensitivity of the bereaved family at this time of crisis and needs to have elementary rules of behavior outlined, such as how long to stay, precisely what to say, whether to show his own feelings about the death, and at what times and how often such calls of comfort may be made.

Our cultural condensation of the period of mourning somehow implies that condolence calls have no place after the initial period of mourning. In this regard Gorer[4] writes of his bereaved sister-in-law: "At the period when she most needed help and comfort from society, she was left alone." Mourning that terminates early of course makes it impossible to condole with a person who no longer grieves. Cultural silence and confusion about the duration of mourning and what the condolence call can achieve positively for the family's readjustment increase the caller's hesitation and awkwardness in making these calls.

3. It is a truism that the sick patient envies a healthy caller his ability to carry out the daily requirements of living, unhampered by physical discomfort. On a fine day, the visitor to the hospital bed knows, although nothing is said, that the patient wishes he, too, could leave his hospital room, and go out to enjoy the sun. In the same way, the one who calls on a bereaved household is dimly aware of their latent feelings of diminished

self-worth and self-esteem, and of their envy, of those who appear to be unhurt and whole.

When we hear, "Why did this happen to me?" what answer can we give? Were we allowed to yield to impulse, the only logical response would be, "Why should you expect to go through this world without sharing in its trouble?" By merely raising the question, the mourner implies that *his* should be a special fate.* In doing so, he puts the caller at an unfair disadvantage. Unless we ourselves die young, all of us have suffered, or will suffer, bereavement. The identity of the bereaved is merely the matter of a point in time. The question itself is that of a childish mind, overwhelmed by an experience beyond comprehension and control. If the caller himself is fearful of death or vulnerable to ill-disguised envy, he becomes uncomfortable. In this frame of mind, he cannot console or comfort others.

For the caller, the solution is to recognize the emotional regression behind the question, and to accept it as one accepts the reaction of an overwhelmed child. Barriers between the bereaved and the sympathizer are not created by the feelings themselves, but by the attempt to deny the feelings.

4. The greatest obstacle to communication between the mourner and the sympathizer lies in the sympathizer's unpreparedness for the mourner's anger. Although a common part of the mourning process, this anger is seldom, if ever, discussed openly. It is hardly to be expected that the average (or even the professional) caller upon a bereaved family is prepared to

---

* The poet, John Keats, raised this question of human trouble in his letters to his brother, George, and sister-in-law Georgiana Keats. According to the writer and critic, Lionel Trilling, Keats resolved the question "with sudden contempt for those who call the world a vale of tears. 'What a little circumscribed notion!' he says. 'Call the world if you please "The vale of Soul-making!" I say *Soul-making*—Soul as distinguished from an intelligence—There may be intelligence or sparks of divinity in millions but they are not Souls till they acquire identities, till each one is personally itself.' "
"There follows a remarkable flight into a sort of transcendental psychology in the effort to suggest how intelligences may become souls, and then: 'Do you not see how necessary a World of Pains and trouble is to school an Intelligence and make it a Soul? A place where the heart must feel and suffer in a thousand different ways.' And the heart is 'the teat from which the Mind or intelligence sucks its identity.' "[8]

recognize or accept the rage he may see in the mourners. On the author's visits to bereaved families, the most frequent initial response she encountered was that of undisguised, open anger. Almost every interview was dominated in tone by expressions of resentment about the death. It is peculiarly painful to be confronted with such expressions of feeling because the caller can do nothing but listen. Until we realize that this is all we can do, we cannot even listen effectively. Through this outpouring and listening, mourner and caller together can express, accept, and understand the helpless anger that often follows in the wake of death.*

Perhaps an unconscious recognition of the mourner's rage and resentment contributes to the continuing difficulties of both parties in resuming normal social contacts after a death. If both mourner and sympathizer could accept that irrational hostility as a universal part of mourning itself, the roles of both would become easier. Both parties would be relieved of any implication that the bitterness expressed and observed is more than a "crisis characteristic," and need not be regarded as a permanent character trait.

WHAT THE CALL CAN CONTRIBUTE

The author believes that the purpose of the condolence call is simple. The call is paid to the mourning family to express sympathy and to give assurance that they are not alone in their grief. Friends of the bereaved have a responsibility to lend what support they can, however awkwardly, in the direction of bringing the bereaved back into the main stream of life. Their task is to help the bereaved relinquish the past, and to adjust to the present. Similarly, no matter how great the loss, it is the duty of the bereaved to go on living, to acquire the "identity" of which Keats wrote.

Most bereaved families know that despite their sorrow, they

* We should make clear that these comments refer primarily to premature deaths, particularly from unnatural causes, not to anticipated death, "in the fullness of time," as the saying goes.

will resume the tasks of daily life because they must do so. They also have considerable awareness of the complexity and ambivalence of their feelings, in relation to daily tasks and to previous associations. By and large, their expectations from these associations are fairly simple. Many bereaved persons who consciously hope for sympathetic support are aware of the problems in themselves which preclude their reaching out for such support, and sometimes even prevent their making use of it when it is at hand.

Understanding breaks down not so much in expectations on the part of either the bereaved or the caller, but because of inability to face underlying feelings such as those we have considered here. This article is a plea for understanding of the underlying feelings which build barriers, so that they may be broken down.

There is nothing unacceptable or shameful in the feelings themselves, only in the attempt to deny them. Feelings of ambivalence, hostility, guilt, and fear have received little attention to date in writings on bereavement, but this silence at last seems to be yielding to inquiry.* Whatever the feelings in response to loss, we believe they should be given opportunity for expression. Although our customs give little assistance to the bereaved or to those who wish to help, art has spoken, where custom is silent. Said Shakespeare,

> Give sorrow tongue;
> The grief that does not speak
> Whispers the o'erfraught heart and bids it break.

More recently, Dylan Thomas wrote:[7]

> Do not go gentle into that good night,
> Old age should burn and rage at close of day;
> Rage, rage against the dying of the light.

* Erich Lindemann discusses this aspect of acute grief, in his well-known paper, "Symptomatology and Management of Acute Grief," which first appeared in the *American Journal of Psychiatry*, in 1944, vol. 101, pp. 141–148. The loss of warmth and the furious hostility described by Lindemann appears on p. 145. Edmund Volkart and Stanley Michael also deal with anger as an aspect of bereavement, in "Bereavement and Mental Health," pp. 299–301.[10]

ACKNOWLEDGMENTS

This work was partly supported by United States Public Health Service Grants MH #02203 and MH #02717, from the National Institute of Mental Health, National Institutes of Health. The work was partly supported also by Eastern Pennsylvania Psychiatric Institute.

REFERENCES

1. BOWLBY, J.: Processes of mourning. *Internat J Psychoanal, 42* (*parts 4–5*):317–340, 1961.
2. COLUM, MARY: *Life and The Dream.* London, Macmillan, 1947.
3. FENWICK, MILLICENT: *Vogue's Book of Etiquette.* New York, Simon and Schuster, 1948.
4. GORER, GEOFFREY: *Death, Grief and Mourning.* New York, Doubleday, 1965.
5. LINDEMANN, E.: Symptomatology and management of acute grief. *Amer J Psych, 101:*141–148, 1944.
6. POST, EMILY: *Etiquette, The Blue Book of Social Usage.* New York and London, Funk, 1937.
7. THOMAS, DYLAN: *Collected Poems.* New York, New Directions, 1953.
8. TRILLING, LIONEL: *The Opposing Self-Nine Essays of Criticism.* New York, Viking, 1955.
9. VANDERBILT, AMY: *Amy Vanderbilt's Complete Book of Etiquette.* New York, Doubleday, 1958.
10. VOLKART, E., and MICHAEL, S.: Bereavement and mental health. In Leighton, A. (Ed.): *Explorations in Social Psychiatry,* New York: Basic Books, 1957.

Chapter 29

THE SOCIAL SERVICE WORKER CAN HELP

ELIZABETH R. PRICHARD

Death was still a few weeks away, yet I could feel its presence in the way the patient's hands clutched mine. They had been stiffened by arthritis, yet the stiffness seemed to ebb as we spoke, and I could sense her resignation towards her coming death. She was old and in pain from an obstruction which was probably caused by cancer. Thirty-five years before she had had surgery for cancer, but she saw no point in undergoing another painful operation. Although she considered herself fortunate to have lived so long, she felt no desire to go on. She displayed dignity and courage as we discussed those whom she wished to see before her death.

Before this patient entered the hospital for the last time, a social worker was able, in a most sensitive and understanding way, to provide whatever help was necessary.

Because of great pain and suffering, many people long for an end to that pain yet they are concerned about the responsibilities which they have not been able to meet fully. This is a cause of sorrow for them and for those they leave behind. One usually sees this in female parents. Thus, the dying words of a widow in her forties were a plea to the social worker to look after her seventeen-year-old daughter, now left alone.

When there are children, the responsibility placed on the physician is heavy, but the social worker can be of great help to him in sharing her observations about what the patient needs and wants to know, and together they can make appropriate plans. Both the physician and the social worker need to be alert for any clues the patient might give. Whether the patient should

249

be told of his impending death, and when, is not easy to determine. A widow was shaken when she learned that she was fatally ill, but nevertheless she was able to make plans for her young children. No one, she said, had the right to deprive her of that responsibility and satisfaction. It eased her suffering to know that she had done all she could. She could face the inevitable and save her waning strength for the moments when her children were with her. Generally speaking, in planning for terminal care the social worker makes every effort to keep the family together for as long as possible. But sometimes the family is against this, and an appraisal of the family relationships may indicate that it would be harmful then, and later, to keep them together. When suffering becomes too painful to bear for the patient and the family, it is best that the patient be cared for in a nursing home or in a hospital.

A woman, twice widowed, had a daughter by her first marriage, and two children by her second. She had been hard-working and her only aim was to be a good mother. She derived much satisfaction from this role although being both mother and father was not easy. Her illness, which proved to be incurable, appeared with little warning and it was a shock for such an active woman to become suddenly and almost completely incapacitated. Her oldest daughter had recently finished high school and had acquired her first job. She was also enjoying the attentions of a young man who wanted to marry her. She was at an age when there is a great need to experience the pleasures of youth before assuming an adult's responsibilities. It was extremely difficult for her to accept the fact that her mother was seriously ill, or to accept the idea that she would be responsible for a seven-year-old sister and five-year-old brother. Time was needed, but would there be enough for her to fully comprehend the situation and prepare herself for it?

Her normal reaction was to flee from reality and to fling herself into the pursuits of youth. She was torn between wanting to help her mother and wanting to be with her young man. Because of the mother's will power, courage and strength, the social worker was able to make full use of the time remaining to prepare the daughter. Arrangements were made to have the mother cared for at home for as long as possible so that she could be with the young children. The social worker continued to help the daughter after the mother's death, since she needed someone to rely on as plans were worked out for the other children.

The finality of death is not easily accepted. Time is needed to lessen the sadness that one feels at the loss of a loved one. A young child cannot comprehend why a mother has left him. He feels that he has done something wrong and is being punished. The relationship of parents and their child is an extremely important factor in the ability of the child to cope with his feelings. The age at which a child loses a parent or a parental figure must be taken into consideration and appropriate help given, otherwise psychological damage may occur. This is a prime factor in working with children. The development of a child goes through many stages in relation to the parents. The two-year-old child's dependency upon its mother requires a different kind of relationship from that of a girl of twelve or thirteen who has a need to identify with a female figure. Thus, grief must be handled in terms of the child's development. Dependency needs not fully met can be a handicap in later years, at which time they may find an outlet in demanding, neurotic behavior or in regression to illness. Social workers have long noted that many patients with regressive illnesses had suffered the loss of a parental figure in their early years. Human beings are infinitely complex; they have physical and emotional needs which must be met to enable them to become healthy, productive adults. The early years of gradual development are preparation for mature future relationships that have the ability to withstand life's difficulties. Such relationships are developed within the family complex, and later with other people.

How do those who are left with the responsibility of the bereft child plan wisely and with sensitivity? A mother or father who has lost a spouse is often too bereaved to give the child all the care and love he now needs. Yet a loving parent can and does respond to the child's needs. The parent who as a young child, suffered the same loss may, depending upon the circumstances at that time, respond in one of two ways: he will either become immobilized by the painful association or be extremely understanding of his child's needs.

Not only death, but separation from a parent through illness or divorce will often cause a child to grieve. The pain is just as great, and the effect is the same. For a long time, the child may have dreams and fantasies about the return of the parent and this situation must be handled with sensitivity. The child who cries out in the night should have comfort and understanding. A nine-year-old child of divorced parents tried to prepare a friend whose parents had just been divorced. To the friend, who had a brother and a sister, she said, "At least there are three of you and you have each other; there is only one of me."

One cannot overemphasize the need for sensitivity and understanding. It does not always have to be put into words, but the child who asks a question should be answered truthfully. One must be prepared to understand and accept his bitterness and anger, which are often displayed in unsocial behavior. The child needs time to sort out his own feelings and to try to cope with what has happened. But even though he cannot understand why it has happened, he will long remember the sensitivity and understanding that are expressed by others. A middle-aged woman still recalls the understanding of a teacher when she returned to class the first day after the death of her sister. A quiet smile from the teacher and the momentary silence of the class gave recognition of her presence and the situation. Nothing more was said, for the teacher knew that at that time the girl could not accept death and could not have borne an effusive outpouring from her or the class.

Grief over a loss is great at any age, but it is almost unbearable for a parent, a husband, or a wife. Although sorrow is always present, the demands of daily living distract the bereaved and help to avert emotional and physical exhaustion. In spite of grief there can be some solace in knowing that one has done all one could. But the guilt-ridden person has a different torment to face. The social worker is guided by such insights whenever help is indicated.

The maintaining of relationships, especially helpful ones, is a primary rule to which all social workers adhere, not only in advising the family but in continuing their own role. They do not force their help upon their patients, but are available and alert to act quickly if the situation indicates it. The bereaved person often cannot talk about the painful reality he is rejecting. He often needs time to come to terms with his sorrow. During this period he may be withdrawn. Those close to him must respect this, yet be ready to respond when necessary. When a child suffers a loss, it is wise to enlist the teacher's cooperation, for the child may frequently appear distracted and do poorly in his school work. If this extended over too long a period, then professional help is indicated. There are those whose anxiety may prompt them to take their problem to anyone who will listen, but this does not necessarily mean that they are ready for advice. They may just be asking for someone to say that this loss has not occurred. The young child may need reassurance that he will not be deserted again, yet he fears that this may happen in future relationships. It is not unusual for the adolescent to shun all those who are closely associated with the parent who has died. The need is urgent to build a life of his own to insulate himself against further pain.

Life must go on. One must meet one's responsibilities. The adult who has been well prepared for life through stable family relationships in his early years, can, in time, meet sorrow and sadness, and carry on. One cannot intrude upon people's feelings. Thus, helping a father to plan for the care of children after the death of a wife must be carried out with sensitivity and under-standing. It is in a situation like this that the social worker is most active, since, frequently, plans have had to be made for a homemaker to care for the children during the mother's last illness. It is important that this service be continued until the father can work out plans of his own. It is wiser to have the social worker help him make plans rather than well-meaning relatives and friends who give advice too freely. Advice is not necessarily needed, but time is, to work through inner conflicts and turmoil.

Social workers plan well ahead whenever possible. They observe and evaluate family relationships to decide who will be able to assume responsibility when death occurs. In the situation of a woman who had been treated for hypertension for several years, the social worker knew that the end would come soon and perhaps suddenly. She wisely set about establishing a relationship with the father of one of the woman's children a few years before the patient died. He was not living at home but he was a frequent visitor. By discussing with him a minor illness of his child, the social worker was able to arouse his concern about the condition of the woman and both children, since the other child—not his—was also hospitalized. Gradually he was helped to take charge of the situation and to take care of both children after her death. This was a helpful arrangement for the patient and provided a stable homelife for the children after her death. Understandably, the man needed help with his feelings and concerns about the possible response and attitude of the children toward their mother's death. After the mother's death, a relative offered to take the children, but since they did not have a close relationship with her, they rejected her offer. The social worker became the female figure with whom the girl who was not the man's daughter could identify, and she helped her choose and and achieve a professional career.

It is not easy for one parent to rear a child. Because he has to cope with his own feelings, he may need help in dealing with the child. Full recognition of one's identity, established through the parents, is of great importance and, although the parent is no longer alive, it has great meaning for the child. That he had a mother or a father and knew what he was like is important in establishing the child's image of himself. During World War II, when some young men leaving for service first learned that they were adopted, the results were shattering (in some instances disastrous) just at the time when they needed the full support of sound family relationships. In working with disturbed and maladjusted adolescents, one, of course, finds the difficulty stemming from the time of early development and from parental relationships. It is not unusual to find that after the death of a parent, the remaining spouse never mentioned the deceased parent. In such a situation, the parent may need help in discussing the deceased parent with the children. The social worker will be able to help the parent with his or her own feelings, so that the child can learn something about the parent he never knew.

The loss of a child is a great tragedy. When death is expected, the social worker and the parents work out plans together. If the parents feel that they have not done all they could, their guilt can be very great. It is of interest to note how helpful close relatives can be at such a time. It is not unusual for parents to want to have the child cared for at home, with the help of relatives. When the child is in the hospital, the continuing presence of the mother to give personal care is of benefit to both the child and the mother. The death of a child through an accident or the carelessness of his parents is a sad situation, and parents usually require or should have a great deal of professional help. Following the death of one child, parents, in their sorrow, often reject, or seem to reject, the other children or, conversely, become overprotective.

When death is expected, some preparation is helpful, although the feelings of the family may make such preparation difficult. Many physicians refer parents and responsible family members to the social worker. One evening a physician gently broke the news to a sixty-year-old woman that her widowed daughter had a serious malignancy and might not recover. He suggested that she see the social worker the next day to help plan for care of her grandchildren. Because she was deeply shocked, she did not fully comprehend everything he said. One of her sons had been killed in an accident and another was now serving in Viet Nam, and she did not know how she could tell her husband of this further sorrow. Feeling the need to talk with someone, she went to the Social Service office at once. A social worker who happened to be there, noted her stricken look, and urged her to discuss her problem. Thus a beginning was made in terms of understanding a problem to be faced by two older people who needed compassion and understanding to help them through their ordeal. Definite plans could not be made at this time nor were they necessary, but a warm, human relationship was established and the assurance of needed help given.

Time, emotional stability and relationship with others are

the factors most needed to help the one who has suffered a loss. We have concentrated on work with children, for many reasons. First, they have not yet been prepared to cope with life, except in the most limited way, and yet are suddenly called upon to face the greatest sorrow of all. Second, their entire future development is affected. The deprivation of a parental figure on whom they are dependent for physical and emotional development can handicap their lives. But we do have sufficient knowledge to prevent, or at least minimize, this damage. Social workers are acutely aware of the role of prevention and that help given in childhood is more effective than that given later. Too often, we see in later years the results of problems which could have been helped in early life. Even though a child has lost a parent through death, the fact that the parent cared, and left the child only for reasons beyond his control is a sustaining force to the child. This knowledge, plus the role of a wise and understanding substitute parent, can help sustain the health which is needed for sound emotional development. Time, patience and understanding are always needed. The need and will to survive are the strongest of all human drives, and provide the basis for building and rebuilding a life which might otherwise be shattered.

Chapter 30

WIDOWERS WITH TEEN-AGE CHILDREN

HELEN WARGOTZ

As Director of the Allied Teenage Guidance Service, I undertook the implementation of a program called "Guidance for
Motherless Homes," to enhance definitive information on the
problems involved in establishing guidelines for fathers in such
circumstances. Through personal and agency sources, I interviewed twenty-one subjects for my investigation. These fathers,
representing an income spread from about $7,500 to approxi-
mately $75,000, worked in many diverse fields—business, the
professions, and industry. They included psychologists, lawyers,
garment industry buyers, an economist, a newsstand owner, a
metals worker, a chiropractor, architect, pharmacist, public relations man, dentist, real estate salesman, car salesman, auto agent
and corporation vice-president.

The youngest father had been twenty-eight when his wife died;
the oldest had been fifty-eight. At the time of the interview, they
had been widowed from one to twenty years. Three of the men
had remarried within two to three years after the wife's death,
but subsequently had been divorced, one after a month, another
after three years, and the third after seven years. Eight children
were involved in the divorces, including an adopted stepchild.
In all, forty-six children were concerned in this study: twenty-
one girls, ranging in age from three to twenty-four, and twenty-
five boys, ranging in age from two to twenty-one at the time of
the mother's death.

I inquired into the effects of the mother's death on the personal, social, scholastic, and interfamilial adjustments of such
families. These were dependent upon how well the fathers were
able to shoulder the tasks involved in raising children without a

257

mother. The first problem concerned the father himself. He had to face up to the inevitability or the unexpectedness of his wife's passing and to cope with the complex feelings of mourning. Even before the end, he had to decide whether or not to share with the children his knowledge of the seriousness of the situation. The father's inability to handle this important task, either from personality limitations or, from a sense of overprotectiveness, can be detrimental to the family's readjustment in functioning after the mother dies.

Children generally feel let down if they are excluded from what is known, and this feeling will have great bearing on their reactions later. The father who shirks his responsibility in this respect leaves a child with no one to talk to. The child is aware of the mother's unavailability and suffers from it without the consolation of sharing knowledge and feelings about it. Parental overprotectiveness is based, of course, on the desire to prevent the child from suffering. However, experts agree that this is not always wise, since it tends to delay emotional maturity in the child and to affect his ability to face the vicissitudes of life. The child's age and his degree of sensitivity must also be taken into consideration, but it is the consensus of opinion that children should be told what is going on. A young child should know that his mother is sick but that the doctor is doing everything possible to make her well. Older ones should be told when the illness is grave. Often this knowledge preserves the child's trust in the adult and gives him an incentive to help in the home. To say the least, a father in danger of losing his wife needs his children desperately at this time, and the sharing of the future grief will obviate any sense of guilt for the child or feeling of abandonment by those whom he loves.

Two fathers in the study had not themselves told the children of the illness of their mother. One had delegated this task to a rabbi. When I saw him eight years later, he was bickering constantly with the girl Rena, quarreling with her as he had with her younger brother, who had been a financial drain and who at the age of eighteen had left home. The father complained bitterly of the lack of communication with Rena. She was lazy in the home, perverse with him, unappreciative and demanding, and would not listen to his criticism of her poor choice of friends. On the occasion of my visit, I had noted her eagerness to speak with me, and her refusal to obey her father's nagging and prodding that she go away and leave us alone. It was clear to me that she was bursting to tell me all about herself and to complain about her father, his demands and his lack of understanding. It seemed probable that a good deal of the lack of communication between this man and his children started when he asked the rabbi to tell them of their mother's serious illness. If Rena's father had been the one to tell them this news, the trouble would have been so much easier to bear. Rena might have found it possible to let him know, as time went on, how lonely and miserable she felt without her mother close by; how much she needed his affection as well as his care. A wall would not have been built up between them. Rena and her brother could have gone to their father yet all the hard work and care he lavished on them was unappreciated; they wanted to be free of him. Would it be too much to say that Rena's reason for wanting to leave home had been the result of his failure to foster communication with her by first confiding in her that her mother was so ill?

The other man who had not told his children that the mother was very ill had a different but no less sad experience. Two and a half years after the mother's death, he had remarried, but the remarriage was unstable and he had sought counseling. At this time, his son was receiving failing marks at school and the father was advised to bring him to the counseling office. During the joint session, the boy told his father that he did not believe he had loved his wife, the boy's mother. Mr. N. E. broke into tears. A good deal of unhappy explanation followed before the true story unfolded itself. The father had not told the boy of his mother's serious condition because the facts had been kept from her, and he was afraid the boy would reveal the truth. The mother died when the boy was nine years old. He understood nothing but that within two months after his mother's death, his father had begun to see other women. The fact was that Mr. N. E. had experienced a period of profound grief and mourning while his wife was still alive; thus, the later period of mourning had been allowed for. The young boy, however, interpreted this as a lack of love for his mother. Had the father attempted to communicate with even so young a child, all the subsequent misunderstanding between them could have been averted. It is notable that most people would think a nine-year-old rather young to be told his mother was in a dying condition, yet he was not too young to entertain by himself the thought that his father did not love his mother.

There is another aspect of this matter which is not often acknowledged but which has undoubtedly caused much childhood suffering. In four families of this group under study, the maternal grandmother and one or more sisters-in-law, in extreme frustration and anger, told the bereaved children that their father was responsible for their mother's death. It is not uncommon for a grandparent to blame the spouse of a deceased person for the death, and to cruelly tell a child that his father has *killed* his mother. One grandmother told a fifteen-year-old boy who subsequently got into trouble with the law for drinking that *he* had killed his mother. The boy revealed this later when he was undergoing psychotherapy.

Evil effects of this nature could have been avoided by simple frankness on the part of the surviving parent. Furthermore, it is entirely natural for any of us, let alone children, to wish someone dead when we are peevish or frustrated. An adult pays little attention to hostility of this kind and soon forgets it. But, if a child has wished a parent harm and the parent dies, the child may possibly construe the illness and death to be the result of his own ill wish and then may develop more or less severe emotions of guilt and remorse. When illness and trouble are unexplained and love and confidence are not displayed by the surviving parent, a child may fail in school, withdraw, feel unworthy, and seek out friendships that may lead him into trouble; some children under these circumstances develop neurotic symptoms. A child who knows what is going on has a better chance to remain stable than the one who is kept in ignorance and unsure of what the reality of the situation is.

One father in our group gave his young children a book on leukemia, since he felt inadequate to tell them about the disease that was taking their mother's life. This is not the most advisable course to follow, but it is certainly better than leaving a child in ignorance of what is going on and what he will soon have to face.

A poor marriage often contributes to ensuing difficulties in family adjustment after the loss has occurred. The more passive and withdrawn a husband may have been with his deceased wife, the greater the likelihood that his troubled feelings will adversely affect his attempts to raise his children alone. He must be sure that he can adequately handle their living with him, during the illness and after his wife's death. He must determine whether he can continue as the breadwinner, keep his family together, and at the same time maintain his inner stability. The addition of a full-time housekeeper or part-time maid to his budget must also be considered. His role in keeping the family together involves more than household routines. His most important task consists of securing the youngster's continued physical and emotional growth. All the elements of care which once were so naturally borne by the mother, now devolve on the father. He must supervise yearly physical check-ups; he must recognize the child with a fever; tend and comfort a child with the measles or other childhood illness; give support to the youngster who is afraid of the dark, and, with older children, particularly girls, he must acquaint himself with and learn to insist upon observance of a proper curfew time, and give his advice on what should be worn on a date. Our culture does not generally prepare or attune fathers to their children's physical or emotional needs. In addition, children, especially young ones, need to see high spirits in adults if they are to view the world and life in positive terms. Not the least of the bereaved father's responsibility is the setting of a good example, for children of all ages require someone after whom to pattern themselves, especially in facing the trauma in their lives.

It is extremely important that the father find the best possible person to run the home. The age of the children, his means, the type of work he does and the amount of time he can give to his family will all have to be considered. Sometimes a relative will be available to supervise the household. If outside help is needed, he will have to be very careful in choosing a house-keeper. The Allied Teenage Guidance Service, for example, will advise a widower about the criteria he should use in selecting help, and has been interviewing and evaluating applicants for such men. One father in our study utilized the homemaking service of a social agency and as a result was able to secure counseling for his children and for himself.

The bane of the motherless family's functioning is its difficulty in maintaining the same full-time housekeeper or maid for any length of time. One father left with young children had employed as many as eight women within a short period of time. Frequent changes in homemakers and household help present a serious problem when the children are under six years of age, for they especially need consistent handling by a warm, interested female. A variety of housekeepers may retard their social and emotional development. Young children cannot say in words what has gone wrong in their environment. Often it must be conceded that the woman who chooses to work as a housekeeper or maid is not the best mother substitute for a young child. A father would do well to consider that instead of planning far ahead to put money aside for his child's education, he might make better use of it during the child's early years for his emotional education for life.

In this survey, two of the fathers left their jobs—one for six months and the other, who gave up his business, for fourteen months—in order to care for the children. Another father, fearing the disruptive influence of having a stranger in the home, placed his 2½-year old child with his mother while he and the two older children—11½ and 14—managed the household themselves. In retrospect, however, he felt that things might have been easier and different if he had been able to "deal with a person who might have other ideas." He and his two children required counseling and psychiatric treatment within a few years of his wife's death.

Another father of three children, very successful in his profession, has a full-time housekeeper who has become a "grandmother figure." He claims that since his household is run so efficiently by her, he is not planning to remarry until his children have grown up and left home, lest he "rock the boat."

In three families, the fathers managed alone with the help of youngsters of adolescent age and younger. In six families, the father, his children and a part-time housekeeper worked out a good system of care for the household. In three other families, a full-time housekeeper saw the children through their adolescence. These were wealthy families, and had the least trouble with changes in help. Nevertheless, the housekeepers were changed on an average of three times in each family.

Relatives were involved in the following situations: In five families, grandparents and an aunt participated in the management of the motherless homes. One maternal grandmother helped out for five months; the other until her death a year later. Afterwards the father and his children managed completely on their own. In two families, paternal grandparents and the widower's sister were involved, one for a short time, and the other for 4½ years, when the children went to live with grandparents until one year after the father's remarriage. As with others, when the grandparents stepped out of the picture, the fathers and children managed by themselves.

The best adjustment was made in three families who had the help of relatives, and a fourth in which the community participated. The first of the three families was one which had the services of both maternal grandparents, who moved in and took over complete management of the home. The widower was at that time twenty-eight years old and had two daughters of 4½ and 8½. These grandparents are still there after eight years. Without question, the children made a very good scholastic and social adjustment. The father was inclined to put the needs of his social and business life before the emotional needs of his children and communicated with them only on a superficial level. Consequently the children's source of emotional gratification came primarily from their grandparents, and in this instance they benefited greatly from this solution to the problem.

In the S. G. family, a very unhappy situation yielded to the influences of an excellent home provided by the grandparents for two boys aged two and six when their mother died. From birth on, they had experienced frequent separations from their mother, who was a mental patient in a hospital. Their father was in Korea, and on his return he changed jobs so often that it was considered best for the children to live with their grandparents. The 4½ years they spent in this environment were productive of very desirable results later, when their father remarried and they went to live with him. The marriage was a poor one; the stepmother was occupied with making a career for herself and did not get along with the oldest boy. Divorce was inevitable, but despite these trying experiences the boys have made a good family, scholastic and social adjustment. This can be attributed to a great extent to the years spent living with their grandparents.

Great credit must be given to the neighbors, landlord, organization brothers and the rabbi of Mr. E. R.'s community. He was critically injured in an accident which took his wife's life. He was on crutches for five months and had been told that he would be an invalid for life. The neighbors and community took over the care of two children, thirteen and sixteen years old. The landlord let Mr. E. R. live rent free for as long as he needed to. Incapacitated as he was Mr. E. R. yet managed to work from his home and earn some money. Six years later, he owned a small business and is now able to walk and even dance. His daughter gets excellent marks in college and his son is in the honor class at school. These youngsters are making an excellent adjustment. Although no doubt the members of the community are responsible in good part, there is no question that the attitude of the father helped greatly in this fortunate result. He was full of courage and love, and had experience in handling the children; he was vitally involved throughout most of his life with the community, had enjoyed marital harmony with his deceased wife, and had deliberately planned to wait four years before he showed any interest in women.

Others of the forty-six children in this study did not fare so well. Despite the fact that they had not been kept in ignorance of the nature of their mother's illness, and despite stability in the management of the motherless home in which they were growing up, a sufficiently large proportion of them were found to be in need of psychiatric treatment. There are many other factors besides these which create a need for help in adjustment, or for preventing emotional problems from developing.

The chief factors which operate in keeping children free of the symptoms of maladjustment appear to be successful work adaptation of the father; active interaction of both parents in the community; family discussions of feelings, events and interests; social activity with neighbors; and close ties to church and synagogue. For members of a motherless home, such exposure to community contacts can provide a pool of relationships from which meaningful ones can develop to compensate for the loss of the mother.

In assessing the emotional adjustments of the children, the criteria used were the personal, familial, scholastic and social adaptations of the youngsters in comparison with usual expectations in children their age. Included were those who would have warranted an evaluation and possibly therapy in years gone by, but because of changed living arrangements, fortunate and sometimes accidental social contacts, and a slower developmental pace, they have regained adequate balance by the time they reached their mid-twenties. They are included because their adjustment might have been achieved much earlier with help, and, under great stress, it is possible that their disturbances might recur.

In seven of the remaining seventeen families, only eight children did not require professional scrutiny either before or following their mother's death. Those who did receive treatment consisted of three boys and five girls. The boys ranged from twelve to fifteen; the girls, from fourteen to nineteen. The reactions, symptoms and behavior that led the fathers to seek aid for them can be divided as follows: among the boys, trouble with the law for drinking; socializing with potential delinquents; failing school marks; giving up athletics; truancy; withdrawing; uncommunicative behavior with other family members; excessive restlessness, nervousness and quick reactions of anger; among the girls, nervous coughing, phobias involving elevators and a fear of remaining alone at home; decline in school grades; over-attachment and dependency on the mother; excessive anxiety and feelings of insecurity; hostility toward the father; premature sexual relations with resultant excessive anxiety reactions; failure at college; hostility towards stepmother; faulty self-image; unrealistic vocational goals; nightmares and insomnia; crying for the dead mother; guilt feelings toward the deceased mother; and inability to socialize.

Other children in these seven families were in need of professional evaluation also, but they had not received any. Four boys between the ages of five and twenty had other problems: decline in high school grades; dropping out of college; nailbiting after mother's death, indicating tension; tendencies to be quiet, retiring, sensitive, uncommunicative about feelings with family members; sullenness, unfriendliness and uncommunicativeness in an adolescent with brain injury. Three girls had these problems: secretiveness about social activities; nailbiting. A 2½-year-old, living with relatives away from her father and siblings, had personality changes.

It is important to keep in mind that although symptoms may disappear in time, the tensions, conflicts and factors generating the tensions may persist, and sooner or later, the youngster's functioning may be affected. Early detection is therefore advisable so that the extent of the trouble can best be evaluated professionally.

The remaining ten families had ten boys and five girls who could profit from such an evaluation. The boys were between five and twenty-one years of age; the girls, between eight and nineteen years old. The danger signals in the behavior of the boys were: truancy; decline in grades; overeating; stealing money from father; socializing with delinquents; hiding leftover food; poor communication with father; dropping out of college; failing to complete musical study although interested in music; inability to have friends; withdrawing and slow reaction-time; reading problems and inability to perform school work; excessive sensitivity; clinging to memory of mother; over-dependence financially; dishonesty; resentment toward mother for her anxiousness; repudiation of religion; disrespect toward older people;

introverted and insecure behavior; underachievement; and dropping out of school.

The problems of the girls were poor self-image; "blue in past two years"; fear of making their father unhappy; overpreoccupation with other children's opinions of her; uncommunicative with father; decline in school grades; uncooperative attitude toward family; sense of loneliness; rejection of father, refusing to eat with him, though previously girl was unable to love either father or mother; resentful of father's interest in a woman; nightmares, inability to sleep for a few months; sudden weight gain when unhappy at a job and after trouble with roommate at college; warnings to father not to get serious with any woman; inability to share reactions regarding death of her mother.

In two of these situations the fathers tried to induce the youngsters to accept help but the offers of help were rejected. In all, thirty of the forty-six children were in need of professional diagnostic evaluation and possibly of treatment. Yet only eight of them received proper recognition of their emotional problems and underwent therapy.

Although in my judgment, nineteen of twenty-one fathers interviewed needed assistance in family or personal planning, only seven, or one third of the twenty-one, sought such help. Two secured aid from social workers and one of them finally was treated psychoanalytically. Five others were treated similarly by a psychologist or psychiatrist. I believe that the twelve other fathers should have considered consulting a professional inasmuch as three second marriages failed and affected eight children.

Another father whose youngster was treated five years after the mother died told me that "In the first year it wasn't easy to get along with even friends or relatives." Yet he had waited five years until his child became severely incapacitated by neurotic symptoms before he reached out for professional guidance for her or himself.

An illustration of this involved a father who sought aid for himself only after his daughter refused to eat with him and after he developed an ulcer and a heart condition. One widower sent his troubled eighteen-year-old only child, a daughter, for treatment, and she married about 1½ years later. Still another father had a disturbed daughter of nineteen but neither he nor his daughter secured help. The daughter's symptoms had already proliferated by the time I spoke with her father.

In conclusion, I would like to offer some practical guidelines for fathers who find themselves in the challenging situation of raising children on their own. They should keep the following in mind:

1. The greater the amount of contact between parent and child, the more easily will the child be helped in adjusting to his new family situation. If possible, therefore, all mealtimes should be spent together. Table talk should be encouraged about activities, interests, ideas, experiences, concerns and problems.

2. In families with very young children, e.g., three through six years of age, and in those with only one child of any age up to twenty, a father should make sound plans for involving substitute maternal figures in the child's life. A maid or housekeeper is generally inadequate in such a role, and cannot be relied upon for the necessary long-term contact with children.

When such maternal women are unavailable from amongst one's family or friends, a specially selected college student (for very young children), a "Big Sister," or a professional counselor should be considered by fathers for regular contact with their children.

3. If not before, the father should within a short time of the mother's passing away, plan a full program of activity for and with his children's participation. The program should involve club, sports and other supervised after-school activities.

4. Weekly socializing with family and friends in their own and other homes should be arranged regularly.

5. Wise fathers will recognize their need for greater understanding in the realm of child rearing. Our society has not prepared them for the traditional maternal role of raising children.

Consequently they should consider a "check-up" study of their family's functioning as great a necessity as the routine visit to their doctor for medical check-up. This has been another service of the Allied Teen-Age Guidance Service in New York.

It may help fathers to know that of the seven men in our study who secured help, the majority were holding high level positions with such organizations as the United Nations, Time Inc., and Metropolitan Hospital. Yet they were able to acknowledge their limitations in the realm of childrearing.

From the data I have available, I believe it is important for fathers generally to consider their manner of socializing with women and their plans to remarry, with the assistance of an objective professional. Children react strongly and unhappily when fathers start dating very soon after a mother dies. In addition, depending upon the children's age and degree of maturity, harm may be done when fathers remain away overnight or go off on weekend trips without informing their children where they can be reached.

In addition, seeing their fathers dating young women often evokes troubled feelings in their adolescent daughters. It is only fair that fathers should build a new life for themselves. Yet while his children are still dependent on him and a part of his household, the father must bear in mind that their feelings will be affected by the manner in which he reconstructs his life.

Children's emotional needs must be considered by the father. Otherwise the family structure, without its other pillar of strength, the mother, is certain to be shaken or fall apart.

Chapter 31

THE PET AND BEREAVEMENT

BORIS M. LEVINSON; JAMES R. KINNEY

Bereavement frequently results in insecurity, anxiety, fear, distrust of the world, and physical discomfort. It brings to a focus, sometimes with explosive force, the underlying tensions, strains, emotions, and inherent weaknesses and strengths of a family. The effects of bereavement vary depending upon the age, conceptual development, and emotional status of the bereaved.

The mature adult realizes that death is a normal phenomenon, that it is part of life, and that it gives meaning to life. However, in many homes, the emotionally immature adult, frozen in his grief, has not himself accepted the reality of death, and in his pathetic efforts to avoid facing the inevitable, will even assure a child that death is, in its essence, a prolonged sleep. Thus, in a sense, he comforts himself.

Even professionals in mental hygiene shy away from the discussion of death. Mankind has practically no advance preparation for the inevitability of death, and hardly any provisions exist for therapeutic experiences that would minimize the effect of death and ameliorate its trauma.[2] The unknown is much worse than the most dreaded reality. When death strikes, sometimes unexpectedly, or a loved one dies, we try to find comfort against the consequent loss of affection and security.

The very young child readily accepts the proffered explanation that death is similar to sleep. Like primitive people,[3] he, too, cannot conceive of death as total destruction. He visualizes death as a very prolonged sleep, as in the story "Snow White." The body does not decay. The person feels, thinks, experiences, senses, yet cannot cry out or move. The dead exist, silently sharing the child's meals, his joys and his sorrows. It is sometimes similar, the child muses, to the game of "cops and robbers," in which the participants are resurrected when the rules of the game require it.

The child feels, however, that this new state of immobilization is much more intense and is not voluntary. He hears vague and confusing explanations that he senses conceal some horrible truth. He becomes sensitized to the existence of a mysterious terror in whose presence his giant protectors tremble. He has already experienced this mystery in his nightmares, when he was frozen with terror. He may develop insomnia and ask to have the light on when he goes to sleep, or have his parent sleep with him. To compound his difficulties, he is reluctant to discuss his fears because he considers them shameful. Since adults are ashamed to talk about such fears, how can he? What he wants most of all is to find something he can love and hold on to, something that will help him integrate his experiences. At this point, having a pet may be most important in giving him help.

The young child thinks of the animal as similar to or perhaps even more important than himself. Young children very readily identify with animals.[1] In children's eyes, the grown-up man, the father, belongs to the animal world.[4] Clinical observations indicate that some children unconsciously believe that they may be transformed into animals and that animals may become children. This is similar to the belief which appears in the hunting cultures, that in "primal times all animals were people."[8]

Other children notice that their pets commit crimes, mate and defecate in public, kill mice, birds and other inoffensive creatures, and still are not punished. They envy them their freedom in engaging in these fascinating but forbidden activities and wonder why their pets escape punishment. They feel, however, that when punishment does come, it will be very severe.

Many children, like members of some preliterate tribes, cannot conceive of death as a natural, lawful event, of its being involuntary. They feel that someone is responsible. For example, Jersild[9] remarks that for children who have been frightened by the thought of an avenging God who punishes youngsters for their sins, death has not only the implication of "annihilation

and nothingness" but is "the ultimate in loneliness and isolation."
Pets usually do not have a very long life span, yet the death of
a pet is interpreted by a child as a punishment for his misdeeds.
Who caused the pet's death? Why was he punished? Where does
the pet's body go? Does the pet have a soul? Finally, the child
may also wonder if he himself will die. Will his parents die? If
so, who will take care of him? These concerns give the child an
opportunity to discuss openly his real or fancied guilt in the
death of his pet and thus to appraise his own feelings about
death, in an effort to come to terms with it.

Children can participate in mock funerals and reenact the
death of their pets in an attempt to master their fear and to
understand their emotions. They bewail their loss, act out their
feelings, learn through their play activities what the realities of
burial are, curb their inordinate fantasies, and try to master
their own anxieties. The idea that death is irreversible and that
the deceased person never returns is unacceptable to the very
young child.[5] He may already have had the experience of the
deceased pet's appearing in his nightmares in the shape of a
ferocious animal. To lay his fears to rest, the young child may
exhume his buried bird or fish and examine the decomposed
body. Thus the fact is impressed upon him that the loss is
permanent. There is no return of the dead. The dead pet will not
return to haunt him in his dreams. As death becomes less mysterious, more understandable, and, in a sense, "palpable," the
associated emotions of fear become more manageable. Other
imaginary figures are cut down to size by the intruding factors
of reality, and the child is able to cope with his grief more
adequately.

Later, when the child replaces his pet, he learns that life must
go on. Just as, when the mother cat died, there was some one
who took care of the kittens, there is usually some one among human beings who can take over and give the necessary support.
The death of a pet, therefore, serves as a sort of emotional inoc-
ulation against the inevitable traumata that will occur when the
loss is that of a person.

The critical illness of a parent usually brings about the mobilization of all of a family's resources. At this juncture, the very young child may feel neglected, and consequently harbor unconscious death wishes against his parent. The young child who has not yet learned the difference between angry wishes and angry deeds may become very anxious when his father dies. He may become terror-stricken, expecting the same fate. Since at this period the child is egocentric,[3] is unable to generalize, and tends to explain death on the basis of the fact that the deceased wished to desert him and therefore died, he may direct his aggression inward and become depressed. He may feel hopeless, stop eating, and wish to die. This is often the result of keeping a child in ignorance of coming sorrow. Whenever possible, the child should be prepared for a parent's death. Serious illness should not be considered a closely guarded family secret but should be discussed in the child's presence in terms he can understand.

The theme of rebirth and reunion after death with the loved one occasionally appears in the fantasies of bereaved children. They may dream of space saucers picking them up and reuniting them with their parents, who have moved to a nearby star. The child fancies that only through death will he be able to achieve his ultimate desire—love through reunion with his deceased parent—thus achieving forgiveness for his evil thoughts and atoning for his guilt. He may also feel that it is not worthwhile to love, that adults betray the trust children place in them by deserting them and leaving them alone just when they are needed most. The love of a pet provides comfort on the plane of reality, thus minimizing the need to escape into fantasy.

Occasionally, a pet is given to a child by a parent and is thus identified with that parent. If the parent later dies, the child may express his anger at the parent's "desertion" by attacking and even killing the pet. This is a frequent occurrence among emotionally disturbed children. It seems as though, by experimenting with death and by inflicting death on an inoffensive creature, the child imagines himself to be the master of life, the conquerer of death. At this critical juncture in the child's life, his needs for affection, support, companionship, and ego gratification are no longer being adequately met. Many an adult depression may be traced to this feeling of desertion in the child's mind.[7]

Perhaps he will turn to the surviving parent, who may either be not ready or incapable at this time of offering any comfort. The parent may be so involved in his own grief that he scarcely pays more than fleeting attention to his child. The child is frequently told not to disturb his parent, the implication being that he is not helpful. He is burdened with the responsibility for being quiet. This serves to deepen the unconscious guilt of the young one, who sees that he is not only deserted by the deceased, but is also neglected by the living, a feeling that may be particularly traumatic at a time when the child has already felt anxious about his relationship with his peers and his standing in his family.

It is at this point, when there is a fundamental change in family dynamics, that the pet may provide a haven. When the entire world seems to come crashing down around the child's ears, the pet is there to share his grief and to offer hope. The child's grief, his tears, his fears and terrors, his feelings of guilt are entrusted to the pet. The pet's silent, nondemanding acceptance of the child's hidden emotions and his unfailing admiration and love for the child are comforting. In his play with the pet, the child may work out his feelings of guilt, fears of punishment, and his attempts to atone for the wrongs he has committed.[11] He is then better able to accept his loss; he does not have to deny it by escaping into a fantasy world. Thus he may be able to emerge relatively unscathed from the traumatic experience, because the pet serves as a warm, stable, and protective bridge between the never-forgotten past and the nebulous future.

Introducing a pet into families that face the threat of the loss of a parent can, in many cases, prove to be a valuable measure of mental hygiene. The pet gives the child a living companion that will not usually be a competitor for the surviving parent's affection. Even more important, "the dog represents a protector, a talisman against the fear of death, which is first experienced as separation anxiety."[6]

It is, in addition, most important for bereaved chidren to go through a wholesome mourning experience, to be provided with an opportunity to assimilate their trauma and break the cathexis with the loved one. This becomes particularly desirable when the surviving parent is unable to accept death as final. Then, the pet may play a crucial role by providing the child with a sympathetic, nonjudgmental listener before whom the child may become immersed in his grief and speak unabashedly and repeatedly about the beloved parent, or evaluate his own guilt in bringing about the death, often with great amelioration of his distress.

B. M. L.

REFERENCES

1. BRILL, A. A.: The universality of symbols. *The Yearbook of Psychoanalysis, 1,* 63–78, 1945.
2. FEIFEL, H. (Ed.): *The Meaning of Death.* New York; McGraw-Hill, 1959.
3. FLAVEL, J. H.: *The Developmental Psychology of Jean Piaget.* New York; Van Nostrand, 1963.
4. FREUD, S.: Analysis of a phobia in a five-year old boy. In *Collected Works,* standard ed. (ed and trans by James Strachey), vol. 10, London, Hogath Press, 1955.
5. GESELL, A.: ILG, F. L.; AMES, L. B.; LEARNED, J., and BULLIS, G. E.: *Child Development.* New York; Harper, 1949.
6. HEIMAN, M.: The relationship between man and dog. *Psychoanal Quart, 25:*568–585, 1956.
7. HILGARD, J. R.; NEWMAN, M. F., and FISK, F.: Strength of adult ego following childhood bereavement. *Amer J Orthopsych, 30:*788–798, 1960.
8. JENSEN, A. E.: *Myth and Cult Among Primitive Peoples.* Chicago, U of Chicago Press, 1963.
9. JERSILD, A. T.: *Child Psychology,* fourth ed. New York, Prentice-Hall, 1954.
10. LEVINSON, B. M.: Interpersonal relationships between pet and human being. In Fox, M. W. (Ed.): *Abnormal Behavior in Animals.* Philadelphia, Saunders, in press.
11. LEVINSON, B. M.: The dog as a "co-therapist." *Mental Hygiene, 46:* 59–65, 1962.

* * *

After the loss of a loved one, there is often a period when the mourner can make no contact with another human being. The solace of a dog or cat (even of a bird or aquarium fish) might well be a bridge back to the world for the bereaved. Jean Stafford, the novelist, has written, "There is no poultice more solacing than the body of a warm, soft cat." A pet, any pet, could bring back warmth, a kind of love, and a will to go on living into the life of the bereaved, and thus provide a unique aid in convalescence.

This should not be interpreted as the substitution of an animal for a loved person. It is the injection of a new stimulus into life by creating a new interest and renewing the sense of caring. The meaningful activities of tending to the needs of an animal provide a respite from depressing thoughts and, in many cases, alleviate the slackening of social pressures that follows bereavement—particularly for the person who must now carry on alone.

J. R. K

Chapter 32

SURVIVOR-BENEFIT-RIGHTS UNDER SOCIAL SECURITY

CHARLES S. FERBER

Social Security survivor benefits are designed to ease the financial burden that descends upon a family when the principal wage earner dies. A program, such as our government's Social Security program, offers some solutions to the practical problems of daily living for those burdened with financial responsibilities and the necessity of providing for themselves and their immediate household. It is our purpose to speak of the available benefits in a general way. No one should attempt, however, to base a judgment on his eligibility or ineligibility solely upon what is brought out here. In every case, survivors are urged to contact a local Social Security office.

The benefits paid help the young widow or widower to keep the family together. Benefit amounts paid are related to the deceased's earnings during his working life. For example, if a young father of two children, both under five, dies, and his average earnings were $450 a month, his widow and children could receive as much as $354 each month. By the time the oldest child reaches eighteen, this family could have received more than $55,000. Children are eligible for additional benefit payments until their twenty-second year if they continue their education. The widow will ultimately be eligible to receive monthly benefits at age sixty or as early as age fifty if she is disabled within the definition of the law. These benefit payments are not subject to Federal income tax.

The income to this family is as secure as the United States Government, which guarantees that every month, without fail, these checks will be issued and mailed to the surviving family.

Behind all Social Security benefits is the basic concept that while a person is working and receiving a salary, he is contributing to a trust fund. When death terminates a wage earner's income, cash benefits are to be paid to his family as a partial replacement for his lost earnings.

Who Is Eligible?

The children of the deceased worker who was the principal wage earner, whether this be the mother or the father, can be entitled to monthly cash benefits. This monthly check will be paid until the child reaches the age of eighteen and, as mentioned above, if he continues his education, until the age of twenty-two. Provision has also been made for the severely disabled child of a deceased wage earner. If he was disabled before his eighteenth birthday, he will be paid benefits as long as his disability continues.

A widow is eligible for monthly benefits at age sixty. Under the latest revision in the law, a *disabled* widow may be eligible for benefits as early as age fifty. However, if she has a child of the deceased in her care, she can receive benefits at any age. Under certain conditions, the divorced wife of the deceased will be paid a monthly check at age sixty, or age fifty if she is disabled.

Survivor payments are not limited to the widow and children of the deceased worker. Many families have the added obligation of supporting older parents. With this situation in mind, the Social Security program provides monthly benefit payments for the parent at age sixty-two, if he had been dependent upon the worker for at least one half of his support.

Although the situation occurs less frequently, monthly benefits are also payable to a widower at age sixty-two if he was dependent upon his deceased wife for one half of his support.

In addition to the above comprehensive scope of monthly benefits, a lump sum payment, designed to help defray the cost of burial expenses, is paid to the surviving spouse if he or she was living with the wage earner at the time of death. In any case, it will be paid to the individual who assumes responsibility for the cost of the burial.

How To Apply For Benefits

Naturally, no benefits can be paid until an application is filed with one of the 750 conveniently located Social Security offices. To avoid delay and any possible loss in benefits, an application should be filed as soon as possible. The application for the lump sum payment for funeral expenses must usually be made within two years after the wage-earner's death. The survivor should bring all the necessary papers and documents when he files his application at the Social Security office: the deceased's Social Security card or a record of his number, proof of age of the individual members of the family (such as a birth certificate or a baptismal certificate), a marriage certificate(if it is the surviving widow or widower who is filing for the benefits), and the certificate of death. Before benefits can be paid to the parents of the deceased wage-earner, proof must be shown that he was providing for at least one half of their support. Generally, this proof must be furnished within two years after the death. Representatives in the Social Security office will explain how the fact of support can be proven.

But, under no circumstances should a person delay in filing his application because he does not have all of these documents. The representatives in the Social Security office will tell him what to do if the necessary documents cannot be located and will help him to secure them, if it is possible. When a person applies, he will be instructed concerning his responsibility to report to the Social Security Administration any event that may affect his eligibility. He should keep all these documents and instructions in a safe place, such as a bank vault, where they can be easily referred to when the need arises.

Many survivors, especially widows, find it easier to adjust to their changed status by finding employment. For these people there is an added consideration. The earnings they may receive from employment or self-employment may affect their eligibility for Social Security benefits. However, even though their personal eligibility may be changed, nothing can affect the eligibility of the other members of the family who are receiving benefits. If the young widowed mother of a family goes to work, her children's checks will still be issued.

The survivor will receive all benefits for the year if he or she earns $1,680 or less in that year. If the earnings exceed $1,680, $1 in benefit payments will be withheld for every $2 of earnings between $1,680 and $2,880. In addition, if he earns more than $2,880 for the year, $1 in benefits is withheld for every $1 of earnings over $2,880. However, the individual will receive a check for any month in which he neither earns wages of more than $140 nor performs substantial work in self-employment—regardless of his earnings for the year. Income from such sources as savings, investments, pensions, insurance, trusts, and legacies is not included in these totals and does not affect the amount of benefit paid by Social Security. Only income from employment or self-employment can affect Social Security.

When a widow or widower remarries, his or her benefit payments are usually terminated. However, the widow who remarries after age sixty, and the widower who remarries after age sixty-two, are still eligible to receive benefits on their first spouse's record.

Although Social Security can in no way fill the emotional void caused by the loss of a loved one, it is a valuable asset. Its benefits assist in keeping the surviving family together and in guaranteeing the necessities of life for them. Its basic philosophy recognizes that, as Thomas Mann so wisely phrased it, "A man's dying is more the survivor's affair than his own."

Chapter 33

AN ELEMENTARY GUIDE TO FAMILY FINANCIAL MANAGEMENT

FRED HELLER

Volumes of books and papers have been written on the subject of family financial management, but the highly specialized problems affecting the bereaved have been relatively neglected. This chapter deals primarily with this group of investors, although many of the principles discussed herein apply to all others who must manage family funds. Therefore, this chapter will try to present an elementary guide for intelligent investment and family financial management.

The bereaved widow finds herself confronted by the challenge of providing for the financial support of her children and herself. If her husband had discussed financial matters with her, she has some knowledge of what is to be anticipated. Whether or not she is familiar with such affairs, she now must analyze her financial situation and make decisions accordingly. The following outline may serve as a basis for such an analysis.

A. List all of the assets that are available to produce income and the amounts of income to be so derived, including the following:

1. Proceeds of life insurance policies.
2. Funds in savings accounts.
3. Funds in checking accounts.
4. Funds to be received from Social Security or pensions, or similar benefits.
5. Value of stocks and bonds owned.
6. Value of real estate holdings and amount of income to be derived from these, if any.
7. Any other assets, such as interests in business, etc.

B. Give consideration to the following three questions to determine whether or not the family income from the above holdings is sufficient.

  1. What are my everyday living expenses? Write down all expenses such as for food, clothing, shelter (rent; or mortgage and real estate taxes on own home); household repairs and maintenance; insurance (health, automobile, fire and theft, personal and household effects, life insurance); medical, transportation, etc.
  2. Is there enough reserve cash remaining which can be left in savings accounts where it is immediately available to meet an emergency or special contingency?
  3. Is sufficient income available for the education of my children, including the continuance, for instance, of music or other private lessons, for college tuition fees, for camp fees, etc.?

If the income to be derived from one's capital, that is the return in dividends, interest, monthly Social Security benefits, and so forth, is sufficient to cover one's usual and hence anticipated, expenditures, one is in a truly fortunate position. If such is not the case, there are certain steps to be taken that can serve to amend the current situation and reduce one's worries about the future.

It must be recognized that both groups must operate within the same framework insofar as making investments is concerned. The primary prerequisites of sound investment management include a clear understanding of one's basic investment objectives, i.e., to obtain maximum income, to assure capital conservation, or to secure maximum appreciation.

If the bereaved's income from all the sources mentioned above is adequate for his living expenses, he may feel that all his resources should be left as they are. Insurance proceeds, paid in a lump sum, may be deposited in savings accounts at the current rate of interest or invested in common stocks which pay some dividends and which also may appreciate in value.

If the bereaved's anticipated income is not sufficient for his needs, steps may be taken to improve the situation. A widow may find that employment hastens her recovery from bereavement and at the same time can help to solve some of her economic problems. And it should be noted that, although her salary may deprive her of some part of her own Social Security benefit payments, her salary income will not interfere with benefits received on behalf of her young children.

Assets may be reinvested to produce the maximum amount of income possible. For example, certain holdings in stocks may be switched to other stocks or to bonds which produce higher yields in the form of either dividends or interest. In such instances greater dividend income will be the primary aim in investing. In the past ten years, more than 85 per cent of the common stocks listed on the New York Stock Exchange have paid cash dividends averaging from 3.3 per cent to 6.1 per cent and there are some sound companies whose stocks have yielded even more.

The three major investment objectives—safety of principal, liberal dividend income, and growth of capital—are not always mutually exclusive. It is possible, for example, to have a relatively high degree of safety combined with a fairly liberal dividend income. And there are some stocks that offer both liberal dividends as well as growth possibilities. However, keep in mind that there is no such thing as the all-purpose stock—one that is completely safe, certain to pay handsome dividends, and sure to go nowhere but up.

From long experience, I have found that too few people have a clear or sound understanding of the fundamentals of investment management. Rather, they are motivated by the quixotic compulsion of "quick gains" that are based on rumor and illusory mob psychology. Such a philosophy generally creates frenzied buying and selling of stocks, many problems, and little in the way of profits. What is gained in one transaction is usually lost in the next.

Financial planning should be done without haste, with much thought, and with the advice of the experts in the field. Security selection can be made to conform to the investor's basic investment objectives. Without practical experience in investing the bereaved would be well advised to proceed cautiously and to pursue a careful and prudent investment policy. A lawyer, or other experienced person, generally will have been delegated the responsibility of administering, or assisting in the administration of the estate. He may help determine what decisions have to be made and when they should be made. There are others too who are trained and are capable of offering professional assistance. Among these is the investment counselor who can assess one's financial needs and determine how they can best be satisfied.

Proper planning and proper investment counsel will often be the keys to reassurance of the bereaved as to her own and her family's future financial security.

PART V

CARE OF THE BEREAVED

Chapter 34

PHYSIOLOGICAL ASPECTS OF DEPRESSION

JEROME STEINER, JOHN F. O'CONNOR AND LENORE O. STERN

In presenting the information which follows, neither the purpose for introducing it nor the implications should be misunderstood or misinterpreted. It is *not* intended as a layman's guide to the practice of medicine, nor as a vicarious excursion into academic medicine; not even as an aid to the interpretation of the symptoms of bereavement—although the material verges on this.

Rather, it *is* intended to provide another insight into the full dimensions of grief and bereavement—through an understanding of which, the surmounting of the bereavement state is enhanced and the timetable of recovery from bereavement speeded. Even more specifically, the reader is encouraged to consider the information which follows as a sensible injunction against self-neglect on the part of the bereaved, who should be persuaded to seek medical advice when he displays symptoms of matching character to those described.

It is repeated emphatically: this material is not provided in lieu of a medical consultation. Also, although many types of professionals are qualified to corroborate the need for medical care and suitably direct the bereaved to a doctor, only a physician can undertake the final diagnostic step to affirm such need and prescribe the definitive therapy. Especially if there is now no one close enough to him who will urge this course, it behooves the bereaved to seek help himself as soon as he can, for there is no merit in lying supine under misfortune. All the implications of such neglect of self are deleterious in the extreme, for they can lead to unfortunate consequences that might have been prevented and which almost certainly will be later regretted.

The information here provided should serve only as an influence leading to medical consultation, the only definitive step which can help differentiate between temporary signs of a physical disorder due to grief and more serious signs of some physical deterioration that ought to be medically investigated.

The person bereaved should look upon the discussion which follows not with apprehension or alarm but with the thought that "a word to the wise is sufficient." Thus he should seek to control his grief by demanding of himself sensible behavior.

A.H.K.

The close relationship that exists between emotion and bodily function has been recognized for centuries; one sees the redness of the face which accompanies anger, the "tension" headache, the paleness which may follow fear, the weakness which may result from a sudden tragic episode. An emotion is instinctive, a state of feeling that has both physical and psychological manifestations. Physical manifestations, being more observable, are more objective in character than are the psychological. The interaction between the psychological and physical has been a subject of speculation since man learned to differentiate the effects of external events from those of his internal experiences.

Most emotional disorders have physiological accompaniments. In depression, the somatic elements are readily perceivable and are generally considered to be a reaction to what is basically a feeling state.

Depression is an internal emotional experience; generally, a response to loss. It may arise from the loss of a person or an object closely related to self; it may consist of a subjective loss of self-esteem, of love or affection. Medically, what is referred to as "depression" is the combined psychological and physical reaction to the setting up of a rather complicated set of defenses against the experience.

In one form or another, loss is a normal part of the life process. People die, loved ones are separated, relationships end, and individuals can be injured both physically and emotionally. A "normal" depression with both somatic and psychological components follows such events. The individual feels despondent, distressed, and, at times, over-irritable. There may be difficulty in eating and sleeping; there may be a loss of interest in normal activities, but usually, routine occupations and relationships are not interfered with. This type of depression is best described as a "grief reaction." It is self-limited and short-lived, disappearing within two to eight weeks and requiring little, if any, intervention by a physician. An awareness of the fact that life continues, that friends remain and that new relationships can develop goes a long way toward making a normal grief reaction tolerable. Such a reaction in varying degrees is familiar to all of us.

The "pathologic" depressions do not resolve spontaneously and require more than time itself for their relief. They are divided into three general types: (1) a retarded depression, (2) an agitated depression, and (3) a depression characterized by somatic or behavioral manifestations, such as excessive alcohol intake, the use of drugs or anti-social conduct.

The retarded depression is best described as a generalized "slowing-down" period. The tone of the individual's feeling is one of sadness and fatigue. He moves and thinks slowly, has difficulty in sleeping and frequently finds that he awakens very early in the morning. His appetite may be poor, and there is usually a significant weight loss of from ten to twenty pounds. This group of symptoms resembles the state which occurs in some of the mammalian species when their food supply is threatened—that is, hibernation. Hibernation is a normal physiologic adaptation in animals to periodically unfavorable environmental conditions, such as cold weather. Food is not readily available, the animal's activity slows down and, therefore, he requires less fuel. Nervous excitability decreases, as do the temperature, blood pressure, respiratory and heart rates. In human beings, one could view the retarded depresssion as a physiological sedation resulting from loss or injury and the ensuing inevitable threat to the satisfaction of needs: personal ambition decreases, physical movement is slowed, appetite fails, sexual desire diminishes or disappears. Insomnia develops, and the individual becomes increasingly tired, with a resulting greater desire for sleep. Unlike hibernation, this constellation of symptoms is not useful to the individual but, nevertheless, it is a coordinated pattern of body reaction which occurs often. Although coping with depressed feelings is more cerebral in the human being than in lower animals, in both there are pre-established physiological systems that come into play.

In the agitated form of a depression, an innate sense of sadness and despondency is mixed with feeling states of fear and anger. Although this syndrome, too, is characterized by autonomic dysfunction, the pattern is markedly different from that seen in the previously described retarded depression. Activity increases and body weight may either be gained or lost as the appetite fluctuates. Dyspepsia is present and, frequently, diarrhea or constipation. Women may stop menstruating and men may become impotent. On the other hand, the individual can well have a marked increase in sexual activity. It is as if there is a need for constant movement in order to discharge the great tension he feels. In the agitated depression, the basic reaction of anger is less under control and much closer to the surface than in the retarded depression. The individual is hyperirritable and tense and at times he will tell you that he is "ready to explode" or to "jump out of his skin." This form of depression typically occurs during the involutional period when sexual powers and attractiveness are felt to be on the wane.

Rene Spitz has compared the agitated state to that which is described by Hans Selye as a "general adaptation syndrome." According to this theory, a stress (which may be the emotional response to loss) upsets the balance of glandular functioning. During the first phase of the syndrome, there is great nervous tension and excitement. If this continues, it can be followed by muscular degeneration and decreased body activity. The final stage of a stress reaction might be equated with a retarded depression. However, if one considers retarded depression to be a physiologic sedative following the experience of loss, agitated depression could be seen as a state of physiological excitement.

The third major type of depression is that wherein the feeling state is hidden and is represented by various somatic symptoms or by antisocial activities. Excessive preoccupation with heart function, digestive system and other body organs is frequently apparent. Careful examination of the individual's physiological functioning and prohibition of the inappropriate behavioral outlets (alcohol, drug ingestion) will reveal the underlying sadness and depressed reactions to loss. When these phenomena substitute for what is commonly known as depression, they are called "depressive equivalents." Typically, the depressed person is felt to be an irritant by the other family members, e.g., they condemn the alcoholic for his "weakness," the middle-aged person for wearing a chip on the shoulder, and the delinquent for showing hostility. Yet all are completely unaware that they are undergoing reactions to loss. This is not to say that all persons who manifest such behavior are depressed; however, when these conditions *are* depressive equivalents, medical treatment must be oriented to the underlying depression. The condition can be treated by the physician with a fair chance of success.

Depression manifests itself through most organ systems:

1. The Skin

Most skin manifestations are secondary to changes in nerve functioning. At times there is excessive sweating. Pallor may occur. Occasionally, psychophysiological reactions such as hives, itching and other rashes are seen in susceptible individuals who are depressed.

2. Muscular System

Muscular coordination can be poor and there is frequently a tremor. There are variations in the speed with which the person can carry out a given act. One research scientist has measured the pattern of electrical excitability of muscles. He has developed an entire theory differentiating depression from other illnesses on the basis of the electrical potential of muscle. This author has been able to find biochemical support for his theory. Again the question might be asked whether the changes in these patterns are secondary to deranged sleep and eating or whether they are primary and definitive of the syndrome.

The depressed person tends, if he is retarded, to slump and walk slowly. There is little tone to his musculature and the response to stimuli is decreased. The opposite is true in the hyperactive, hypertonic and hyperexcitable agitated person.

3. Cardiorespiratory System

The depressed patient will occasionally have some breathing difficulties. These are mainly related to excessive sighing associated with feelings of shortness of breath as a result of excessive concern or concentration on the process of breathing. Most commonly, this is seen in the retarded depression or when the feeling state is being handled by denial. On the other hand, the agitated person will experience the hyperventilation syndrome. In this case, due to overbreathing, the patient builds too high an oxygen level in the blood, causing decreased stimulation of the respiratory center in the brain, and there is a subjective feeling of shortness of breath (although the opposite is true). Dizziness, numbness of the extremities, chest pain, and occasionally unconsciousness follow. This is a self-limiting set of symptoms and is rarely dangerous to the individual.

The depressed person frequently becomes aware of a rapid, strong heart beat—"palpitations." He may at times feel that he is having a heart attack and feels as if the blood is not reaching the tips of his fingers and toes, which tingle and "fall asleep." He may become excessively concerned with his own cardiac status. Blood pressure can rise or fall depending on the individual's susceptibility. Most somatic preoccupations disappear with alleviation of the depression.

4. Digestive System

All depressives are subject to gastrointestinal disturbances. In the retarded depression, an individual may lose his appetite. In an agitated state, he may try to "calm his nerves" by overeating. Gastrointestinal disturbances have their own consequences—weight fluctuates, indigestion is common and, not infrequently, there are the complications of a malnourished state. Because of dietary changes or perhaps nervous and hormonal dysfunctions, the individual may either be constipated or develop diarrhea. These bowel disorders further complicate the physiological picture by upsetting the organism's salt and water balance and the ability to handle waste products.

5. Genitourinary System

The depressed person may complain of burning on urination or of urgency that is unrelated to any infectious process. Frequently, a woman's menstrual period becomes irregular or ceases completely. It appears certain that these irregularities are secondary to hormonal changes.

6. Endocrine System

Frequently seen is a depressive reaction following the normal hormonal changes which occur in late middle-age. One also sees depression following the birth of a child. This, too, is a period of great hormonal change and readjustment. Recent work indicates that there are hormonal changes which occur during a depressive reaction. It has been shown that in severe cases there is an increase of the hormone secreted by the adrenal cortex. However, these studies have not been standardized, and research at various laboratories yields apparently contradictory results.

Disorders of thyroid function are often accompanied by depression. However, it is unlikely that depression causes thyroid dysfunction or that this is a regular accompaniment of the feeling state.

The role of endocrine imbalance in depression remains vague. Although probably not a precipitating factor, it still may be responsible for converting a grief reaction into depressive illness.

7. Nervous System

A sleep disturbance is always present. Early morning awakening is typically characteristic of the retarded depression. The agitated depressive is likely to have more difficulty in sleeping through the night. Careful studies using brain wave and dream patterns have shown that all depressions are accompanied by objectively observable changes. Any depressed individual is more wakeful and more responsive to sound stimulation in all stages of his sleeping than is the nondepressed individual; he sleeps less than usual, spends less time in a deep sleep, and has greater difficulty in falling asleep.

It is theorized that nerve cells, which are continually bombarded by stimuli, in this case as a result of depression, become fatigued and therefore are less able to transmit the necessary impulses for normal brain conduction. This theory would account for disturbances in memory and attention, in muscular functions, in sleep and various other manifestations.

The attention span of the depressed person is shortened. He is easily distracted and has difficulty in the interpretation of sensory impulses. Either touch, taste, hearing, and sight are bombarding him or he does not register all of their stimulation. Often he feels that he has grown hard-of-hearing, that all foods taste the same, that his eyes burn or refuse to focus and his hands cannot identify objects as readily as before.

TREATMENT

Depression is a definitely treatable entity with a good chance of successful outcome. Familiar to most persons are environmental change and counseling. Psychotherapy is frequently effective. Many new drugs are available as well as other forms of physical treatment. The role of female (estrogenic) hormones remains unclear, except, perhaps, in the management of involutional depression in the female. As an adjunctive form of treatment, the use of hormones can help to alleviate such physical manifestations as hot flashes, but they have no demonstrable effect on the psychological symptoms.

In summary, depression may be described as a feeling state of sadness, fear or fatigue, or combinations of these, accompanied by sleep disturbance, digestive disorders, nervous and muscular impairment and various other somatic complaints. This collection of symptoms is not unique, and the physician must differentiate true depression *per se* from other medical illnesses. There is no doubt that depression is not just a "state of mind." It is a generalized illness which follows the rules defining all other medical illnesses and, like others, it is both incapacitating and painful. Fortunately, there are various forms of treatment available that have proven effective in its amelioration.

Chapter 35

MEDICAL CARE DURING BEREAVEMENT

GEORGE A. HYMAN

In this brief summary of the medical and psychological needs of close family members of the deceased, three significant time periods must be taken into account. They are,

1. That period of time which shortly precedes the death event, in cases of terminal illness and in those cases where imminent death is predictable by clinical prognosis.
2. The four-week period immediately following the death event.
3. The period of time after the four-week period, which can be approximated at eight weeks (second and third month after the death event).

During the time interval including periods one and two it is not unusual that all persons virtually immersed in the care of the dying patient and subsequent responsibilities which immediately follow the death event *do not care for and ignore their own health and medical needs.* Danger signals of serious illness in some cases have been neglected to the extent of producing noncurable later conditions.

Family members must make every effort to guard physical and emotional health, to obtain adequate nutrition and rest as a means of fortification for the debilitating responsibilities that lie ahead. The physician in attendance should administer mild hypnotics, when indicated, such as 15 mg phenobarbital three times daily; nightly sleeping medication if needed, and special attention to medical conditions such as hypertension, diabetes and cardiac disease is recommended. The task of pursuading attendant relatives to accept immediate hospitalization for their own needs in this time of crisis is most difficult, but must be accomplished when at all possible. Neglect of these necessary surgical situations at this time can result in untold misery and further death events in an already stricken family.

During period two, stronger tranquilizers are often required, together with antidepressants in some cases. Librium® (10 mg three times daily) or Tofranil® (25 mg four times daily) may be needed. (Meprobamate, 400 mg four times daily, may also be given, although it is less potent than the preceding medications, and may also be somewhat depressing.) Severely reactive depression may require the use of stimulants, such as Dexedrine® or Ritalin® in the mornings, and stronger sleeping medications may now be indicated (Seconal,® Tuinal® or Placidyl® in appropriate dosages).

It is in this time period that all presenting symptoms of near relatives should be discussed with the personal physician, by telephone, at least, if not in person. In many cases, reassurance may be given by telephone and an opportunity is thereby given to make necessary evaluations, if needed, without further delays. The relative should be made to understand by the physician that he need feel no guilt at intelligent concern for his own health at this time.

In the third period of time, it is wise for the near relatives of the deceased to visit their physicians on a regular basis, in order to discuss all symptoms that may possibly have appeared within the course of all three time periods. It is also possible, at this time, to discuss with the physician the various aspects of individual anxiety and doubt with which they are invariably beset. The family member in consultation with the physician would do well to pave the way for other members of the family (sons and daughters, etc.) to visit their physicians as well, in order that symptoms (new) and neglected danger signals of serious illness may be checked. It is vital that all family members receive routine physical checkups, and it behooves the physician to express the concept of good physical health as an aid to recovery from grief and bereavement.

Chapter 36

NUTRITION DURING BEREAVEMENT

FREDERICK STARE

𝒩 utritional needs, both physiologic and psychologic, continue during periods of grief, whether the grief be due to the loss of a loved one, loss of hope, or loss of one's mental or physical well-being. But I am not aware of any particular nutrient, combination of nutrients, or foods or diets that have any unusual preventive or therapeutic effect on grief. On the other hand, I do not know of any specific nutritional researches on this important and common problem.

The cells of the body require nourishment in sorrow as in happiness. They need protein, glucose, the various vitamins, minerals, essential fatty acids, and water—the fifty some specific nutrients that make up good nutrition, the balanced diet. To obtain them, variety in food consumption is the key: (1) milk or its products; (2) meats, fish, poultry, or eggs as sources of nutritionally superior protein; (3) fruits and vegetables, and (4) cereals. Variety not only among these four basic food groups, but variety within these groups each day and at each meal is needed.

Portion size or quantities consumed can be small, but that they be consumed is important.

While the physiologic needs for nutrients are not known to be affected by grief, it is possible, in fact likely, that the psychologic values of food may be of increased importance. Eating has always been one of the pleasures of life as well as a necessity. Eating is comforting. Eating provides a sense of security. The giving and taking of food is a sign of affection and love. It is possible that during periods of grief five or six small meals rather than our customary three may help dispel or lessen the depth of one's grief.

It is important, most important, that the grief-stricken individual force himself, if necessary, to eat—to provide for the physiologic and psychologic needs of his body and soul.

Chapter 37

PSYCHOPHARMACOLOGICAL TREATMENT OF BEREAVEMENT AND ITS COMPLICATIONS

DONALD F. KLEIN; H. ROBERT BLANK

Medical practice today is indeed drug oriented. Fortunately, even overly severe and prolonged bereavement states have responded favorably to drug therapy, often as an adjunct to psychotherapy.

A preceding chapter developed the pattern of over-reaction to grief, and its effects on body function. In the following chapter, another pattern, that of pathological emotional involvement, is examined.

In offering the reader the information which follows, again it must be understood that neither the purpose for introducing these facts nor their implications should be misinterpreted. This information is intended solely to provide deeper insight into the full dimensions of grief and bereavement as well as, more specifically, to indicate an often appropriate method by which management of inordinately intense bereavement states can be accomplished; for in this context the use of therapeutic agents can be of great value in surmounting the bereavement state and speeding the timetable of recovery from bereavement. Even more specifically the reader is encouraged to consider this information for the purpose of discerning any unfavorable signs in his own grief. And, if these match too closely those spelled out in the following chapter, the bereaved should at least consider the advisability of consulting with his physician.

A.H.K.

The term *bereavement* is commonly limited to refer to the death of a loved one. The symptomatology of acute grief consists of a tendency toward sighing respiration, complaints of exhaustion and lack of strength, anorexia, feelings of unreality, increased emotional distress, and intense preoccupation with the image of the deceased. The bereaved often feels guilty, hostile, irritable, restless, unable to sit still, and is constantly searching for something to occupy time, although showing a painful lack of ability to initiate and maintain organized activity.

Such states of acute grief and mourning appear to be a necessary phase for a lasting, balanced detachment of the bereaved from the deceased, and the repatterning of his life to compensate for the loss of the beloved person. The links with the lost person are repeatedly reviewed, with much painful affect. Attempts to block the mourning process by means of heavy sedation seem to be futile for limited use, and unwise for prolonged administration. However, mild sedation or so-called minor tranquilization is often necessary, since patients in a severe mourning state may easily exhaust themselves and become prone to such disease states as may follow in consequence. Severe insomnia, in particular, should be treated, since deprivation of sleep has an extremely unstabilizing effect upon the central nervous system. Hence, the use of certain minor tranquilizers in moderate dosage is indicated at such times, for example, meprobamate (400-800 mg) three or four times daily or Librium® (10-25 mg) four times daily.

Minor tranquilizers are preferable to barbiturates, since suicide is much more difficult to accomplish with these drugs. The use of major tranquilizers or antidepressants is not indicated in simple bereavement and should be avoided unless the bereaved is suffering from a mourning state of a pathological nature.

COMPLICATIONS OF THE MOURNING PROCESS

All the states described below require skilled psychiatric management, experience and skill, the approach combining both psychotherapy and drug therapy.

Affect Block

Not infrequently, bereaved people who have been raised with a stoic code, in particular, males, pass into a state of marked emotional rigidity, woodenness, and tension, and are unable to relax and mourn for fear they might break down. This fear of being overwhelmed and unmanly is frequently severe, and attempts to engage these patients in exploration and discharge of feelings may be bluntly rejected. In these circumstances, the use of minor tranquilizers seems specifically indicated, since they reduce anticipatory anxiety, and the bereaved patient may engage in the mourning process without becoming overwhelmed. Paradoxically, these patients may appear more upset during "tranquilization."

Agitated Depression

Agitated depression, characterized by tension, agitation, and insomnia may stem from mourning. Marked guilt feelings and bitter self-accusations occur; the mourner may occasionally demonstrate a need for punishment, and have suicidal thoughts. The distinction between an agitated depression and an acute grief state is more than one of degree. The grief-stricken person is preoccupied with the image of the lost person and frequently spends much time crying and sighing. The patient suffering from an agitated depression is preoccupied with himself, his own feelings of mental pain, emptiness, and powerlessness, and often has no ability to cry or mourn. The first issue in the treatment of agitated depression, as with all potential psychoses, is evaluation of the risk to the patient or his environment caused by his illness. The most obvious concern is suicide. However, the patient may also cause marked damage to his business, social, or personal life and incur long-lasting intrafamilial difficulties. The degree of risk that can be tolerated is directly proportional to the structure and support that can be supplied. Obviously, patients who either live alone or with people who reject and misunderstand them are exposed to considerably more risk than patients surrounded by well-meaning, intelligent, and informed relatives.

Agitated depression responds quickly to active drug therapy utilizing major tranquilizers and the major depressants. Often, beneficial effects on agitation and insomnia occur even within the first few days of treatment.

The patient's depressive complaints eventually lose vigor. After two to three weeks of treatment, the depressive complaints diminish and may disappear altogether, to be replaced by denial and minimization of difficulty. However, after the patient has experienced one month of feeling relatively well, the medication may be reduced toward a standard maintenance dose.

Medication should not be discontinued for at least three to six months following remission. When it is discontinued, the patient should nevertheless remain in regular therapeutic contact so that the onset of recurrence, an all too frequent happening in this type of situation, may be detected. At present, we are ignorant of the precise indications for discontinuing the medication. Therefore, in view of the disruptive effects of relapse, conservative treatment should be maintained for a longer rather than a shorter period of time.

Psychotherapy and Milieu Treatment

Psychotherapy and environmental care are of marked importance in the care of the patient with agitated depression. In particular, life should be so structured as to prevent withdrawal, brooding, or ruminating. You cannot simply tell someone not to ruminate. What is required is structured distraction to force the bereaved patient's focus of attention outside himself, into the environment. This requires active patient participation. It is far more efficacious for a patient to be directed into some simple or even menial activity (e.g., scrubbing floors, washing windows), than to permit him to passively watch television, an activity from which he can rapidly become disengaged, introverted, and brooding. The agitated depressive should be directed to tasks which are simple, easily completed, and that have a clear goal in sight. Social support and interaction are of marked value. Supportive psychotherapy is probably best considered a specialized form of social support. Exploratory psychotherapy is largely ineffective during the depressed state, and attempts to engender insight are regularly misinterpreted as a severe reproach. For instance, it is not uncommon practice for patients with depressions to be told that they harbor tremendous hostility which they are turning against themselves. This interpretation, predicated on insight, regularly leads to further demoralization; the patient becomes convinced that he is a time bomb waiting to go off, and manifests consequent further reduction of engagement with the environment. For instance, one depressive patient complained of feelings of inadequacy about driving. It was suggested to her that this was due to her unconscious homicidal impulses, an "interpretation" which caused the patient to give up driving altogether.

Retarded Depression

Not infrequently, patients will pass from a mourning state through a mild agitated depression and into an unrecognized moderate retarded depression, characterized by chronic apathy, feelings of being overwhelmed, and demoralization. Such patients may become socially ineffective recluses. Effective intervention may require the use of a major antidepressant as well as psychotherapy. Such patients frequently misinterpret their pathological emotional state as the natural outcome of their loss and will consequently resist treatment.

Elation

A surprising reaction to bereavement may be one characterized by over-activity, no sense of loss, and expansive, adventurous, and oftimes foolish behavior. Such bereaved patients may invest unwisely, give away belongings, and lose friends and professional standing.

This behavior, which frequently has deleterious consequences to the patient, is often psychiatrically interpreted as a manifestation of guilt and self-punishment. It should be emphasized that this is an extremely serious matter in that the ill person may well, in addition, ruin himself socially and financially. Active intervention by means of drug therapy is absolutely mandatory.

Phobic-Anxious States

Another psychopathological state that can be a consequence of bereavement is the development of acute panic attacks related to the belief that the bereaved himself is in danger of dying. These panic attacks cause the patient to restrict his activities out of fear of being overwhelmed when alone. Such patients will not travel by themselves, and are frequently restricted to their home. They become extremely demanding of the attention of their family and utterly dependent.

Anticipatory anxiety is the fear that such a panic state may occur. Phobic reactions are characterized by a high level of anxiety and, consequently, the person will avoid all situations that may trigger a panic, e.g., being alone, traveling, etc. These patients are prone to addictive behavior with sedatives, alcohol, and stimulants. Psychotherapy as well as drug therapy is of major importance in the recovery of these bereaved persons. The minor tranquilizers are moderately effective in reducing anticipatory anxiety, although they rarely succeed in erasing it entirely. Antidepressant medication is essential for control of the panic states.

SUMMARY

In summary, grief and mourning are normal emotional consequences of profound loss. They usually do not require psychopharmacological intervention, although minor tranquilizers prevent extreme distress and exhaustion. However, a number of abnormal emotional states, that may occur as a consequence of bereavement, may require and will greatly benefit from psychopharmacological intervention.

D. F. K.

❂ ❂ ❂

MEDICATION FOR THE SYMPTOMS OF ACUTE GRIEF

Drugs are no substitute for the presence and availability of the physician for emotional support and counseling. Yet drugs frequently are useful, even life-saving. In my experience, insomnia is the most important target symptom. I often tell acutely depressed patients, "It is one thing for you to sweat out your painful depression and anxiety during the day; it is too much to expect you or anyone else to add insomnia to the ordeal." It is important to bear in mind that, in this age of pill-taking and addiction, one frequently finds resistance to taking prescribed medication among depressed persons, who typically have prominent guilt feelings and self-punitive tendencies.

Tranquilizers and antidepressant drugs also have their indications, particularly in the following types of cases:

1. When the bereaved is suffering from: cardiac illness, arthritis, hyperthyroidism, etc.

2. When the bereaved has learned of his loss suddenly, as in the case of accidental death, and the bereaved is first seen by the physician in a state of shock, or in such a state of acute grief that he is unable to communicate or take care of his personal needs.

3. Similar states seen in prolonged and pathologic mourning. If a man is unable to return to his job because of difficulty in concentration or other symptoms two weeks after his bereavement, and he is not under medical care, a trusted friend, relative or clergyman should arrange for medical consultation. An antidepressant or a combination of antidepressant and tranquilizer for such a person might make the difference between a chronic disabling depression and normal mourning while meeting one's work responsibilities. The physician can determine whether psychiatric consultation is required.

In talking about return to work within a week or two, I am not implying that the bereaved should be able to resume his work at peak efficiency. The fact is that most men and women feel like getting back to work in a week or two, and uniformly I get their report that they feel better working. Hence, if they cannot go back to work, it is wise to assume that certain symptoms are interfering, and that medical treatment might relieve these symptoms.

H. R. B.

PART VI

REBIRTH OF THE SPIRIT

Chapter 38

TIME

AUSTIN H. KUTSCHER

When one suffers a most grievous loss, many well-intentioned relatives and friends make attempts at consolation. Almost invariably, the classic cliche "time will heal the wound" is offered.

Although time has been, still is, and doubtless will continue to be, a great healer, time, for the bereaved, is a commodity which is, at best, a matter involved in the far distant future. It can neither be grasped in terms of present reality, nor does it have meaning at all in any catch-phrase or proverb, however well-intended. The good hearted purveyors of these platitudes (fortunately, indeed, for most of them) have obviously not been touched by the tragedy of deep loss.

It is, however, unrealistic to assume that nothing can be done except to wait for time to heal the wound, in whatever chance way this may come to pass. There are, simply, some right things to do in this situation—and some wrong ones. In point of fact, the firm conviction that planning—not drifting—is a better approach to the innumerable problems of grief, forms the basis for this multicontributor, multidiscipline volume.

Exhaustive material pertaining to the many-faceted aspects of time (physical, psychological, theological, philosophical, and so forth) appears in the literature. These brief remarks are in no way intended as competitive. They are merely an attempt to define several concepts of time, as these relate specifically to the subject of bereavement.

One thought remains acutely pertinent to time and grief: one cannot and should not expect that the passage of time itself will heal the wound in the shortest and best manner. Time does heal some of us in time, in and of itself; we are not denying

309

that. But in the terms of our work within this volume we must take the time concept further and insist that it is what the bereaved *does and accomplishes with this time* which determines how long it will take the wound to heal, and how successful the healing will be.

The therapeutic use of this time involves the reshuffling of old thoughts, the introduction of new thoughts and plans, the exploration of new trails in the company of old and new friends, a process of weaving the old life with a new one; immersion in all of life's interests, activities and responsibilities. Finally, it involves new relationships centered about persons (or one person) to care for, to give to . . . to love.

When these active, *not* passive pursuits—these energies, positive, *not* negative—have come to pass within the framework of a suitable period in time, the therapeutic results will be positive as well. Hope, and with it, *life* can be rekindled to a bright flame by that magic which is all too often referred to as "time alone."

Chapter 39

RENEWAL

AUSTIN H. KUTSCHER

So closely allied are the varied aspects of grief and bereavement that thought can scarcely be given to any one of them without touching upon a goodly number of other factors. In this volume, thus far, we have reflected upon the entire subject of grief resulting from bereavement, beginning with each facet of the individual's confrontation with life and death; from his realistic involvements to his psychological reactions. We have taken him through the labyrinth of emotional response to the inevitable conclusion . . . acceptance.

We must now proceed to the more tangible and practical areas and explore those means by which the bereaved can help himself to proceed successfully through the subsequent stages of his grief, toward his ultimate goal of complete recovery . . . his reentry into life and the pleasures of living. Far from being an act of disloyalty, or a sign of love forgotten, a return to living (no matter how tentative or hesitant the first steps may be) is, in truth, the greatest tribute the bereaved individual can pay to the memory of his loved one.

It is well within the realm of possibility, therefore, that within a relatively short space of time the bereaved may return to living in the terms so powerfully stated by Dryden:

> For all happiness mankind can gain
> Is not in pleasure but in rest from pain.

With the introduction of this concept, the theoretical concept of pleasure, at least, once again becomes tenable.

In what manner, then, can the bereaved bring himself to look (albeit reluctantly) upon pleasure? He must first rid himself of

311

the conviction that his present life *must* be devoid of all human joy. In the earliest stages of grief he finds himself deeply troubled by guilt and self-reproach. His loved one is gone, while *he* remains alive, daring even to think of peace, happiness and pleasure! This is the first obstacle to be met, complicated by added pressures imposed by his conscience, by his relatives and by the social structure of the culture in which he lives. Few bereaved persons are able to escape the social pressures from without or those inner, subconscious pressures which urge them to conform to a generally accepted timetable applying to grief and bereavement. These obstacles can and must be overcome, according to the approbation of clergyman, physicians, psychiatrists, psychologists and social scientists who have elected to advise the bereaved.

The world offers an endless array of diversions: reading, music, art, theatre, motion pictures, radio and television, sports, travel, crafts and hobbies, to name but a few. It matters not by what means the initial disengagement from a state of total bereavement is accomplished; when the mind of a bereaved person is opened in readiness to begin living again, the major step has been taken.

He must first consider whether he wishes to become involved in a chosen activity merely as a spectator, or, rather, as an active participant. Does he wish to read, or to write? He may be inclined to visit many museums of art; on the other hand, he may find special pleasure in one particular museum and prefer to revisit it. Perhaps he has a talent for painting. He may wish to study piano, or find that he enjoys music in the form of recordings or concert; there is, too, the symphony, opera, ballet and the musical theatre. A devotee of sports will find many avenues open to him, the events appearing regularly on television being the most conveniently accessible. Some people, however (provided that the physical activities involved are not too taxing), may need to expend their energies by flinging themselves into active sports participation. Golf, tennis, bowling, swimming . . . there are many sports from which a suitable selection can be made. Each individual must determine for himself which of these activities will afford him the most satisfying release from the tensions of his bereaved state.

One of my own tentative steps toward recovery from grief was to order tickets for myself and my sons to see the New York Mets play baseball. The season was not scheduled to open for several months, yet the mere thought of taking this step toward a pleasurable event, though still months away, was unbelievably painful. For me, the simple task of writing the letter for the tickets was the beginning.

The reader may well ask, at this point, "But how shall *I* begin?" The answer to this question is . . . there is no single way. There are myriad ways. I found one, and everyone can find one for himself, if he will but search it out and grasp it firmly when it comes into view.

Some bereaved persons may find, as I did, that music offers spiritual comfort. Music was the first outside influence that I found tolerable as a concomitant to my grief. Not being an opera or ballet devotee and finding the symphonic classical repertoire inexpressibly depressing at that time, I turned to the recordings of the musical theatre. The themes, as well as the music and lyrics, of the music dramas "Carousel" and "West Side Story" had always, for me, seemed poignantly sad. These were music dramas that did not offend my personal sensitivities, and I truly felt that they could not possibly offend others about me, nor would they heap upon my head accusations of improper, unloving or disrespectful conduct during a time of early bereavement. I was reintroduced to this music at my children's insistence that we watch together the showing of "Carousel" on television. How sad, yet how exalting is the music and the lyric of the song, "You'll Never Walk Alone." Thus, music, theatre, television, all intruded themselves, and, as time passed, they were to become increasingly *welcome* intruders.

If one has the means, travel may well be the turning point. There are many therapeutic aspects to travel. It can be regarded as escapism, a search for excitement, the gratification of a desire for exploration and adventure in new lands, an educational device and so forth. It is of interest to note, however, that a great many persons, traveling alone in a state of relatively recent bereavement, are taking journeys that were once a part of husband and wife planning (or, parent and child planning, in some cases).

Though now alone, the bereaved traveler can often enjoy the blessing of a strong spiritual bond with the departed, while, at the same time, taking that vital step forward to regain the pleasures of living. It is also well known that the special friendships acquired during these travels very often endure for a lifetime.

The bereaved who has an interest in a craft may find that what was once merely a hobby is, suddenly, a Godsend; and, there is always reading. Many suitable works are included in the bibliographics of this volume, as well as in the brief anthology of literature. If the individual wishes a broader variety of subject matter upon which to expand his reading, a trip to his public library can provide absorbing material in any field which may be of interest to him.

In time, these beginnings of renewal will lead to increased powers of enjoyment. The senses begin to reawaken . . . even, for example, so elemental and primary a sense as that of hunger. One begins to give thought, not merely to the taste of food, but to the symbolic breaking of bread as it used to be. Eating at home has no doubt remained a more or less perfunctory ritual; as the horizons of living widen, the taking of meals with relatives and friends reminds one of the modern custom of dining out. The first thoughts of dining at a restaurant pose new problems, very likely to express themselves by these questions . . . How can I dine there without my loved one? Shall I go to new places? Will it be the same? The answer to these and many other questions may safely be left to the decision (best come to, perhaps, by trial and error) of the individual.

One need not search too far for other opportunities to provide respite from grief and renewal of life. Close at hand may be a child with a fine report card, arousing conflicting feelings of pride and of great sadness that the loved one is not sharing this moment with you. There will be times when a friend or relative will engage you in a completely absorbing conversation, drawing you out so that you begin to feel almost like your former self. These pleasures will eventually cease to yield to feelings of self-reproach at the thought that you are permitting yourself to move out of the abyss of pain and sorrow.

A pet may again become a source of comfort. People who have never cared to own a pet may now find that they are, surprisingly, both pleased and delighted to have one . . . a puppy, for instance, in need of care as well as affection.

The television set provides much diversion and entertainment in almost every household. You may struggle against merriment in response to a television comedian, but a time will come when the laughter from the audience and that of your family will not intrude as harshly upon your mood. You will begin to think in these terms. . . . "Is it wrong to smile just a little, even at a time of grief? Should I not welcome a smile as a sign of some recovery? Will my friends continue to seek me out if my sorrow is forever mirrored in my face?"

You will now begin to consider the satisfactions of companionship and will gradually seek it. Whereas, until this point in time, you have barely been able to tolerate yourself, you begin to understand that renewed sociability is imperative . . . that family, friends *and* new acquaintances alike must be accorded a place in your life. Each person naturally gravitates to those who are most interesting to him, and you will find new friends of both sexes companionable and comforting. Eventually, you will enjoy being among people for longer periods of time; perhaps one day you may even come to love one particular person . . . a companion whose presence fills you with happiness.

Whenever the bereaved can bring himself to consider the subject of remarriage, an important step in recovery will have been made. Initially, every bereaved person believes this to be an impossibility, but some thought, at least, must be given to it, difficult though it may be. He will, I think, at this point in his convalescence from grief, realize that his greatest source of comfort has come from love itself: the love of his children, the love of his parents, the deep love of friendship. So that, when that special person appears . . . the right person . . . once more can he experience fully the joy of living with someone with whom he can share his life through remarriage.

Remarriage, as we have stated earlier in this volume, has the deeply considered, authoritative approval of all groups who have studied the subject. The clergy, sociologists, psychiatrists, philosophers, the testimony of the Bible and the God-given inclinations of man attest to the reality of two basic human requirements: the need for love and the need to love.

It may be said, in the final analysis, that whenever and by whatever means one learns anew that happiness is more than the mere absence of pain, he will have regained, with greater appreciation than ever, the pleasures of living.

Chapter 40

CREATIVE GRIEF

JOSEPH BESS; GENE E. BARTLETT

All normal patterns of grief are closely related in terms of their final transcendence of grief. Creative grief, however, represents a different path in the direction of such recovery. Creative grief might be considered both as a reflection of an abiding love for the deceased as well as the response of a bereaved person who does not content himself with only the usual "work of mourning." It encompasses a certain purpose or goal to be sought and finally attained.

It is a realistic hypothesis that everyone has within himself a seed of creativity. The bereaved, in addition, experiences a catastrophic event that may cause such seeds to germinate and may flower into a truly beneficent response to his bereavement. Creative grief may be expressed, among other ways, by bequeathing a memorial monument, a hospital bed, a personally assembled art collection or a museum exhibit, a library; by organizing a permanent group or society or foundation; by undertaking or sponsoring a research program befitting the circumstances, and so forth. In still another context, such grief might take the form of an artistic creation such as a symphony, a song, a book, or a poem inspired by the loved one's memory.

However, it is pertinent to question whether the presence or existence of tangible productive works, monuments, or grief-inspired gifts to mankind are the *sine qua non* of creative grief. What of him who lacks artistic talents, material wealth, and intellectual interests but who nonetheless experiences genuine grief to the depths and core of his being?

In answer it should be stated categorically that an adequate description of creative grief extends beyond the tangible. We must also consider acts of the human personality as expressions of creative grief, acts which result in the enrichment of the human spirit, heart or soul—those acts which have a real and enduring inspirational influence on the lives of all who are touched by them.

The above should provide us with a better understanding of the individual who expresses grief in this fashion. While resolving his own grief, he ensures the continuation of the joy and sorrow of the past. Through his creativity he transcends his own individual grief and transforms it into a universal good.

J. B.

* * *

ACHIEVING CREATIVE GRIEF

Will the grief absorb the person or will the person absorb the grief? If the former, then the life of the bereaved virtually comes to a standstill. There is loss of energy, a progressively demanding grief, a mounting self-absorption whose issue is a misery as intense as any known to man. But if, in due time, it is the person who absorbs the grief, then whole dimensions are added to his remaining years, dimensions which come only through the conquest of suffering.

We will never be able to measure that amount of the world's work for human welfare which has been made possible by the energies first released in sorrow. Perhaps it is motivation like that of the great Quaker philosopher Rufus Jones, who is reputed to have kept near him for forty years the portrait of a son who died as a small boy. Closest friends say that the philosopher never lost the sense that he must be a father whose life would be respected by a growing boy.

In whatever form it may appear, the outlet for our sorrow often may lie in ministry to the wider needs of the world or in the unending battle against injustice. A world marked by such needs offers many saving outlets to those who must ask, Where do I use the passion of my grief?

G. E. B.

Chapter 41

REMARRIAGE

FREDERIC HERTER, JOSEPH C. LANDRUD, ELIZABETH L. POST,
ROSE N. FRANZBLAU, ROBERT MICHELS, AND RALPH OBER

𝓝o consideration of this entire area of concern would be remotely complete without earnest elaboration on the subject of remarriage. What we would like to bring to the reader's attention has all been succinctly discussed in the book *But Not to Lose* (Austin H. Kutscher, Editor, Frederick Fell, New York, New York, 1969). Hence, we present here, in lieu of restatements, the following direct quotations:

A.H.K.

A PHYSICIAN'S VIEW

Frederic P. Herter

It has been my observation that the happily married individual is the first to become remarried after the loss of husband or wife. This appears at first paradoxical, but I think the explanation can be found in the fact that these people have become dependent on a totally shared existence for their happiness. Grief at their loss is soon supplanted by a renewed need for both giving and accepting love, and it is not surprising to find that these second marriages are usually extremely happy ones. It is also not surprising that a certain degree of guilt accompanies the second courtship and the initial phases of the remarriage. Months before, it seemed quite inconceivable that any further personal relationships could ever be entered into. To love another, fully and with intensity, appeared impossible. Did not such a new relationship, in fact, lessen or negate the validity of the shared happiness of the first marriage? Was not that first love a hollow and transitory liaison, to be forgotten and violated at the first opportunity?

319

Could not a new attachment be construed as gross infidelity? The answer of course lies in the fact that the capacity for love is infinite in its scope and must find some vehicle for expression; it does not die with the death of a loved one, but rather reroutes itself into other channels. Such is the essential nature of man.

SEXUALITY AND BEREAVEMENT

Robert Michels

Death and sex are two topics that are extremely difficult to discuss openly in contemporary society. Both involve strong emotions deeply rooted in the most private areas of one's life.

The death of a loved one, any loved one, invariably affects one's attitudes, feelings, and behavior insofar as sex is concerned. But the death of a spouse or the sexual partner produces a more direct and dramatic effect.

Grief over the loss of any loved person not only affects attitudes toward personal sexual behavior but also influences basic sexual drives. An individual who has suffered a recent loss has little interest in his usual activities, including sexual activities. This diminished interest in sex is accompanied by an increased desire for tender, loving contact with the sexual partner. An understanding partner can provide this contact and, as the bereaved individual experiences a return of his normal sexual drives, he can gradually restore the relationship to its previous pattern.

The relationship between *husband and wife* is the most intimate and all encompassing one in our society. When death severs this relationship, the surviving partner often reacts in an exaggerated form. He no longer has a sexual partner to whom he can turn. His pain is intensified since the loss has deprived him of the usual mechanism of repair. Even the thought of seeking affection or physical love elsewhere makes him feel guilty.

This problem, like death itself, seems insoluble. The individual may attempt to deny his sexual feelings or to gratify them by means of loveless relationships or masturbation. Even in the absence of bereavement such behavior may often be associated with guilt and anxiety. In the setting of grief these responses are accentuated. The bereaved's preoccupation with his loss makes is impossible for him to take the first necessary step toward the development of another sexual relationship until, at the least, he has achieved partial recovery from the pain of the loss.

There is no easy solution. It is useful, however, to regard this problem as inevitable and face it openly. The individual must maintain his social and family relationships for emotional support during the crisis. He must realize that his transiently-diminished sexual impulses will be restored and that one of the problems which he faces is to find a way to gratify them. He must recognize that any possible solution may include patterns of behavior which might, consciously or unconsciously, lead to anxiety and guilt. He must strive to gratify his sexual needs with a minimum of distress and to continue his life as fruitfully as possible.

A MINISTER'S VIEW

Joseph C. Landrud

As we experience release from paralyzing guilt, it is natural that we return to life with a steadily increasing eagerness and zest. We emerge from the cold deep well of self-confinement into the warming sun of revitalizing personal relationships. Before we know it, we may even find ourselves in love again. This is both wonderful and frightening. It is wonderful because it is unexpected, unplanned, yet we have the happy realization that the void in our lives is filled with new love. But it is frightening to acknowledge that it has actually happened, frightening to admit to ourselves that we are in love again.

Such a new love may seem to minimize or even cheapen the love we felt for our now-deceased mate. True, by this time we are freed of the guilt in connection with that earlier death. But now, by virtue of our new love, we may begin to feel guilty about not feeling guilty.

The way out of this seeming impasse is to return in meditation to the *quality* of our love relationship with the departed. Was that love relationship truly free, spontaneous, self-giving and life-affirming? If so, it is without end and nonlimiting. It is no healthy testimony to the quality of our love for someone to say that when he or she died our ability to love also died. Authentic love which, in its deepest form is the love of God expressed through us to all, without limit and without end, could certainly find a new object in the world around us. It is this deep and limit-less love that truly makes us free.

A PSYCHOLOGIST'S VIEW

Rose N. Franzblau

Where there has been a good first marriage, the chances for a good remarriage are greater. In the original loving relationship, tensions, disagreements and hurts are worked out amicably. Differences are taken in stride because the love for the other is great and real, and guilt over unresolved conflicts is minimal.

The person needs to adjust step by step and area by area to a life without the departed loved one. When the reality that the beloved partner will never return has been accepted, the bereaved can feel free to face life again and to want a new love and a new marriage. It can be like a cherished theme of love, played now as a reprise.

Engaging once again in a lovelife gives them a reason for living and strengthens their drive to survive. In a remarriage, each brings a lot of the past, old memories, feelings, and attitudes relating to the first marriage, into the new union. Often a most important living part and symbol of the past is the children of their first marriage. These are constant reminders of the first love in the other's life.

A pair who remarry feel that life has favored them, and that they are fortunate to be wanted in love, all over again. After all, to the couple it is a new and gratifying experience which is expressed physically, emotionally and psychologically.

Awareness of the normal problems that take place in such a remarriage is the first step toward happy adjustment. The second is acceptance of these problems as characteristic of such situations, and not implying any reflection upon themselves or others. The third and final step is putting this awareness and acceptance into action, by working out all difficulties lovingly and patiently.

Just as the new couple are adjusting to each other, the family and friends must adjust to them. They, too, need time to do so.

When the youngsters in the family see their parent's new life continuing and blossoming, their faith in the continuity in life and happiness is reaffirmed. Then they can give up the feeling, born of their tragedy, that when the life of their beloved parent ended, all hope of happiness in their own life came to an end as well. In giving renewal to each other, the couple also gives new hope and a love of life to their children.

PARENTS WITHOUT PARTNERS

Ralph Ober

It becomes a cruel fact of life that the single parent faces various kinds of discrimination. The prejudice takes numerous forms. The welcome one has when he is a married parent is quickly dissipated, once a mate is lost. Married friends show in many ways that they would rather not maintain a close relationship with a person now widowed, divorced, or separated. To the married woman, a single female parent represents a kind of threat to her own marriage. The lone woman might lure away her husband. To the married man, the converse is true. The unattached, formerly married male friend might have covetous eyes for his wife.

As for children living in one-parent homes, they are made aware in many ways that they are different. They feel a special status in the community and in school. Their playmates may poke fun at them or look down on them because they do not have two parents. Married parents of their playmates may lock the door to them for various reasons. A number of colleges and private schools about the country pry into the lives of children who come from single-parent homes. One major state university in New York queried applicants applying for admission on their parents' marital status.

Facing such problems and recognizing the need of single parents and their children to find a kind of "way station" in their period of adjustment following the dissolution of a marriage, Parents Without Partners set about the task of developing activities and programs which would serve a common purpose.

The purposes of the organization are basically educational. Professional help is employed in numerous chapter activities, which include discussion groups on various subjects of special concern to single parents and their children. Therapy for both parents and their children is made available. All chapters must conduct a broad program of children's activities to comply with the requirements of the international by-laws in addition to programs for the social and recreational needs of single parents.

ETIQUETTE

Elizabeth L. Post

The question of whether a bereaved person wishes to marry again is, of course, a purely personal one. Many people cannot conceive of living with anyone other than the one they have lost. Others feel this way at the moment of bereavement, but gradually change their minds as time heals their wounds, or their loneliness increases. Still others realize shortly after the death occurs, or even beforehand in the case of a prolonged illness, that they undoubtedly will want to marry again. This is often true of people who have been very happily married and enjoyed a relationship of mutual trust and understanding. Although they realize that a second marriage may not provide exactly the same relationship as the first, they are fully aware of the joy and companionship that a good marriage brings, and do not wish to go through the rest of their lives alone.

There is no longer any objection, as far as etiquette is concerned, to a widow's or widower's starting to see members of the opposite sex as soon as he, or she, wishes. It may be with remarriage in mind, or it may be that one enjoys the company of the opposite sex. But to become publicly engaged very shortly after a bereavement would show little respect for the deceased. In ordinary circumstances, a bereaved person should wait nine or ten months before announcing an engagement, and approximately a year before remarrying. Of course there are perfectly acceptable reasons for shortening these times, such as the imminent departure of one or the other for overseas military service. But under normal circumstances, a reasonable wait serves several purposes: it softens the shock which the family of the deceased may feel when they are told of the proposed remarriage; it allows any children involved to come to know the future step-parent; it indicates a respect for the deceased; and, most important, it allows the bereaved person sufficient time to be sure of his, or her, own emotional stability and rational approach to remarriage.

PART VII

A SELECTED ANTHOLOGY
OF THE
CLASSICAL LITERATURE

Great literature gives no sterile promise of comfort to man, no concise solutions for insoluable suffering, no easy formulae for the ageless enigma of death, no single philosophy for living and dying, loving and grieving. Rather, the great literature of every age fuses all that life contains—worlds of light and darkness, illusions and realities, beauty and ugliness, promises and deceptions, imprisonment and freedom. It is the distillation, expansion and transcendence of life. New meanings, insights, and dimensions are brought to consciousness.

Anguish of the soul wants no easy comforters nor false prophets of joy and peace. Perhaps it is the full acknowledgment of utter despair and the total confrontation with complete aloneness that matters the most to the bereaved and must be understood. The anguished soul rejects the cry of "Peace, peace; when there is no peace." Most importantly, perhaps, the anguished soul needs and craves the echo and reflection of its own grief and sorrow.

Certain works of tragedy, comedy, poetry and drama reflect the varieties of grief and, at the same time, represent the continuing voices of life. Within each successive stage of bereavement, man's grief is in turn deepened, assuaged, heightened, mitigated, absolved and immortalized by the voices of the poets. And gradually and steadfastly, the rhythm and rhyme of life begin to pulsate again and to be felt once more. In the eternity of time, there remain the resonant and elegaic refrain, the haunting melody, the quavering recitative, the spectral image of the lost love, the lost dream, the lost world.

(O lost, and by the wind grieved, ghost, come back again)

BEHIND THE VEIL

A Literary Mosaic of Grief

SANDRA BESS

Dissolve, thick cloud and rain; that I may say
The gods themselves do weep!

WILLIAM SHAKESPEARE, *Antony and Cleopatra*

Is it nothing to you, all ye that pass by?
behold, and see if there be any sorrow
like unto my sorrow.

OLD TESTAMENT, *Lamentations*

You say that she is dead.
    How can that be?
When life himself is dead
    Tell that to me.
You could as soon divide
    Mountain from mountain side.
It is the world that died.
    It is not she.

CHAUNCEY DEVEREUX STILLMAN, *Bereavement*

O life as futile, then, as frail!
    O for thy voice to soothe and bless!
    What hope of answer or redress?
Behind the veil, behind the veil.

ALFRED LORD TENNYSON, *In Memoriam*

Alas; that all we loved of him should be,
But for our grief, as if it had not been,
And grief itself be mortal! Woe is me!
Whence are we, and why are we? of what scene
The actors or spectators? Great and mean
Meet massed in death, who lends what life must borrow.
As long as skies are blue, and fields are green,
Evening must usher night, night urge the morrow,
Month follow month with woe, and year wake year to sorrow.

PERCY BYSSHE SHELLEY, *Adonais*

. . . I will not hold back
these mad cries of misery, so long as I live.
For who . . . who that thought right
would believe there were suitable comforting
words for me?
Forbear, forbear, my comforters.
These ills of mine shall be called cureless
and never shall I give over my sorrow,
and the number of my dirges none shall tell.

SOPHOCLES, *Electra*

Thus, thus, and thus, we compass round
    Thy harmlesse and unhaunted ground,
And as we sing thy dirge, we will
            The Daffodill
And other flowers lay upon
The altar of our love, thy stone. . .
Sleep in thy peace, thy bed of spice,
And make this place all Paradise . . .

ROBERT HERRICK, *Dirge of Jephtha*

Then shall the dust return to the earth as it was; and the spirit shall
return unto God who gave it.

OLD TESTAMENT, *Ecclesiastes*

(O lost, and by the wind grieved, ghost, come back again)

Men search out God and searching find him.

AESCHYLUS, *Agamemnon*

Ye cannot find the depth of the heart of man,
neither can ye perceive the things that he thinketh:
then how can ye search out God, that hath made all
these things, and know his mind, or comprehend his
purpose?

THE APOCRYPHA, *The Book of Judith*

How may son of dust find words,
so pure, so light, so luminous,
that they can rise up from the earth?
. . . translate for me,
this lamentation into speech
fit for Immortal ears.

AUGUST STRINDBERG, *A Dream Play*

I shall come to one place, I shall pray there, and before I have time
to grow used to it, to love it, I shall go on further. And I shall go on
till my legs give way under me and I lie down somewhere, and reach
at last that quiet, eternal haven, where is neither sorrow nor sighing! . . .

LEO TOLSTOY, *War and Peace*

. . . And if by prayer
Incessant I could hope to change the will
Of him who all things can, I would not cease
To waery him with my assiduous cries;
But prayer against his absolute decree
No more avails than breath against the wind,

Blown stifling back on him that breathes it forth:
Therefore to his great bidding I submit.

JOHN MILTON, *Paradise Lost*

What *is* the Almighty that we should serve him?
and what profit should we have, if we pray unto
him?

OLD TESTAMENT, *Book of Job*

Call it, then, what thou wilt,—
Call it Bliss! Heart! Love! God!
I have no name to give it!
Feeling is all in all:
The Name is sound and smoke,
Obscuring Heaven's clear glow.

JOHANN WOLFGANG VON GOETHE, *Faust*

. . . what in me is dark
Illumine, what is low raise and support;
That to the highth of this great argument
I may assert Eternal Providence
And justify the ways of God to man.

JOHN MILTON, *Paradise Lost*

. . . and see that man's ways, even at his best
are far from God's as earth is from the heaven
whose swiftest wheel turns above all the rest.

DANTE ALIGHIERI, *The Purgatorio*

(O lost, and by the wind grieved, ghost, come back again)

. . . And thus the heart will break, yet brokenly live on . . .

LORD BYRON, *Childe Harold's Pilgrimage*

For it so falls out
That what we have we prize not to the worth
Whiles we enjoy it, but being lack'd and lost,
Why, then we rack the value; then we find
The virtue that possession would not show us
Whiles it was ours.

WILLIAM SHAKESPEARE, *Much Ado About Nothing*

Ay, go to the grave of buried love and
meditate! There settle the account with thy
conscience for every past benefit unrequited—
every past endearment unregarded, of that
departed being, who can never, never, never
return to be soothed by thy contrition!

WASHINGTON IRVING, *Rural Funerals*

Away! we know that tears are vain.
That death nor heeds nor hears distress:

Will this unteach us to complain?
Or make one mourner weep the less?
And thou—who tell'st me to forget,
    Thy looks are wan, thine eyes are wet.

        Lord Byron, *Oh! Snatch'd Away in Beauty's Bloom*

When you and I behind the Veil are past,
Oh but the long, long while the World shall last,
    Which of our Coming and Departure heeds
As the sea's self should heed a pebble-cast.

        Edward Fitzgerald, Jr., *Rubaiyat of Omar Khayyam*

    As for man, his days are as grass:
as a flower of the field, so he flourisheth.
    The wind passeth over it, and it is gone;
and the place thereof shall know it no more.

        Old Testament, *Psalms*

    O, call back yesterday, bid time return!

        William Shakespeare, *King Richard II*

(O lost, and by the wind grieved, ghost, come back again)

And hope, against my will, slipped into my heart

> JEAN BAPTISTE RACINE, *Phèdre*

     . . . he, within
Took measure of his soul, and knew its strength,
And by that silent knowledge, day by day,
Was calm'd, enobled, comforted, sustain'd.

> MATTHEW ARNOLD, *Mycerinus*

Man by suffering shall learn.
So the heart of him, again
Aching with remembered pain,
Bleeds and sleepeth not, until
Wisdom comes against his will.

> AESCHYLUS, *Agamemnon*

O hope, misery's comforter,
Don't make such a din in my ears

With all thy marvelous promises
That only deceive a heart in pain.

CHARLES D'ORLEANS, *Chanson*

. . . yes, in spite of all,
Some shape of beauty moves away the pall
From our dark spirits . . .

JOHN KEATS, *Endymion*

Tho' much is taken, much abides; and tho'
We are not now that strength which in old days
Moved earth and heaven; that which we are, we are;
One equal temper of heroic hearts,
Made weak by time and fate, but strong in will
To strive, to seek, to find, and not to yield.

ALFRED LORD TENNYSON, *Ulysses*

. . . O Wind,
If Winter comes, can Spring be far behind?

PERCY BYSSHE SHELLEY, *Ode to the West Wind*

(O lost, and by the wind grieved, ghost, come back again)

. . . As the west wind lifts up again the heads of the wheat which were bent down and lodged in the storm, and combs out the matted and dishevelled grass as it lay in night-locks on the ground, so we let in time as a drying wind to the seedfield of thoughts which are dark and wet and low bent. Time restores to them temper and elasticity . . . new hopes spring, new affections twine and the broken is whole again.

RALPH WALDO EMERSON, *The Tragic*

. . . Living tones are we, we sound
together in thy harmony, Nature! . . . what,
then is death and all the woe of men?
. . . Like lovers' quarrels are the disso-
nances of the world. Reconciliation is
there, even in the midst of strife, and
all things that are parted find one
another again.

FRIEDRICH HÖLDERLIN, *Hyperion*

. . . it seems to me that love of some kind is the only possible explanation of the extraordinary amount of suffering that there is in the world.
I cannot conceive of any other explanation. I am convinced that there is
no other, and that if the world has indeed . . . been built of sorrow, it
has been built by the hands of love, because in no other way could the
soul of man, for whom the world was made, reach the full stature of its
perfection. Pleasure for the beautiful body, but pain for the beautiful soul.

OSCAR WILDE, *De Profundis*

Joy and woe are woven fine
A clothing for the soul divine;

Under every grief and pine
Runs a joy with silken twine.

> WILLIAM BLAKE, *Auguries of Innocence*

Grief melts away,
Like snow in May,
As if there were no such cold thing.

Who would have thought my shrivel'd heart
Could have recover'd greenesse? It was gone
Quite underground; as flowers depart
To see their mother-root . . .

> GEORGE HERBERT, *The Flower*

Now, as the spring grows warm, Time, revolving in its perpetual round, again calls back the west winds. Mother earth, refreshed, puts on her brief youth and now, loosened from frost, the ground turns green and sweet. Am I deceived, or is my power of song also returning, and has inspiration come to me through the bounty of spring? Through the bounty of spring it has come and again gains strength . . .

> JOHN MILTON, *Elegy V: On The Coming of Spring*

For, lo! the winter is past,
the rain is over and gone;
the flowers appear on the earth;
the time of the singing of birds is come,
and the voice of the turtle
is heard in the land.

> OLD TESTAMENT, *The Song of Solomon*

(O lost, and by the wind grieved, ghost, come back again)

Another book was opened
Which is the book of life

NEW TESTAMENT, *Revelation*

What though the radiance which was once so bright
Be now forever taken from my sight,
      Though nothing can bring back the hour
Of splendor in the grass, of glory in the flower;
        We will grieve not, rather find
        Strength in what remains behind;
        In the primal sympathy
        Which having been must ever be;
        In the soothing thoughts that spring
        Out of human suffering;
        In the faith that looks through death,
In years that bring the philosophic mind.

WILLIAM WORDSWORTH, *Intimations of Immortality*
from Recollections of Early Childhood

The smallest sprout shows there is really no death,
And if ever there was it led forward life, and does
      not wait at the end to arrest it,
And ceas'd the moment life appear'd.
All goes onward and outward, nothing collapses . . .

WALT WHITMAN, *Song of Myself*

Ah, happy, happy boughs! that cannot shed
   Your leaves, nor ever bid the Spring adieu;
And, happy melodist, unwearied,
   For ever piping songs for ever new;

More happy love! more happy, happy love!
For ever warm and still to be enjoyed,
 For ever panting, and for ever young;
All breathing human passion far above,
That leaves a heart high-sorrowful and cloyed,
 A burning forehead, and a parching tongue.

JOHN KEATS, *Ode on A Grecian Urn*

Death, be not proud, though some have called thee
Mighty and dreadful, for thou art not so;
For those, whom thou think'st thou dost overthrow,
Die not, poor Death, nor yet canst thou kill me . . .
One short sleep past, we wake eternally,
And Death shall be no more; Death, thou shalt die.

JOHN DONNE, *Holy Sonnet X*

. . . And thus we, night wanderers through a stormy and dismal world, if we bear the lamp of Faith, enkindled at a celestial fire, it will surely lead us home to that heaven whence its radiance was borrowed.

NATHANIEL HAWTHORNE, *Night Sketches*

Angels are bright still, though the brightest fell.

WILLIAM SHAKESPEARE, *Macbeth*

Look homeward, Angel, now . . .

JOHN MILTON, *Lycidas*

(*O lost, and by the wind grieved, ghost, come back again*)

THOMAS WOLFE, *Look Homeward Angel*

PART VIII

REFERENCES

GRIEF AND BEREAVEMENT: A SELECTED ANNOTATED BIBLIOGRAPHY OF BEHAVIORAL SCIENCE AND PSYCHIATRIC WRITINGS

RICHARD A. KALISH

A n annotated bibliography on bereavement, unavailable elsewhere, is presented here primarily for the benefit of the considerable number of bereaved persons who are engaged in or oriented to the health sciences and paramedical areas, and to whom such reading matter is both accessible and of interest.

A.H.K.

INTRODUCTION

The origins of the following bibliography can be traced to the fall of 1964, when the present compiler mimeographed and distributed a bibliography of 340 titles, partially annotated, covering the entire topic of death and bereavement; a few months later a supplement of sixty-eight titles was issued. The winter 1965 issue of the *Journal of Human Relations* published a slightly augmented version, although without annotations. Smith, Kline, and French reproduced and distributed both the initial compilation and the supplement.

Continued efforts to keep the bibliography up to date have resulted in the addition of innumerable new items. What was once a bare trickle of articles has become a healthy stream. Many of these newer writings have been abstracted and cited in *Omega,* a quarterly newsletter co-edited by the author and Robert Kastenbaum, Ph.D. The bibliography in this volume is only a small fraction of the entire collection dealing with the topics of grief and bereavement.

Only English-language publications have been abstracted: only the topics of psychology, sociology, and psychiatry are scrutinized thoroughly. Anthropology, nursing, general medicine, gerontology, mental health, and theology have all made major contributions to this compilation.

Many people have aided in this final product. Among the more notable have been Drs. James Averill (University of California, Berkeley), Lenin Baler (University of Michigan), Robert Fulton (University of Minnesota), Peggy Golde (Stanford University), and Alex Portz (Huron Valley Child Guidance Clinic), all of whom have published bibliographies from which I borrowed freely; also Mrs. William Blau, Mrs. Barbara Kalish, Mr. Murray Kane, Miss Katherine Langston, Miss Ann Johnson, and Mrs. Marian Selvin, who have shared the responsibility for gathering materials and writing many of the abstracts.

An additional source of bibliographic material should be noted. In his book, *Modern Man and Mortality* (Macmillan, 1964), Dr. Jacques Choron has presented a bibliography of some 400 titles dealing with death and bereavement. Taking a more historical and philosophical stance, Dr. Choron's sources have relatively little overlap with those presented here. Also, many non-English sources are cited in this book.

R.A.K.

ALDRICH, C. K.: The dying patient's grief. *Journal of the American Medical Association, 184*:329–331, 1963.

Criticizing the traditional determinants of a person's ability to accept death, this study explains the psychology of the dying patient from the perspective that loss of personal interrelations is more important than fear of dying. The effects of this approach are explored with respect to who should be told of impending death; the resulting interface with grief of others for the dying patient; the denial-acceptance spectrum; and the consequently defined role of the doctor.

ALVAREZ, WALTER C.: Care of the dying. *Journal of the American Medical Association, 150*:86–91, 1952.

A physician relates from his own experience techniques in dealing with the dying patient and the family. Frankness, honesty, kindness, compassion, and comfort are the keys to easing the suffering of these patients as well as encouraging them to make the most of the time left to them.

ARCHIBALD, HERBERT C.; BELL, D.; MILLER, C.; and TUDDENHAM, R. D.:

Bereavement in childhood and adult psychiatric disturbance. *Psychosomatic Medicine,* 24:343–351, 1962.

This article is another statement of the important bearing of psychic trauma in childhood on the mental health of the adult. The incidence of childhood bereavement was determined for a serial sample of 1000 patients in a Veterans Administration mental hygiene outpatient clinic and compared with normative incidence estimates obtained by the Metropolitan Life Insurance Company and with results of other investigations of childhood bereavement. The group studied, in agreement with other reports, showed an appreciably greater frequency of bereavement in childhood generally than did the general population. The authors believe that the loss of a parent in early life constitutes a "nonspecific trauma" whose effects depend upon complex interactions among such variables as sex, biogenetic vulnerability, parent surrogates, type of loss, availability of compensatory supports, and developmental status. There remains the possibility that with enough cases and a finer age classification, it may be demonstrated that psychiatric vulnerability is greatest at specific developmental stages.

ARTHUR, BETTIE, and KEMME, MARY L.: Bereavement in childhood. *Journal of Child Psychology and Psychiatry,* 5:37–49, 1964.

An intensive case study of the families of eighty-three disturbed children who had experienced the death of a parent revealed a high incidence of both intellectual and emotional problems either directly or indirectly related to the loss. There was both transitory and permanent disruption of the child's pattern of adaptation.

BALER, LENIN A., and GOLDE, PEGGY J.: Conjugal bereavement: a strategic area of research in preventive psychiatry. *Working Papers in Community Health (Harvard School of Public Health),* 2, 1964.

A discussion of theoretical and research implications of recently bereaved widows as a source of information regarding crises. A seventeen-page bibliography is included.

BARRY, HERBERT JR.; BARRY, HERBERT III, and LINDEMANN, ERICH: Dependency in adult patients following early maternal bereavement. *Journal of Nervous and Mental Disease,* 140:196–206, 1965.

Characteristics of adult psychiatric patients, from both mental clinics and private practices, who suffered a bereavement early in life (between 3 and 48 months old) were compared to those of other psychiatric patients who suffered a later bereavement (between 11 and 17 years old). Comparison of symptoms, personality features, sex, age, marital status, and socioeconomic status showed a statistically significant difference in the dependency character. Dependency was a prominent characteristic of thirteen of the first group, and of only four of the second group (each group numbered 15 persons).

BARRY, HERBERT, and LINDEMANN, ERICH: Critical ages for maternal bereavement in psychoneuroses. *Psychosomatic Medicine*, 22:166–181, 1960.

Maternal bereavement was found to be significantly more frequent in a series of 947 psychoneurotics than in the total population. The impact of the maternal death was most pronounced in early childhood and in female patients. In females, especially those under nine years of age, the effect was traumatic; when the child was under three, it was even more severe.

BECKER, HOWARD: Some forms of sympathy. *Journal of Abnormal and Social Psychology*, 26:58–68, 1931.

Sympathy is a term with a long and varied history; but, instead of gaining in precision and definiteness, it has gradually become one of the vaguest concepts with which the social psychologist has to deal. The author feels that a point has now been reached where it must either be discarded or given a precise limited meaning. This paper, in an attempt to do the latter, becomes an exercise in semantics. In the course of analyzing the various facets, factors, and components involved, the following types of "sympathy" have been distinguished: compathy or emotional solidarity; mimpathy or emotional imitation; sympathy or emotional participation; transpathy or emotional contagion; empathy or emotional intuition; and unipathy or emotional identification. According to the author, these are only some of the forms usually lumped together under the term *sympathy*.

BECKER, HOWARD: The sorrow of bereavement. *Journal of Abnormal and Social Psychology*, 27:391–410, 1933.

Exposition of the theories and empirical principles of sorrow, with illustrations drawn from case studies made by the writer. The variety of expression shown includes the type that gives free vent to its violence in outward behavior; the type that is tearless and mute; the type that sinks under the sense of weakness and discouragement; and the type that engages in activity approaching frenzy.

BECKER, HOWARD: Separation anxiety. *International Journal of Psychoanalysis*, 41:89–113, 1960.

Because of their survival value, instinctual responses that the mother satisfies, such as crying, smiling, sucking, clinging and following, result in mother-child ties. Thus attachment results. When the mother is not available, protest behavior and separation anxiety result. Separation anxiety, grief, and mourning are intrinsically related because they are the result of the temporary or permanent loss of the mother-figure. Liability of feeling, separation anxiety, and grief are the unavoidable risks of attachment to a loved object.

BECKER, HOWARD: Grief and mourning in infancy and early childhood. *Psychoanalytical Study of the Child*, 15:9–52, 1960.

This article demonstrates the reality and duration of grief and of the psychological processes of mourning in very young children, from six months of age onward, and the intimate relationship that grief has to separation anxiety. Bowlby questions the common assumption that in regard to future capacity to make object relations, loss of breast at weaning is the most significant loss sustained by the infant and young child. Role of weaning needs to be evaluated afresh in the light of more systematic evidence and should not be allowed to obscure the significance of loss of the mother figure during the early years.

BECKER, HOWARD: Separation anxiety: A critical review of the literature. *Journal of Child Psychology and Psychiatry*, 1:251–269, 1960–1961.

An examination of the literature shows that there are, at present, six main theories to account for separation anxiety. These are the theories of Transformed Libido, Birth Trauma, Signal Anxiety, Depressive Anxiety, Persecutory Anxiety, and Primary Anxiety. Whereas three of them (Birth Trauma, Signal Anxiety, and Primary Anxiety) were developed explicitly to account for the observation that young children are anxious when their mothers leave them, the other three had different origins and only later came to be applied to the data regarding separation anxiety.

BECKER, HOWARD: Childhood mourning and its implications for psychiatry. *American Journal of Psychiatry*, 118:481–498, 1961.

This article tries to trace the psychological and psychopathological processes that commonly result from loss of mother (and to a lesser extent, father) in infancy and early childhood. The reaction of children so deprived is characteristic of all forms of mourning, i.e. the sequences of protest, despair and detachment. It is concluded that loss of a mother in early childhood (up to five years) is generally more traumatic than such a loss at a later period in the child's life.

BECKER, HOWARD: Process of mourning. *International Journal of Psychoanalysis*, 42:317–340, 1961.

Grief and separation anxiety intimately related. Describes basic psychological processes of mourning, as divided into three phases: urge to recover lost object; disorganization; subsequent reorganization. Mourning responses of animals show what primitive biological processes are at work in human beings, with other features specific only to human beings. Pathological mourning has the persistent seeking of reunion with a permanently lost object as its main feature. Infants who lose mothers show symptoms typical of pathological mourning. Thus they are more apt to develop personality disturbances.

BECKER, HOWARD: Pathological mourning and childhood mourning. *Journal of the American Psychoanalytic Association, 11*:500–541, 1963.

Fifth in a series exploring theoretical implications of behavior of young children who have been removed from mother figures, this article puts forth two theses: (1) separation anxiety results, grief and mourning are set in motion; (2) mourning processes in early years often predispose future psychiatric illness.

BREWSTER, HENRY H.: Grief: a disrupted human relationship. *Human Organization, 9*:19–22, 1950.

Case history providing clear demonstration of the interactional problems to be found in a grieving person, including interdependence of two partners in a human relationship and how behavior and subjective state of the survivor changes when relationship has been broken by death; and the need for bereaved to release emotional tie to deceased subsequent to replacement of the type of interaction lost. If there is an inability to tolerate attending emotional distress, morbid grief reaction develops, in which distress of grief is hidden by a protracted state of emotional preoccupation and impairment of mental functioning. Thus a neurosis results, requiring psychiatric help.

DEUTSCH, HELENE: Absence of grief. *Psychoanalytic Quarterly, 6*:12–22, 1937.

Observations from cases in which the reaction to the loss of a beloved object is a complete absence of the manifestations of mourning. Author is convinced that death of a beloved person must produce reactive expression of feeling in the normal course of events; that omission of such reactive responses is to be considered just as much a variation from the normal as excess in time or intensity; and that unmanifested grief will be found expressed to the full in some way or other.

EDELSON, STUART R., and WARREN, PORTER H.: Catatonic schizophrenia as a mourning process. *Diseases of the Nervous System, 24*:527–534, 1963.

The Psychoanalytical theories of melancholia of Freud, Bowlby, and others are explored in an effort to understand the relationship of catatonic Schizophrenia to mourning. Psychic mechanisms found in a part of these theories are discussed by viewing catatonic illness as one process of mourning. Protest, common to both the illness and mourning, is seen as the first stage of this process, with despair and detachment following. Implications of this hypothesis are outlined for treatment and therapy.

ELIOT, THOMAS D.: The adjustive behavior of bereaved families: a new field for research. *Social Forces*, 8:543–549, 1930.

Every twenty-three seconds someone dies, equivalent to twenty-six deaths in ten minutes. Sex is no longer a loathsome subject for discussion, while death remains so. Although the sex taboo has been broken down, the death taboo has not. Each represents a life-crisis, bringing out intense emotions seeking expression in unusual actions. Death may come to be accepted as something involving normal stresses with a minimum of abnormal distresses. As proper sex education is important, so is proper death education. Remainder of paper elucidates proposed research in this new field.

ELIOT, THOMAS D.: The bereaved family. *Annals of the American Academy of Political and Social Sciences*, 160:184–190, 1932

Bereavement is not found outside groups involving affective attachments, and is typically a family crisis, concerned with family interaction of primary and secondary effects. Some primary effects are sense of unreality, shock, self-injury, grief. Secondary effects include behavior patterns which take time and social interaction to form, such as escape, compensation, introjective identification. Familial changes resulting from bereavement are seen to include disturbance of family unity, necessitating reshaping of roles; consensus of family regarding new roles; possible decreased family solidarity, possible increased family solidarity; maturity of children. Remembrance of deceased may activate behavior of family.

ELIOT, THOMAS D.: Bereavement as a field of social research. *Bulletin of Society for Social Research*, 17:4, 1938.

Suggests that a shift in focus from the dead to the survivors may be helpful in evading resistance of taboo against researching attitudes toward death. Literature of objective analysis in this field is small but growing, including cultural analysis of bereavement phenomena, social-process analysis of bereavement, and social-psychological analysis of bereavement.

ELIOT, THOMAS D.: "—of the shadow of death." *Annals of the American Academy of Political and Social Science*, 229:87–99, 1943.

Investigating in what respects attitudes toward death are different in World War II from those in the preceding "peace," and World War I. Nothing definitive is mentioned and it is concluded that few facts are available.

ELIOT, THOMAS D.: Attitudes toward euthanasia. *Research Studies, State College of Washington*, 15:131–134, 1947.

Brief paper giving main points of a small study on people's reactions toward arguments for or against legislative proposals of periods of agitation, such as 1947 campaign to legalize euthanasia in which 46.1 per cent expressed willingness to permit a physician to hasten death, 45 per cent were unwilling, with remainder doubt-ful or blank. If processes were legalized, 68.3 per cent would not aggressively object and 31.1 per cent would.

ENGEL, GEORGE L.: Is grief a disease? *Psychosomatic Medicine,* 23:18–22, 1961.

Uncomplicated grief takes three phases: shock and disbelief; awareness of the loss; restitution and recovery. The author reviews various attitudes pro and con towards regarding death as a disease, stating advantages in such a consideration (e.g. study by medical scientists).

ENGEL, GEORGE L.: *Psychological Development in Health and Disease.* Philadelphia, Saunders, 1962.

This book was written primarily for medical students and psychiatric residents. It is divided into two parts, the first dealing with all the factors and considerations in the individual's psychological development and the second part demonstrating how these psychological factors operate within the framework of health and disease. Chapter 26, entitled "Psychological Responses to Major Environmental Stress," is pertinent to this bibliography. A discussion of grief and mourning deals with all the general responses to loss of objects as represented by persons, job, valued possessions, home, country. Object loss is "compared to a wound and mourning to wound healing. Like wound healing, preexisting and previous conditions will influence or change the course of the process and sometimes prevent it altogether." The author outlines the course of normal grief and mourning and describes specific forms of unresolved grief and mourning (and describes pathological aspects thereof).

ENGEL, GEORGE L.: Grief and grieving. *American Journal of Nursing,* 64: 93–98, 1964.

Given that a systematic knowledge of grief process aids nurses in coping with bereavement situations, the following topics are studied, along with suggestions for application: importance of grief; sequence of events; normal/pathological distinction; interplay of social, biological, and psychological factors as they make up series of events; factors influencing successful mourning; and practical considerations for communication of death, for relatives, etc.

FREUD, SIGMUND: Mourning and melancholia. In *Complete Psychological Works of Sigmund Freud.* London, Hogarth, 1917, pp. 152–170.

Correlation of melancholia and mourning is justified by the general picture of the two conditions. Mourning is the reaction to the loss of a loved person or an abstraction which has taken the place of one. As an effect of the same influences, melancholia, instead of grief, develops in some people. Unlike mourning, melancholia is regarded as a pathological state, with an extreme diminution of self-regard. It is postulated that the self-reproaches are reproaches against a loved object which have been shifted away from it on to the patient's own ego. Melancholia borrows some of its features from mourning, and others from the process of regression from narcissistic object-choice to narcissism. An analytic explanation of melancholia is extended to mania as well.

FULTON, ROBERT: *Death and Identity.* New York; Wiley, 1965.

A collection of readings on death and bereavement with extensive editorial commentary by the author, a sociologist. In Western culture, the question of identity posed by death has traditionally been answered within the framework of sacred doctrine. In our modern secular society, death is now viewed as a private disaster, a noxious disease which has become a taboo subject and as such the object of much disguise and denial as well as of raucous and macabre humor. This book is a collection of recent and pertinent research conducted by psychiatrists, psychologists, sociologists, and medical personnel on various facets of death. The author hopes that by this compilation a basis can be established for better comprehension of the dynamics and dimensions of death.

GORDON, NORMAN B., and KUTNER, BERNARD: Long term and fatal illness and the family. *Journal of Health and Human Behavior,* 6:190–196, 1965.

The effects of fatal and long-term illnesses of children on family-life stability are discussed. First, the evolution of sets of parental behaviors and attitudes to cope with the problem is detailed, including short- and long-term adjustments; outward practical consequences; and inward self-attitudes and intrafamilial relations. Second, the duty of the physician in such cases is outlined; care of initial traumatic reaction and understanding of problem on part of parents. Finally, the determinants of the crisis are suggested, such as the nature of the illness, and also of the child, and the conditions of the illness.

GREER, INA M.: Grief must be faced. *Christian Century,* 62:269–271, 1945.

The message of this article is that grief must be undergone. It can be denied, postponed, distorted, or expressed in the form of imaginary or psychosomatic symptoms, but it eventually must be experienced. The church can help by offering opportunities for the mourner to continue to interact with the lost one by prayers for the dead and days of remembrance. Friends can help by being understanding and supportive. Help from an internist and/or psychiatrist is necessary when physical or mental disease occurs.

HAMOVITCH, MAURICE B.: *The Parent and the Fatally Ill Child.* Los Angeles, Delmar, 1964.

This book reports a parent participation project in a hospital pediatrics department. The project, funded by a grant from the National Institute of Mental Health to the City of Hope Medical Center, focused primarily upon situations in which parents were faced with predicted early death of a child due to either leukemia or sarcoma. The project proposed to demonstrate that a hospital program providing for full participation by the parents in the care of these children can mitigate the traumatic effects of such a crisis upon the children and the parents. It was proposed also to demonstrate the feasibility of such a hospital program for full parental participation. The results of the study demonstrated that, in general, this program was successful in mitigating the trauma associated with these illnesses. Hamovitch concludes that this experience can serve as an incentive to other hospitals to modify their concepts of the role of relatives in the care of hospitalized patients, many of its principles having applicability to general pediatrics wards and to catastrophic illnesses that strike in any age group.

HINTON, JOHN M.: *Dying*. Baltimore, Penguin Books, 1967.

The rational and irrational emotions associated with death are discussed by a psychiatrist who has long been concerned with patients suffering from incurable illnesses. He attempts to take from the contemplation of death some of its more frightening magnetism. Chapters include fear of death and dying, physical distress in the terminal illness, speaking of death with the dying, prolonging life and hastening death, and reactions to bereavement.

JACKSON, EDGAR N.: Grief and religion. In H. Feifel (Ed.): *The Meaning of Death*. New York, McGraw-Hill, 1959, pp. 218–233.

Emotions of grief cluster around three main psychological processes: (1) incorporation: the individual becomes in part the deceased person; (2) substitution: the individual attaches his emotion to somebody or something outside himself, resolving his feeling by such an external attachment; (3) guilt: ambivalence involved in love relationship; when the object dies, the feelings are set free and thus cause guilt. Religious function is to protect bereaved individual against destructive fantasy and illusion by surrounding fact of death with a framework of reality that is accepted by grieving individual and supporting community. This makes legitimate and more easily possible a reinvestment of emotional capital in the continuing relationship of life.

JACKSON, EDGAR N.: *For the Living*. New York, Channel Press, 1963.

Answers to questions that are frequently asked regarding death, bereavement, and funerals.

JACKSON, EDGAR N.: *You and Your Grief*. New York, Channel Press, 1964.

A brief statement by a minister to the mourner on dealing with his own grief and that of his children.

KALISH, RICHARD A.: Dealing with the grieving family. *R. N.*, 26:81–84, 1963.

The nurse is likely to be involved with grieving members of deceased patient's family. "Guideposts" are given to help her deal with and perhaps ease their grief, including: most grief-stricken people need to talk; privacy may be the immediate need; resentment and guilt feelings are common; expression of nurses' emotion may be necessary.

KRAUS, ARTHUR S., and LILIENFIELD, ABRAHAM M.: Some epidemiological aspects of the high mortality rate in the young widowed group. *Journal of Chronic Diseases*, 10:207–217, 1959.

The relationship was reviewed between marital status and mortality appearing in statistical data published by the National Office of Vital Statistics on deaths and death rates in 1949–1951 by marital status, age, color, and sex. The main feature was the lower death rate in the married group than in the single, widowed, or divorced at every age. The outstanding excess of mortality among the young (under age 35) widowed was noted. Three hypotheses were suggested to explain what appears to be a genuine association between young widowhood and subsequent mortality. These were called the "mutual selection of poor-risk rates," "joint unfavorable environment," and "effect of widowhood" hypotheses. Further studies were suggested to assess these hypotheses.

KRUPP, GEORGE R.: The bereavement reaction: A special case of separation anxiety—sociocultural considerations. *Psychoanalytic Study of Society*, 2:42–74, 1962.

This article centers on adult bereavement in contemporary America, its symptomatology, pathology, and significance. The individual's reaction is conditioned by early infantile neurosis and by biological adaptive mechanisms as well as by the cultural milieu. The intimate nuclear family, the long dependence of children, emphasis on youth and vitality, and the urbanization characteristic of American culture are factors which may account for extreme bereavement crisis.

KRUPP, GEORGE R., and KLIGFELD, BERNARD: Bereavement reaction: A cross-cultural evaluation. *Journal of Religion and Health*, 1:222–246, 1962.

This article deals with the reactions to the loss of a loved one (bereavement reaction) in different regions of the world at different times. It is noted that there is present in almost all cases an attempt to regain the lost love object, and/or the belief in an afterlife where one can rejoin the loved one. In preliterate societies, bereavement pathology is less common than in more "civilized" societies.

LANGER, MARION: *Learning to Live as a Widow*. New York; J. Messner, 1957.

This book deals with a specific form of bereavement, widowhood. Its purpose is to provide women with guidance and assistance in their efforts to master their grief and to find new ways to live a well adjusted and rewarding life. The book is written in such manner that not only those who are bereaved may find help to better solve their problems, but also those who are happily married now may think ahead about dealing effectively with widowhood if and when it occurs. A resource appendix provides guidance to all kinds of services that may be needed or helpful to widows.

LEHRMAN, S. R.: Reactions to untimely death. *Psychiatric Quarterly, 30:* 564–578, 1956.

Grief reactions are more normal when death occurs in an aged person and when it has been expected. Under such circumstances, the work of mourning is accomplished quickly because a certain amount of it has already preceded the event of death. Pathological reactions to death are more frequent when the death is untimely and sudden. Other conditions and etiological factors also contribute to the formation of these pathological reactions. This paper is concerned with some variants of pathological reactions to untimely death, their origin and meaning. The clinical material consists of five case histories. Reactions to untimely death tend to follow the pattern of grief reactions which represent a defense against unbearable, painful affect or a defense against serious internal ego-threat such as suicide.

LINDEMANN, ERICH: Symptomatology and management of acute grief. *American Journal of Psychiatry, 101:141–148,* 1944.

Observations are presented which were gleaned from 101 patients recently bereaved, or close relatives. The hypothesis that acute grief is a definite syndrome with psychological and somatic symptomatology is presented, and several individual cases are discussed in this light. Both normal grief and morbid grief reactions are dealt with. It becomes apparent that a realistic acceptance of the new role with the bereaved, a coming to grips with guilt feelings, and an acceptance of the grieving process are all important aspects of the resolution of grief.

LINDEMANN, ERICH: Psychological factors as stressor agents. In TANNER (Ed.): *Stress and Psychiatric Disorder: Mental Health Research Fund Proceedings*. Oxford, Blackwell Scientific Publications, 1960.

Bereavement is concrete illustration of a response to a form of social stress. This is a stressful situation brought about by the cessation of interaction with an emotionally relevant other person. It leads to patterns of response with physiological, psychological, and social facets. The response may be well-adapted and lead to an adequate solution of the problem. It may also be maladapted leading to disorganization, failure to resolve the problem, and even to disease. Such social stress presents a hazardous situation to people who will respond differently depending on physiological, psychological, and particularly on social system determinants. The reorganization of the social system is an essential part of the problem-solving process.

MARRIS, P.: *Widows and Their Families.* London, Routledge and Kegan Paul, 1958.

MUNRO, ALISTAIR: Childhood parent loss in a psychiatrically normal population. *British Journal of Preventive and Social Medicine, 19:69–70,* 1965.

This study investigates childhood parent loss in a group of persons with no history of serious psychiatric disorder. The results suggest that parental bereavement may normally be a much commoner event than generally assumed. The author, in trying to establish a basis for comparability of study results, defines terms used in studies of childhood parental loss: parental bereavement, loss, deprivation; parental absence; disturbed relationship with parent; childhood. The findings of this study indicate that parental bereavement *per se* is of questionable value in assuming a predisposition for mental illness.

MUNRO, ALISTAIR: Parental deprivation in depressive patients. *British Journal of Psychiatry, 112:443–457,* 1966.

The author contends that there is meager evidence for the connection between childhood bereavement and psychiatric illness in later life. His study demonstrates that there is no apparent justification for regarding parental deprivation as an etiological factor in depressive illness, using a group of depressive in-patients with a control group of the psychiatrically normal. In a review of the literature he observes that samples used were by and large depressed, instutitionalized children and that the loss of the father is seldom taken into account, parental deprivation being assumed synonymous with maternal deprivation.

NATIONAL ASSOCIATION OF SOCIAL WORKERS. *Helping the Dying Patient and his Family.* New York, National Association of Social Workers, 1960.

PARKES, C. MURRAY: Effects of bereavement of physical and mental health—a study of the medical records of widows. *British Medical Journal, 2:* 274–279, 1964.

The effects of bereavement and grief—seen as a psychological reaction to the loss of a loved object—is measured on forty-four widows in terms of their complete medical records. With the number of medical office consultations per six months as the unit, the results showed an increase in consultations and in morbidity. Some effort was made to isolate that part of the increased morbidity relating to recent bereavement. The analysis further compared psychiatric and nonpsychiatric complaints; effects on widows over sixty-five and under sixty-five; and effect six, twelve, and eighteen months after bereavement.

PARKES, C. MURRAY: Recent bereavement as a cause of mental illness. *British Journal of Psychiatry, 110*:198–204, 1964.

Examines incidence of recent bereavement in pre-illness histories of psychiatric clinic patients, relating volume of incidence of bereavement among clinic population to that expected by chance. Of the ninety-four mental patients who experienced bereavement not more than six months before presenting illness developed, seventy-eight had lost a parent or spouse. Loss of spouse was 6 times chance; of parent only a fraction above chance. Study of age, sex and diagnostic information concludes the article.

PARKES, C. MURRAY: Grief as an illness. *New Society*, April 9, 1964, p 11.

The symptoms of grief are well known, following a stereotyped and predictable course. This, coupled with the fact that its cause is known, makes grief unique among functional mental disorders. A study of it, it is hoped, may throw light on the pathology of less clearcut disorders, though there has been little research into the effects of bereavement on the adult human being. Three types of grief are described and the differences explained using case histories.

PAUL, NORMAN L., and GROSSER, GEORGE H.: Operational mourning and its role in conjoint family therapy. *Community Mental Health Journal, 1*:339–345, 1965.

The operational mourning technique is designed to involve the family in a belated mourning experience with extensive grief reactions resulting in empathy and understanding of the origins of the present relational difficulties. Includes a case illustration.

SHOOR, M., and SPEED, M. H.: Death, delinquency, and the mourning process. In Robert Fulton (Ed.): *Death and Identity*. New York, John Wiley, 1965, pp. 201–206.

Abnormal reactions tending to delinquency are presented as case histories of several young persons, each suffering the loss of a close family member, somehow discouraged from regular mourning patterns, and previously conforming to social expectations. Substitutions for accepting the loss, reviewing memories of deceased, making deceased a "living memory," and transferring affection elsewhere included such diverse reactions as burglary, running away from home, sexual misbehavior, and general depression and under-achievement. Youths, of both sexes, ranged in age from fourteen to seventeen years.

SIGGINS, L.: Mourning: A critical survey of the literature. *International Journal of Psychoanalysis,* 47:418–438, 1966.

With Freud's model of mourning as a springboard, a model delineating intrapsychic aspects of adult reactions to the death of a loved one is shown. Reactions are distinguished as normal, pathological, and clinically recognizable psychiatric illnesses precip-itated by bereavement. Normal mourning reactions include guilt, anger, relief, and internalization of relationship to the lost one. Reactions include positive and negative aspects of the relation-ship. Where reaction is markedly exaggerated as failure to deal with the reality of death, mourning is pathological. There follows a discussion of similarities and differences between adult and child-ren reactions to death. A lengthy bibliography is included.

STERN, KARL; WILLIAMS, GWENDOLYN M., and PRADOS, MIGUEL: Grief reactions in later life. *American Journal of Psychiatry,* 108:289–294, 1951.

Bereavement reactions in later life are studied in twenty-five subjects, and the tendency toward somatic illness in these subjects is explored. Developing after a spouse's death, these symptoms often are attended by a relative paucity of overt grief and conscious guilt feelings. Other features of this study are mentioned also and the application of psychological dynamics of old age are discussed.

VOLKART, EDMUND H., with MICHAEL, STANLEY T.: Bereavement and mental health. In A. H. Leighton, J. A. Clausen, and R. N. Wilson (Eds.): *Explorations in Social Psychiatry.* New York, Basic Books, 1957, pp. 281–307.

The thesis is advanced that the category of bereaved persons is culturally defined, as is the form of bereavement. The emotions of a bereaved person vis-a-vis the deceased, consist of various degrees and intensities of the sense of loss, hostility, guilt, and the like. When these are minimal in strength, the bereaved person has a very low initial vulnerability to any mental health problems. When these are maximal and complicated, the person (unless he has a correspondingly high ego strength) has a high initial vulner-ability to mental health problems in bereavement.

YOUNG, MICHAEL; BENJAMIN, BERNARD, and WALLIS, CHRIS: The mor-tality of widowers. *Lancet,* 2:454–456, 1963.

Previous studies suggest that the shock of widowhood might weaken the resistance to other causes of death. An exploration of this suggestion was made by the authors using a sample of widowers.

The cohort chosen was of 4,486 widowers of fifty-five years and older whose wives died in 1957. The cohort was followed for five years at the time this article was written, and all deaths of widowers were recorded. The conclusion is that there is excess mortality in the first six months (an increase of about 40 per cent). This increase is eventually followed by a fall back to the level for married men in general. It is speculated that there will be a further rise in mortality at later durations of widowhood. Further light, it is hoped, will be thrown on this speculation.

ZELIGS, ROSE: Death is part of life. *California Parent-Teacher,* 36:7, 1959.

A child's reaction to the death of a pet is reported in this article. Most parents would like to spare their children the harsh reality of death, but that is impossible. A child should be taught that death is a natural part of life for all things. Ideally such learning should be gradual and in the course of daily experience, absorbing ideas and attitudes from the adult world around him.

ADDITIONAL REFERENCES

DOROTHY HOWARD AND LEE M. OLSON

THE WOMAN ALONE

BERELSON, BERNARD, and GARY A. STINER: *Human Behavior.* New York, Harcourt, 1964.

DEUTSCH, ALBERT: *Our Rejected Children.* Boston, Little, 1950.

EGLESON, JIM: *Parents Without Partners.* New York, Dutton, 1961.

FRANKL, VICTOR E. *Man's Search for Meaning.* New York, Washington Square, 1964.

JACKSON, EDGAR N.: *Understanding Grief, Its Roots, Dynamics and Treatment.* New York, Abingdon-Cokesbury Press, 1957.

LIEBMAN, JOSHUA L.: *Peace of Mind.* New York, Simon and Schuster, 1946.

MICHALSON, CARL: *Faith for Personal Crises.* New York, Scribner, 1958.

ROSENTEUR, PHYLLIS I.: *The Single Woman.* Indianapolis, Bobbs-Merrill, 1961.

TOURNIER, PAUL.: *The Meaning of Persons.* New York, Harper, 1957.

TOURNIER, PAUL.: *The Whole Person in an Broken World.* Translated by John and Helen Doberstein. New York, Harper, 1964.

WESTBERG, GRANGER E.: *Good Grief.* Philadelphia, Fortress Press, 1962.

ZAPOLEON, MARGUERITE WYKOFF: *Occupational Planning for Women.* New York, Harper, 1961.

THE FATHERLESS FAMILY

FREUDENTHAL, KURT: Problems of the one parent family. *Social Work,* IV:44–48, January 1959.

JONES, EVE: *Raising Your Child in a Fatherless Home.* London; Collier-MacMillan Ltd., 1963.

ROCKFORD, ELBRUN. *Mothers on Their Own.* New York, Harper, 1953.

REMARRIAGE

BERNARD, JESSIE: *Remarriage, A Study of Marriage.* New York, Dryden Press, 1956.

MEN, WOMEN AND SEX

Fromm, Erich: *The Art of Loving.* New York, Harper, 1956.

Marcuse, Herbert: *Eros and Civilization.* Boston, Beacon, 1955.

Mead, Margaret: *Male and Female: A Study of the Sexes in a Changing World.* New York, Morrow, 1949

FAMILY LIVING

Anshen, Ruth N. (Ed.): *The Family: Its Function and Destiny.* New York, Harper, 1949.

Ellis, Albert, and Robert Harper: *Creative Marriage.* New York, Lyle Stuart, 1961.

Feldman, Frances Lomas: *The Family in a Money World.* New York, Family Service Association of America, 1957.

Benedict, Agnes E., and Franklin, Adele: *Your Best Friends are Your Children: A Guide to Enjoying Parenthood.* New York, Appleton, 1951.

English, Oliver Spurgeon, and Foster, Constance J.: *Fathers are Parents Too: A Constructive Guide to Successful Fatherhood.* New York, Putnam, 1951.

Gesell, Arnold, and Ilg, Frances L.: *The Child From Five to Ten.* New York, Harper, 1946.

Jackson, Edgar N.: *Telling a Child About Death.* Des Moines (Iowa); Meredith, 1946.

Charles L. Allen: *When You Lose a Loved One.* Westwood (New Jersey); Fleming H. Revell Company. (Library of Congress Catalog Card Number: 59-5995.)

Paul Weiss: *The God We Seek.* Southern Illinois University Press, 1964. Library of Congress Catalog Card Number: 64-13476.)

A Treasury of Comfort, Edited by Sidney Greenberg: New York, Crown, 1954.

INDEX